Music and Sound in Docu

This collection of twelve essays provides a rich and detailed history of the relationship between music and image in documentary films, exploring the often overlooked role of music in the genre and its subsequent impact on an audience's perception of reality and fiction. Exploring examples of documentary films which make use of soundtrack music from an interdisciplinary perspective, *Music and Sound in Documentary Film* is the first in-depth treatment on the use of music in the nonfiction film and will appeal to scholars and students working at the intersection of music, film and media studies.

Holly Rogers is Senior Lecturer in Music and Director of the Research Centre for Audio-Visual Media at the University of Liverpool. She is the author of *Visualising Music: Audiovisual Relationships in Avant-Garde Film and Video Art* (2010) and *Sounding the Gallery: Video and the Rise of Art-Music* (2013).

Routledge Music and Screen Media Series

Series Editor: Neil Lerner

The **Routledge Music and Screen Media Series** offers edited collections of original essays on music in particular genres of cinema, television, video games and new media. These edited essay collections are written for an interdisciplinary audience of students and scholars of music and film and media studies.

Music and Sound in Documentary Film

Edited by

Holly Rogers
University of Liverpool

Routledge
Taylor & Francis Group

NEW YORK AND LONDON

First published 2015
by Routledge
711 Third Avenue, New York, NY 10017

and by Routledge
2 Park Square, Milton Park, Abingdon, Oxon OX14 4RN

Routledge is an imprint of the Taylor & Francis Group, an informa business

Library of Congress Cataloging-in-Publication Data
Music and sound in documentary film / [edited by] Holly Rogers.
    pages cm — (Routledge music and screen media series)
    1. Motion picture music—History and criticism. 2. Film soundtracks.
    3. Documentary films—History and criticism. I. Rogers, Holly
    (Professor of music), editor. II. Series: Routledge music and screen media series.
    ML2075.M8755 2015
    781.5'42—dc23
    2014019564

ISBN: 978-0-415-72861-4 (hbk)
ISBN: 978-0-415-72866-9 (pbk)
ISBN: 978-1-315-85155-6 (ebk)

Typeset in Goudy and Gill Sans 10/12
by codeMantra

Senior Editor: Constance Ditzel
Senior Editorial Assistant: Elysse Preposi
Production Manager: Mhairi Bennett
Marketing Manager: Emilie Littlehales
Project Manager: Francesca Monaco, codeMantra US
Cover Design: Salamander Hill Design

Contents

Series Foreword

While the scholarly conversations about music in film and visual media have been expanding prodigiously since the last quarter of the twentieth century, a need remains for focused, specialised studies of particular films as they relate more broadly to genres. This series includes scholars from across the disciplines of music and film and media studies, of specialists in both the audible as well as the visual, who share the goal of broadening and deepening these scholarly dialogues about music in particular genres of cinema, television, videogames and new media. Claiming a chronological arc from the birth of cinema in the 1890s to the most recent releases, the *Routledge Music and Screen Media* series offers collections of original essays written for an interdisciplinary audience of students and scholars of music, film and media studies in general and inter-disciplinary humanists who give strong attention to music. Driving the study of music here are the underlying assumptions that music together with screen media (understood broadly to accommodate rapidly developing new technolo-gies) participates in important ways in the creation of meaning and that includ-ing music in an analysis opens up the possibility for interpretations that remain invisible when only using the eye.

The series was designed with the goal of providing a thematically unified group of supplemental essays in a single volume that can be assigned in a variety of undergraduate and graduate courses (including courses in film studies, in film music and other interdisciplinary topics). We look forward to adding future volumes addressing emerging technologies and reflecting the growth of the aca-demic study of screen media. Rather than attempting an exhaustive history or unified theory, these studies—persuasive explications supported by textual and contextual evidence—will pose questions of musical style, strategies of rhetoric and critical cultural analysis as they help us to see, to hear and ultimately to understand these texts in new ways.

Neil Lerner
Series Editor

Preface

Bill Nichols

Bill Nichols is the pioneering theorist of documentary film. It therefore makes perfect sense for him to introduce this book, which is the first collected volume of essays on the sound and music of the genre. As you will see, not only has he been responsible for some of the most influential texts in documentary studies, he also has many thoughtful ideas about the ways in which music works on a documentary audience. Here he introduces some of the main new directions signalled in this book.

– Holly Rogers

I know firsthand how important music is to documentary. For several years my university had a 16mm print of Dziga Vertov's *Man with a Movie Camera* (1929). The print had no soundtrack at all. It was truly a silent film, even though most silent films were accompanied by music. When I projected it in class, students fell asleep. The onslaught of rapidly edited images began to feel arbitrary and inconsequential. This wasn't true for every single student, but the impression of a less than rapt reception remains vividly in my mind.

Then, in 2003, the Alloy Orchestra, which has created soundtracks for quite a number of films, released a new version of the film with their remarkable music, performed on a striking mix of non-traditional and traditional instruments, as accompaniment. Reception changed overnight. The film took on a vitality and coherence it had had all along that the completely silent version eviscerated. The Alloy Orchestra's music gives tempo to the day that structures the film; it gives vitality to the machinery that awakens and begins to produce the goods that will benefit the people; it organises an effective response to the film that makes the editing cohere in a way it did not do when it was simply a visual cascade without any soundtrack at all.

Examples multiply. Consider Werner Herzog's extraordinary film, *Grizzly Man* (2005), an examination of the life of Timothy Treadwell, a nature cinematographer and defender of Alaska's grizzly bears whose own stunning footage of solitary life among the bears comprises a significant part of Herzog's film. The film possesses a haunting quality and would not do so as powerfully were it not for the unforgettable music composed by Richard Thompson, formerly of Fairport Convention. The guitar solos that punctuate the film add a deeply-felt resonance that enhances the sense of tragedy and loss that Herzog meditates on (Treadwell and his girlfriend wound up being killed by a bear).

A kindred documentary spirit to Herzog is Errol Morris. (They served as co-producers of Joshua Oppenheimer's *The Act of Killing*, 2013). Morris's third film, *The Thin Blue Line* (1988), utilised a score by Philip Glass to convey something of the eerie, almost somnambulant world of guilt and innocence that surrounds the murder of a Texas policeman. Glass had previously created the music for Godfrey Reggio's poetic *Koyaanisqatsi* (1982), a film composed solely of stunning images and memorable music that stresses the need for balance and harmony in our relation to the earth. For *The Thin Blue Line*, Glass gave the sometimes surreal images that Morris mixes with more straightforward interviews even more potent impact. Nothing was what it seemed, or almost nothing. Morris contradicts the criminal justice system to show that the real killer escaped prosecution and that the wrong man was awaiting execution on death row. The tendency of Glass's music to possess a tonality that is both hypnotic and repetitive gives effective embodiment to the sense that the police and prosecution had circled around and around the events, repeating their own mantra of assumptions and convictions, only to let the truth slip through their fingers like the elusive spirit that hovers near but not quite in Glass's music.

So far, this parade of examples of music that makes a difference in documentary may seem to only prove that it is a valuable support to the underlying and more fundamental aim of the film that the images convey. I want to take the argument further, as Holly Rogers does in her Introduction. Music may be considered a supplement, valuable, or even invaluable, to information carried by images if we take documentary to be a form of film that conveys facts and makes arguments. Some documentaries do, though many such films might be better labelled instructional, informational or educational (in the limited sense of servicing an educational market that may not always seek out the best of documentary filmmaking to meet curricular needs). Much journalism leans toward facts, reports and descriptions and in these cases music can be a valuable complement to bring the argument alive, to give it greater intensity, to engage the viewer to the point of heightened attention, but it seldom fulfills so much as complements the primary goals of the filmmaker.

But what if this is not the fundamental goal of those documentaries that have stood as the most notable and most influential documentaries through the decades? What if there are other goals at work? What if documentaries aren't simply informational but rhetorical? What if they aren't only rhetorical but also poetic and story driven? We then begin to drift toward the territory Rogers invites us to investigate: fiction. Here, too, facts and information have a place but a subordinate one to tone, style, structure and effect. I've elsewhere described documentaries as 'a fiction (un)like any other' as a way to suggest that many of the same techniques and structures occur in documentary as in fiction. But beyond techniques, the two forms also share another common goal: to give sensory embodiment to a representation that will engage us, a representation that is more imaginary than not for fiction and a representation that is more historical than imaginary for documentary. (By historical I mean that documentaries address the physical world we occupy whether it is a previous incarnation of this world, the historical past, or some aspect of its present condition.)

What does giving sensory embodiment to the historical world mean? On the one hand, it means finding a way to represent reality so that we will entertain if not adopt a particular way of understanding or explaining some aspect of this world. A recitation of facts does not a documentary make. Documentaries engage us as ways of seeing the historical world, much as fictions do by means of their imagined representations of some aspects of human experience. The best documentaries give us a vivid sense of what it feels like to live in or reflect on the world from a particular perspective. And few things help us to better understand what it feels like to be in a particular time or place, in the midst of a specific challenge or situation, than music. In this sense, music is not a supplement, a filling in or colouring of an outline already sketched, but part and parcel of what we come to understand it feels like to be, to live and perceive and act and dream in a particular way.

This is why the examples I've cited and the many other examples the contributors to this volume cite serve as testimony to the vital role of music in giving sensory embodiment to what it feels like to spend a day in 1929 Moscow (in *Man with a Movie Camera*), to be only a few paces from huge, carnivorous grizzly bears and hundreds of miles from any other person in *Grizzly Man*, to be snared in a legal maze of contradictory but prevailing judgments that may suffice to kill you in *The Thin Blue Line* and to encounter the thousands of other situations and dilemmas documentaries attend to.

Music is part of the heart and soul of a film form that strives to represent what it feels like to experience the world from a particular angle, with specific people, in specific places and at specific times. It takes the concreteness of such images and imbues them with a more timeless emotional glow. It brings them alive in a way similar to how our own bodies and sense organs receive the world around us as far more than a conglomeration of facts and much more as a force field of intensities and lures, focal points and empty spaces. Music may make the world go round, but it also makes documentaries that represent this world come alive in compelling, memorable ways.

The essays that follow will demonstrate how this is so from a variety of perspectives and over the span of documentary film production. Holly Rogers has given us the first and no doubt not the last book to take up the far too long neglected topic of documentary film music. But it is not simply first; it is also supremely well conceived and executed. It provides a solid foundation for the work that has yet to come.

Bill Nichols
April 2014

Acknowledgments

This project would not have come about without the dedication and hard work of the contributors, who all embraced the topic of music and sound in documentary film with such great enthusiasm. Their ability to produce excellent and original research was matched by their endless patience and good humour, which made the task of editing this book an immensely enjoyable one. I extend my thanks to the series editor Neil Lerner for his help and encouragement and to Constance Ditzel and Elysse Preposi at Routledge for their support and professionalism.

The idea for this project arose during an afternoon pastry-eating session with Bill Nichols in a San Francisco coffee shop and I'd like to thank him for his support. My interest in documentary film was nurtured during a US/ UK Fulbright Commission scholarship to the DocFilm Institute at San Francisco State University, where I had the pleasure of teaching, learning from and befriending an inspiring class of documentary filmmakers. I'm sure I learned way more than they did. My education continued during several sessions on documentary music with my students at the University of Liverpool, who continue to surprise me with their original thought and insightful comments. I'd like to thank the Fulbright Commission for their financial help and the students on both sides of the pond for their inspiration.

As usual, this book is dedicated to my parents John and Polly; to Jigs; to the rest of my family; to my creatures old and new; and to the one who will shortly be with us.

Introduction

Music, Sound and the Nonfiction Aesthetic

Holly Rogers

Music in fiction film helps the audience to relax and fully engage with the stories unfolding before them. With this in mind, theorists have developed a rich and productive discourse that demonstrates the unique narrative, emotional and practical power of music in fiction film. But what happens when the images presented are promoted as 'real'; as a (mediated) representation of the world beyond the camera? What can be the role of music in such a world? As soundtracks become an increasingly important part of documentary filmmaking, questions of authenticity, authorship, audibility and reception are pushed into the foreground.

A great deal of critical attention has been paid to the fragile boundaries between fiction and nonfiction cinema. But attempts to identify a clear and consistent documentary aesthetic have often been thwarted by the porous nature of the borders that distinguish films that document real-world events from those whose imagined landscapes promise fictional escapism: 'Documentary as a concept or practice occupies no fixed territory' writes Bill Nichols. 'It mobilises no finite inventory of techniques, addresses no set number of issues, and adopts no completely known taxonomy of forms, styles, or modes'.[1] Elsewhere, however, Nichols acknowledges a constant that initially appears to underpin many nonfiction feature films: 'The documentary tradition relies heavily on being able to convey an impression of authenticity'.[2]

This notion of 'authenticity' – a word so heavily laden that I use it here with extreme caution – critiques the use of music and creative sound design in many documentary features, as the inclusion of a voice from beyond the filmed world can call into question what is being shown. Many working in the early *cinéma vérité* tradition or adhering to the direct or observational styles of documentary filmmaking, for instance, were particularly astute in their drive for an 'impression of authenticity', promoting minimum creative intervention in order to produce the illusion of a naturalistic chain of events that appears to have little to do with the presence of a director: events would have unfolded in this way, these directors imply, with or without the presence of a camera. The freedom of movement enabled by the more-recently available lightweight, hand-held cameras made the move from studio-based practices to location shoots with small crews easily attainable in the late 1950s and early 60s; and the development of synchronised sound equipment encouraged not only a greater sonic fidelity, but also a closer relationship between filmmaker and subject. Albert Maysles, for instance, recalls how he refrained from using techniques such as shot-reverse-shot to ensure that the images unfolded in a way similar to that of human sight in order to achieve what he describes as 'a closeness to what is going on'.[3] With a similar intent in mind, Indian documentarian Rakesh Sharma explains how he prefers to shoot people that 'I've never met in my life before' in order to achieve a truthful and immediate view of events: his use of a 'tiny handicam', along with the avoidance of external microphones or artificial lighting, helps to make his subjects 'completely comfortable', in order to give them the space to act in as natural a way as possible.[4] Such forms of apparent non-intervention have been taken to extremes recently in films such as *Restrepo* (Sebastian Junger and Tim Hetherington, 2010), a documentary shot on hand-held cameras that follows a small troop of soldiers on location in the military occupation of Afghanistan and offers a highly guttural (and, at times, disturbing) form of authenticity. When combined with a lack of voice-over or music, such observational techniques create film that 'appears to leave the driving to us' (Nichols).[5]

But what role does music have within the realist, unmediated aesthetic of such documentary practice? For many filmmakers, the answer is simple: it has no role. If nonfiction film must document, why place an outside voice against the factual representation of the images? According to the dictates of *cinéma vérité* and direct cinema, for instance, only synchronous – or what is known as diegetic – sound was permissible (that is, sound created from within the filmed world rather than sound-effects added in postproduction); this could include music so long as it was created within the camera's frame – think of Frederick Wiseman's *Titicut Follies* (1967), where the prisoners engage in various forms of music making (figure 1), Barbara Koppel's *Harlan County U.S.A.* (1976), in which diegetic folk music and songs by local artist Hazel Dickens highlight the plight of the miners, the rapping army recruits in Nick Broomfield and Joan Churchill's *Soldier Girls* (1981) or, more recently, the guitar-playing soldier in *Restrepo*. By contrast, dramatic music – or what is commonly referred to as nondiegetic music – as an element of postproduction, is an addition that can jar with the present tense of nonfiction filmmaking. Although source music has always been employed, then, dramatic music is less common. It is feared that music may contradict the apparent spontaneity and naturalism of the documentary aesthetic. Although Stan Neuman has made several documentaries that make use of music, for instance, he has also made others 'where there's very little, because I think the documentary image doesn't support music that well. Music within a documentary tends to diminish the image'.[6] Michel Brault, direct cinema pioneer and cameraman for *Chronicle of a Summer* (Jean Rouch, 1960), is even more clear in his dislike for dramatic scoring, explaining that for him, 'Music is an interpretation, it's the filmmaker who says, alright I'm going to make you listen to music here on top of these images to create a

Figure 1 The prisoners perform in *Titicut Follies* (Frederick Wiseman, 1967).

certain impression. It's impressionism. I don't think documentary is a form of impressionism. It's realism, and music has no place there'.[7] Brault's separation of realism (he was a promoter of the hand-held camera) from sonic representation is misguided in several ways. First, documentary may be underpinned by a realist aesthetic, but it often remains persuasive, subjective, emotional and narrative. As soon as an aesthetic decision is made, the line between the real and the fictional begins to flex. Second, our understanding of realism in relation to sound and music in the digital age has become highly complex. Ubiquitous music in our everyday lives, in shops, on TV and on mobile media has highly attuned our sonic awareness. In addition, the saturation of music in fiction cinema has formed audiences highly accomplished in processing images with the help of musical signification. Lastly, music in film is one of the most powerful illusory persuaders that what we are watching is, in fact, yet rather paradoxically, as real as possible. Unlike fiction film, documentary rarely tries to conceal itself as a constructed product. The role of music, as it is understood by many mainstream fiction film directors and composers, is therefore obsolete and can 'diminish' the 'realism' being presented; an audience does not need to buy into the fiction of the images. However, although pertaining to an 'impression of authenticity', documentary film is, for many, about persuasion. And the emotion, historical referents and rhythmic persuasion of music make the use of creative sound an extraordinarily compelling device for many nonfiction filmmakers.

Of course, music does not stand alone in its ability to add a creative, transformational adjunct to the filmed image. Despite techniques to give the illusion of non-interference, in truth most documentarians exercise a great deal of control over the variables of any given situation. For this reason, Werner Herzog, a director proficient in both fiction and documentary styles, has often warned that 'the word 'documentary' should be handled with care'.[8] Non-intervention, even in the fly-on-the-wall style, is always compromised: the choice of shot, angle, focus, point-of-view; the lingering camera; the ways in which those being filmed change their behaviour when confronted with a camera, however small and discrete; and the creation of dramatic trajectories and character development in the editing room. Such interventions belie, at various levels, a creative directorial presence. Because of this, other directors have considered an objective viewpoint impossible to achieve and have aimed instead for a more poetic relationship with their subject matter: 'I really don't believe in *cinéma vérité*', claims Agnès Varda, 'instead I believe in a sort of *cinéma mensonge*'.[9] Errol Morris embraced the idea of a *cinéma mensonge* in his 1978 film about a pet cemetery business, *Gates of Heaven*, for instance, when he designed an office for one of the cremation bosses that existed only as 'part of his fantasy world', giving us not what was actually there, but rather providing a glimpse into the mind of one of the key protagonists.[10]

The difficulties of objective representation have provided the starting point for many theoretical explorations into the documentary aesthetic, from John Grierson's famous promotion of documentary in the 1930s as the 'creative treatment of actuality', to Nichols's understanding of the form as a 'representation of the world we already occupy' rather than as a *'reproduction'* of it:[11]

> Were documentary a *reproduction* of reality, these problems would be far less acute. We would then simply have a replica or copy of something that already existed. But documentary is not a *reproduction* of reality, it is a representation of the world we already occupy. Such films are not documents as much as expressive representations that may be based on documents. Documentary films stand for a particular view of the world, one we may never have encountered before even if the factual aspects of this world are familiar to us.[12]

Along similar lines, Michael Renov has described the representational qualities of documentary film in terms of four overlapping functions: to record, reveal, or preserve; to persuade or promote; to analyse or interrogate; and to express. Underpinning these functions are interventions that result from the creative vision that transfigures reality through the location, duration, lighting, sound environment and *mise-en-scène* of the finished film; 'moments at which a presumably objective realisation of the world encounters the necessity of creative intervention' as though the spheres of fiction and nonfiction *'inhabit'* one another'.[13]

The blurred styles of documentary and the fiction feature encourage what Paul Arthur calls a 'tangled reciprocity' of aesthetic intent and reception.[14] Fiction films that feature untrained actors (*Battleship Potemkin* (1925), *Bicycle Thieves* (1948), *Shadows* (1960) and *Beasts of the Southern Wild* (2012)) can create a greater sense of 'authenticity' or gritty realism, for instance, while the hand-held camera style and lack of dramatic music in *The Blair Witch Project* (Daniel Myrick and Eduardo Sánchez, 1999), *Cloverfield* (Matt Reeves, 2008), *The Hurt Locker* (Kathryn Bigalow, 2008) and *Argo* (Ben Affleck, 2012) create a deceptive sense of unmediated vision (during its early release, the jittery shots and improvised dialogue of *The Blair Witch Project* allowed its directors to promote it as real, found footage from an abandoned video camera, thus creating a degree of hysterical fear amongst its audiences, this author included).

But, as we have seen, the necessity for creative invention in the documentary feature opens a reciprocal flow of influence and stylistic elements from mainstream cinematic traditions can be found in many works of nonfiction. From the self-reflexive, essay-style of modernist documentary, through to the performative, interactive and democratised phase of digital nonfiction work, the subjective has become a welcome and established part of the process for many documentarians, securely enmeshing the 'two domains' (Renov) of documentary and fiction.[15] But while observational styles promote the realistic possibilities of documentary, others lean more heavily on the inventive, or poetic, possibilities inherent in the 'tangled reciprocity'. Many of the most successful documentary films have a style that pertains to the condition of the mainstream fiction film: highly edited, expensively-shot competition documentaries such as *Spellbound* (Jeffrey Blitz, 2002) and *Mad Hot Ball Room* (Marilyn Agrelo, 2005), for instance, make use of well-used narrative and musical structures to create highly marketable dramatic arcs familiar to fiction film, forms of tension and release that forge a new, hybrid nonfiction style dubbed the 'docutainment'.[16] At the other end of the spectrum, poetic ruminations move the profilmic into a highly creative and personal realm. During a retrospective at the Minnesota's Walker Art Center in 1999, Herzog – one of the most outspoken of the poetic documentarians – issued his *Minnesota Declaration: Truth and Fact in Documentary Filmmaking*, a 'somewhat tongue-in-cheek' list of 12 points that demonstrated his dislike of *cinéma verité* and its superficial 'accountant's truth'.[17] The fifth point encapsulates his understanding of authenticity and truth particularly well: 'There are deeper strata of truth in cinema, and there is such a thing as a poetic, ecstatic truth. It is mysterious and elusive, and can be reached only through fabrication and imagination and stylisation'.[18] In many cases, for instance, Herzog's fly-on-the-wall approach is clearly staged, something that draws attention to the highly mediated quality of his documentaries: 'I rehearse and I shoot six times over, like in a feature film' explains the director; 'And sometimes I create an inner truth. I invent, but I invent in order to gain a deeper insight'.[19] It is at such moments of 'fabrication and imagination' that creative sound design and music become particularly noticeable.

Figure 2 Marine biologists playing in *Encounters at the End of the World* (Werner
       Herzog, 2007).

Not only are Herzog's documentary images propelled by intricate and audible
soundtracks: at pivotal moments, the visual narrative stalls to make room for
musical tableaux; for music in and of itself (notable examples include *Death for
Five Voices*, 1995, which includes numerous scenes of music performance and
listening and *Encounters at the End of the World*, 2007, where Henry Kaiser fulfils
the dual role of underwater cameramen and composer: figure 2). Herzog's promotion of filmic artifice brings him closer to documentary's etymological root
in the Latin *docere*: his aspiration is not to show but rather to teach, something
articulated in the fourth point of his declaration, which states that '[f]act creates
norms, and truth illumination'. The desire to reach for a 'poetic' truth that lies
beyond, or within, the filmed world can be found in many other personal and
highly musical nonfiction works that also question the nature of authenticity
and historicity, from the audiovisual, found footage poems of Jonas Mekas, to
Iain Sinclair's prosaic journey films and to musical escapades, such as Godfrey
Reggio's environmental tone poem *Koyaanisqatsi: Life Out of Balance* (1982),
with its insistent, driving score by Philip Glass.

Several documentaries have played with these boundaries in explicit ways.
Joshua Oppenheimer's *The Act of Killing* (2012) explores the memories of a
group of small-time Indonesian gangsters, led by Anwar Congo, who became
part of a fully-fledged death squad responsible for the execution of over a million people in the 1960s. The director explains that his film is 'about killers
who have won, and the sort of society they have built. Unlike ageing Nazis or
Rwandan génocidaires, Anwar and his friends have not been forced by history

to admit they participated in crimes against humanity. Instead, they have written their own triumphant history, becoming role models for millions of young paramilitaries'.[20] Obsessed with cinema, the executioners would use techniques seen in their favourite films: and in this documentary, Oppenheimer invites the now elderly squad to reenact their atrocities in the style of gangster movies, westerns and, significantly, musicals. 'We created a space in which they could devise and star in dramatisations based on the killings, using their favorite genres from the medium', Oppenheimer says. 'We hoped to catalyse a process of collective remembrance and imagination. Fiction provided one or two degrees of separation from reality, a canvas on which they could paint their own portrait and stand back and look at it'.[21]

Music and the Documentary Aesthetic

When these instances of 'ecstatic' truths and 'collective remembrance and imagination' include music, an entirely new and highly interdisciplinary realm of meaning and discourse opens up. Speaking of nonfiction film, Nichols reminds us that '[t]he centrality of argument gives the sound track particular importance in documentary … most documentaries still turn to the sound track to carry much of the general import of their abstract argument'.[22] For Nichols, the soundtrack resonates with the spoken word in the form of voice-over commentary or dialogue taken on-site. But, more significantly, it is the unspoken moments that hold the most power in the construction of documentary persuasion.

The mediation of the profilmic through various 'strata of truth' (Herzog) is *always* at play when creative sound and music are employed in a documentary film. Since its earliest days, fiction film has been awash with music; its role, it has often been theorised, to lessen our awareness of the technological construct that unfolds before our eyes; to encourage us, the audience, to enter into a contract and believe, on some level and temporarily, that what we are watching is real. To do this, edits, geographical and temporal cuts and evidence of the mechanics behind the film, have to be concealed, something easily achievable through a continual flow of synchronous sound. In addition, well placed music can draw out a narrative, highlight the aesthetic strands between scenes, focus attention on one thing to the exclusion of others and help promote intense aesthetic bonding with certain characters or themes. Whether music is concealing editing cuts, or heightening emotion, however, its main role is to remove an audience from the auditorium and transport them into the heart of the story. And herein lies the paradox: our everyday lives are not ordinarily accompanied by music (we can recall Hitchcock's question to David Raskin, composer of his 1944 film *Lifeboat* 'But they're in a lifeboat out in the middle of the ocean; where's the orchestra?', to which Raskin replied 'behind the camera!'); and yet, in fiction film, music is used to help us believe that what we are watching is real and encourage us to develop empathy with the characters.[23]

But, as we have seen, the documentary feature, although 'enmeshed' with fiction film, leans towards a completely different aesthetic. Documentary is often reactive, created in the moment. Recording actual events, nonfiction filmmakers do not need to erase awareness of the materiality of their projects; camerawork frequently responds to unexpected action and can be jittery, unfocused and fast moving; the director can be in shot; and the people being filmed are invited to break the fourth wall and directly address the viewer. Such gestures are all apparent signifiers of authenticity and objectivity. Like documentary images, sound recorded on location is similarly responsive and can operate very differently to the heightened and clear points of audition that characterise the highly post-produced sound worlds of fiction film. Documentary directors either work the sound equipment themselves, or perhaps use a single sound person who must be quick on her feet, as Chilean director Patricio Guzmán explains: 'There's nothing better than being in tune with your cameraman and soundman. When you're united by an invisible cable, it's amazing, it's like jazz'.[24] British filmmaker Kim Longinotto speaks in similar ways about audiovisual harmony: 'I think that sound is like the heartbeat of a film, if the sound isn't good then the film's thin ... the sound is where you get the emotion of a film'. Speaking of her attempts to film in the noisy and chaotic classrooms of Hold Me Tight, Let Me Go (2007), for example, Longinotto describes how her soundwoman had to perform like a 'ballet dancer' in order to capture the relevant sounds while attempting to physically stay beyond the limits of the camera's viewfinder.[25]

Nevertheless, the result can be confusing. The distinctions between sonic background and foreground are difficult to negotiate under such circumstances, even with the use of shotgun or directional microphones, as Jeffrey Ruoff reminds us:

> One of the major stylistic characteristics of documentaries that use sounds recorded on location is the lack of clarity of the sound track. Ambient sounds compete with dialogue in ways commonly deemed unacceptable in conventional Hollywood practice. A low signal-to-noise ratio demands greater attention from the viewer to decipher spoken words. Slight differences in room tone between shots make smooth sound transitions difficult. Indeed, listening to many of the scenes of observational films without watching the screen can be a dizzying experience. Without recognizable sources in the image to anchor the sounds, we hear a virtual cacophony of clanging, snippets of dialogue and music, and various unidentifiable sounds, almost an experiment in concrete music ... While Hollywood sound tracks are typically easier to understand than sounds in everyday life, documentary sound tracks are potentially more difficult to follow than sounds in everyday life.[26]

As Ruoff points out, it is easy for sounds recorded under such conditions to become dissociated from their points of visual reference; visual and aural points of view may not be the same and, as sounds coalesce in the aural middle ground, run the risk of becoming not only 'more difficult to follow than sounds in every-day life', but also, and rather strangely, less realistic to ears attuned to the arti-ficial sonic clarity of the fiction film. Sound design in fiction film ensures that the relevant information is always audible; and the supporting sounds are in no way confusing. In documentary, noise often operates at the opposite end of the spectrum. And, as all sounds coalesce into the middle ground, they run the risk of becoming dislocated from their visual points of reference, moving instead into the non-referential realm of music, as we shall see in the chapters to come.

Dramatic music can be used by documentarians for many reasons. It can help to add spatial depth to chaotic actuality sound, but it can also operate in ways very similar to those of mainstream fiction film, from the earliest examples of composed scores (such as Virgil Thomson's lavish and highly filmic scores for Pare Lorentz, or Aaron Copland's music for Ralph Steiner and Willard Van Dyke's 1939 documentary, The City, as we shall see in Julie Hubbert's chapter) to the more recent instances of compiled music, which introduce previous his-tories and cultural resonances (most notably the prominent ragtime and boogie-woogie soundtrack of Terry Zwigoff's Crumb (1994), James Marsh's choice of Michael Nyman's pre-existent music to heighten the tension in his Oscar-winning Man on Wire (2008), as John Corner shows us later in this collection, and the songs from Radiohead's back catalogue that populate Jon Shenk's 2011 film, The Island President).[27]

Music can hold things together and tell the story; it can lead viewers into narrative and emotional positions in a way akin to mainstream fiction film soundtracks; and it can help to turn each visual representation into a highly personal vision. As we shall see throughout this book, choices such as musi-cal style, instrumentation, structure, texture, mode, history and genre, familiar-ity, text/lyrics and audiovisual synchronicity or dissonance can fundamentally change the reception of the unfolding images. Narrative or aesthetic strands can be forged between scenes, an audience can be compelled to focus on one character or emotion in particular, even within a crowded image, and strong empathy can be encouraged with certain viewpoints or personal endeavours.

The power that music holds over an audience's interpretative juices is per-haps most obvious within documentary films of persuasion. Music has frequently been used as a powerful propaganda tool, for instance, propelling many exam-ples of early documentary such as The Triumph of the Will (Leni Riefenstahl, with a soundtrack compiled from Wagner's music, 1935) and many World War II films, which were scored by well-established concert hall composers such as Benjamin Britten (Harry Watt and Basil Wright's Night Mail in 1936) and Gail Kubik (William Wyler's Memphis Belle (1943), George Gercke's Men and Ships (1940), Sam Spewak's The World at War (1942) and Jerry Chodorov's Earthquakers (1943) amongst others), who insisted that 'the use of creative music in the docu-mentary film is based upon the premise that creative music, like any other creative art, has the power to move people ...'.[28] His scores, maintained Kubik, contributed to the fight for democracy represented in the images via the very process of creative composition: 'Music in the documentary film aids democracy to the extent that it is creatively composed music ... Music *really* aids democracy to the extent that it reflects the feelings of a free and unrestricted personality'.[29] In these instances, the persuasive abilities of music are paramount: and yet, music also holds an ambiguous role in the presentation of nonfiction images.

As we have seen, the 1960s saw a move towards a more observational aesthetic, a search for (at least an illusory) non-intervention that led to a silencing of the musical soundtrack. Documentary entered a period of non-musical synchronous sound, although the rise in popularity of the music documentary and the concert film ensured that many nonfiction films still remained highly musical (as Jamie Sexton reminds us in chapter nine): think of the Maysles Brothers' *What's Happening! The Beatles in the U.S.A.* (1964) and *Gimme Shelter* (1970), Richard Leacock's *Stravinsky Portrait* (1964), D. A. Pennebaker's *Don't Look Back* (1966) and *Monterey Pop* (1968) and Michael Wadleigh's *Woodstock* (1970). When documentary filmmakers again began to include music in their work, the reinstatement of a soundtrack became highly noticeable and, as a result, increasingly cinematic. In his work on music in documentary film, John Corner makes two insightful observations regarding the function and techniques most common to soundtracking the nonfiction image. First, he points out that dramatic music is more copiously included in films about travel and animals where the message is less political and the tone less persuasive, declaring that 'a strong tendency has been for music to be employed more frequently the 'lighter' the topic and/or treatment. Right from the 1950s, this can be seen in documentaries seeking to place a comic, sentimental or lightly ironic framing on their subjects'.[30] Some recent examples are George Fenton's opulent scores for David Attenborough's *The Blue Planet* (2001) and *Planet Earth* (2006), which will be explored by Mervyn Cooke in chapter six and Alex Wurmen's (re-)scoring of *March of the Penguins* (2005), which currently sits second in the lifetime gross list for documentary film. By this reasoning, the scores of Fenton and Wurmen are not designed to lead spectators into certain narrative positions, but rather, they are intended to accompany and highlight the images, replacing location and actuality sound with highly evocative, sweeping scores that seek, in places, to humanise the creatures depicted and to familiarise the otherness of the filmed wilderness for an audience located on warm sofas many miles away: to create empathy and to promote a stronger form of engagement with the rhythmic alignment of audiovisual elements (such programmes come closest to the Mickey-Mousing aesthetic found in many cartoons); and to blend together transitional sequences and montages to enable a greater flow in programmes that frequently jump between terrains and activities. This last point is particularly important. Music's ability to stitch things together is especially welcome for filmmakers working with footage caught on the run. 'A documentary film can sustain far more gaps, fissures, cracks and jumps in the visual appearance of its world even though it represents the familiar, historical world', writes

Nichols. 'People and places can appear in a manner that would be disturbingly intermittent in fiction. An intermittent representation of people and places, based on the requirements of a logic, can, in fact, serve as a distinguishing characteristic for documentary'.[31] In such cases, music that spans several scenes can help to alleviate the disquieting potential of visual rupture.

However, Corner also points out a prevalence of music for 'programmes which operate confidently within a sense of themselves as artefacts, as authored "works". This need not mean a claim to high aesthetic status, it simply indicates a level of self-consciousness about the crafting and styling of the account, the degree of creative and imaginative freedom exercised in its construction'.[32] Music, he argues, performs two roles in documentary film: it can add a sense of fun, or comedy; but it can also signify a departure from actuality or reportage and a movement towards the 'illumination' and personalised depiction sought by Herzog above.

The notion that music can readily be found in an 'authored' documentary, in which the director's presence or signature style is clearly evident, is supported by the prevalence of music in feature documentaries that have been commercially successful. Box office hits often hover, at least in terms of available technology and budget, between fiction and documentary styles. As we have seen, *March of the Penguins*, with its sumptuous score, currently sits second only to *Fahrenheit 9/11* (Michael Moore, 2004) in terms of its lifetime gross, while other successful documentaries that feature a prominent nondiegetic soundtrack to suture together scenes, encourage empathy with certain characters or emotional states, or emphasise a particular narrative trajectory of tension and release include *Hoop Dreams* (Steve James with Ben Sidran, 1994), *Spellbound* (Jeffrey Blitz with Daniel Hulsizer, 2002), *Touching the Void* (Kevin Macdonald with Alex Heffes and Bevan Smith, 2003) and *Cave of Forgotten Dreams* (Herzog with Ernst Reijseger, 2011).[33] In *The Act of Killing*, the most devastating re-enactments are the musical scenes, in which Anwar, explains Oppenheimer, 'was very much in the driver's seat: he chose the songs and, along with his friends, devised both scenes'.[34] In one scene, for example, the characters dance in front of a waterfall to a version of Matt Munro's 'Born Free', originally used for James Hill's 1966 film of the same name. Paradoxically, the cinematic excess provided in these opulent scenes produces a particularly uncomfortable reminder of the unutterable truth that lies beneath the music.

The use of music to provide a connective web around disparate scenes and locations – of 'intermittent' representation – is a technique common to the fiction film and the nature documentary; but also one familiar to the narrative nonfiction film. Several recent examples demonstrate the connective power of music by presenting complex and fragmented visual narratives that progress without the help of voice-over. In Thomas Balmès's creative documentary *Babies* (2010), for instance, the original score by Bruno Coulais takes centre stage, vying only with occasional dialogue and diegetic sound to suture together and promote poetic and cultural connections between the snippets from the

Figure 3 The four protagonists of *Babies* (Thomas Balmès, 2010).

lives of four youngsters growing up in different parts of the world (figure 3). Similarly, Antonio Pinto's haunting soundscape for *Senna* (Asif Kapadia, 2010) helps to conceal the technological and stylistic differences inherent in the collage of newsreels and race footage used to construct the Brazilian racing driver's story, while the eclectic variety of home footage that populates the crowd-sourced YouTube film, *Life in a Day* (Macdonald, 2011), is made less jarring by the consistency of Harry Gregson-Williams and Matthew Herbert's composed sound world (although this too includes raw crowd-sourced sound). Music, in other words, can heighten a nonfiction world in ways reminiscent of the construction of fantasy in mainstream cinema.

But as we have seen, music in mainstream fiction film assumes the paradoxical role as a tool with which to add verisimilitude to moving images, despite the lack of soundtrack in many people's everyday lives. It can make us less aware that what we are watching is fiction and allow us more readily to empathise with the characters we have just met. In documentary film, spectators do not need to be drawn into an imaginary world, and yet there are moments when a form of transportation is required. One particularly popular musical technique that can initiate such a transformation is the use of music to suggest a move back in time in the form of a re-enactment to illustrate the recollection of an interviewee. Although this form of musical suture is also prevalent in the fiction film style, from Max Steiner's reworking of 'As Time Goes By' in *Casablanca* (Michael Curtiz, 1942) to Ennio Morricone's score for *Once Upon a Time in the West* (Sergio Leone, 1968), in documentary the passage is not only temporal, but also takes the viewer away from actuality and into a state of imaginative recreation. Despite his desire to both penetrate and reveal, Errol Morris, for instance, insists that the aim of nonfiction film is to document. 'The truth', he says, is not 'up for grabs'.[35] And

Figure 4 The policeman looks into the camera in *The Thin Blue Line* (Errol Morris, 1988).

yet he famously displays a penchant for recreation, a fondness for re-enactment perhaps most clear in his investigation into the 1976 shooting of Dallas policeman Robert W. Wood in another box office hit, *The Thin Blue Line* (1988), in which the move between an observational style and that of a mainstream aesthetic is immediately obvious (figure 4). Here, interview scenes and talking heads are interspersed with highly interpretative, even poetic, escapades that suggest how the murder may have unfolded (it turns out that Morris's theory – that the wrong man had been incarcerated – was in fact accurate). For Morris, re-enactments are details, or moments of contemplation: 'The re-enactment is not re-enacting anything, it's there to make you think about reality, about what we take to be reality, what we think is reality, what claims to be reality', the director says. ... 'I like going after odd details ... and those are constructive, but underneath it all is some pursuit of truth'.[36]

An original score by Philip Glass is heard throughout the film; however, the heavy and highly persistent minimalist track is particularly audible leading into, and during, these re-enacted scenes: 'I don't like music that is supposed to tell you what to think', Morris says. 'But I do like music that creates a bed where things are driven forward. The soundtrack to *The Thin Blue Line* is, I think, one of the best things that Philip has ever done. It is essential to the movie. If this is a nonfiction film noir, that idea of inextrability, that idea of being trapped in a web of fate, those ideas are really driven home by the soundtrack, by the Philip Glass score'.[37] But whose musical voice is this? And what does it do to our relationship with the unfolding images? Is this fact or fiction? The music signifies that we are no longer in the present tense; but also that the subjective opinion of the director is now taking precedence.

Still a popular technique, the use of music to heighten and distinguish re-enactments from nonfiction elements of a film can be seen in *Touching the Void*, a film about two mountaineers attempting to scale a monstrous peak in the Peruvian Andes. The film, explains director Kevin Macdonald, combines 'some elements of drama with elements of documentary'.[38] As the mountaineers reminisce about their terrifying adventure, their recollections are played out via opulent and highly realistic re-enactments. During these re-enactments, the use of sound and music is particularly compelling. The film had two composers: Alex Heffes provided the acoustic score; and Bevan Smith the electronic music. Sound designer Joakim Sundström (who later worked on Peter Strickland's 2012 sonic extravaganza, *Berberian Sound Studio*) then wove the two musical voices together. At the start of the film, we hear a soundscape created from voices, wind sounds and highly ambient electronica; but after several minutes, the electro-acoustic sounds gradually morph into an increasingly symphonic acoustic track. At other times – and particularly towards the end of the film – we are left with real-world sounds that have been enhanced into a disturbing musical wash. Here, actuality sounds (or those created in the studio to appear thus) are elongated into a musical score, thus leading the viewer into the fictional recreations by softening the edges between the documented and the fictional (Marion Leonard and Robert Strachan explore this form of sonic elongation in more depth in chapter ten).

And yet, despite the attempt to conceal the imaginative realm in *Touching the Void*, the inclusion of a voice as strong as music that emanates from beyond the screen world nevertheless questions the role of an emotional artform in factual programming. Music after all (and as our colleagues working on the soundtracks of fiction film have amply demonstrated) is never neutral. By using the techniques of 'suggestion', or technical effacement, common to the cinematic use of music in the fiction film, feature documentaries remove themselves from the observational fidelity of the unmediated image. What is it that we are hearing? If our eyes are given real events, what happens when our ears are offered a sonic elsewhere? In fiction film, both image and music are conjured forth from another place, but in nonfiction features, the elsewhere signified by music appears to conflict with the present tense of the images. This can be put another way: in fiction film we have to suspend our disbelief; in documentary, we have to keep it activated and hold together in our minds two worlds at once. But when dramatic music is used in documentary film, this form of activation is problematised.

Music and Sound in Documentary Film

Those attempting to contextualise and theorise documentary film have often shied away from the sonic aspects of these mediated presentations. And yet, the paradoxical combination of 'real life' images with the openly fictional narrative voice of music opens up a significant area of theoretical investigation that could fundamentally change how we think about the documentary aesthetic: once music is taken into account, in other words, the radical and much theorised divide between documentary and fiction film needs to be revisited.

The authors in this collection work in various related disciplines, from music to documentary, from communications and new media to cultural studies. Their chapters trace the merging of music and image in nonfiction audiovisuality from the earliest examples of documentary film to the most recent forms of expanded technology and explore the fragile and mobile boundaries between music, sound-effects and voice, which are so important to the construction of a nonfiction, audiovisual aesthetic. Does music bring documentary film closer to its fictional counterpart? Or does it create different modes of engagement? Does music contradict the apparent spontaneity and naturalism of documentary? And how can real-world sounds assume an emotional and narrative role akin to a musical soundtrack?

Acknowledging the role of music and sound as integral to the creation of the documentary aesthetic, *Music and Sound in Documentary Film* formulates a multi-faceted theory of audiovisual narration for realist and factual programming. Some chapters consider documentaries that are about, or promote, musical performances; others focus on nonfiction works with sumptuous soundtracks that problematise the very nature of documentary and question exactly what it is that is being documented; and the remaining explore the boundaries between the creative treatment of real-world sound and traditional musical scores.

Carolyn Birdsall opens the book with an essay on the city film. She posits the city as a site through which to understand the aesthetic uses of sound in urban documentaries from the late 1920s through the early 1930s. Using the idea of the 'symphonic' motif and the creative elongation of urban sounds, Birdsall explores the differences between early outdoor and studio recording techniques in the work of Dziga Vertov, Joris Ivens, John Grierson's GPO Film Unit and Walther Ruttmann. The symphonic structure of these urban documentaries, she argues, can be mapped onto a metaphor for the social body, a structure that opened the doors for the development of a new and highly experimental form of documentary sound and music.

Taking a different approach to early documentaries, James Deaville traces the inclusion and 'fetishisation' of sound and music in the first sound newsreels for theatrical release in the U.S. (1927–1929). With the newly-emergent sound-on-film technology, newsreel producers—and those working on the Fox Movie-tone newsreels in particular—showed a keen interest not only in including diegetic sounds in their work, but also for embracing extended scenes of musical performance. In fact, popular music, jazz and band performances featured so heavily in these early nonfiction products that Deaville is able to suggest that the American awareness of the world at this time was in part shaped by these (most often staged) musical scenes, which lent heavily towards entertainment value in an attempt to sensationalise the news and shape public opinion.

Moving forward to the 1940s, Julie Hubbert concentrates on the documentary depiction of ideology, place and race, tracing the ways in which the American nonfiction film style evolved before and during World War II. With reference to the rediscovered documentary *One Tenth of Our Nation* (Film Associates, 1940), a rare example from this period of a film that explicitly tackles the problems of race, Hubbert investigates the role that music played in early American documentaries, an investigation that feeds into a bigger discussion concerning the appropriation and quotation of folk song and spirituals in contemporary music of the time.

Working in the same decade, Thomas F. Cohen turns his attention to postwar British educational films and takes a contextual look at the links between documentary as a pedagogical tool and as a marker of developing reforms in education. Educational films are notable for their fidelity to what is in front of the camera and are characterised by strict audiovisual synchronicity in contrast to the creative treatment of locational sound that Birdsall uncovers in the Symphony film. Cohen's two examples – *Instruments of the Orchestra* (Muir Mathieson, 1946) and *Science in the Orchestra* (Alex Strasser, 1950) – offer contrasting views on the musical arts in post-war Britain: the first aims to encourage children to engage with music while reasserting the social order from a previous age; the second responds to the cultural and political climate by using music to recruit potential scientists.

Orlene Denice McMahon takes a different approach to film sound in her investigation of documentaries by Chris Marker created in mid-twentieth century Paris. With reference to two travelogues – *Dimanche à Pékin* (1956) and *Lettre de Sibérie* (1958) – and two political essay films – *Description d'un combat* (1960) and *Cuba sí!* (1961) – McMahon explores the ways in which sound and music can be used to play with visual perception in documentary filmmaking. Marker's ironic placement of sound against image and his unusual treatment of voice-over opens up a larger discourse about the objectivity of the documentary tradition in general and the essay film in particular.

Mervyn Cooke's chapter acts as a pivot point in the book, propelling us from the 1950s – Jacques Cousteau's *Le Monde du silence* (1953) – to the early 2000s – *Deep Blue* (Alastair Fothergill and Andy Byatt, 2003) – in the first of our maritime investigations. In his comparison of the musical tropes that have become associated with the maritime documentary and the similar soundscapes of ocean-located fiction films, Cooke notes the overwhelming presence of harp glissandi and the use of circus-like music or waltzes to capture the dance-like nature of the underwater kingdom. His discussion feeds into several of the book's larger considerations. First, the relationship between locational sound and dramatic music forms a compelling entry point into the films discussed. Cooke identifies many instances in which instruments mimic real-world (or, rather, those imagined to be true) noises, a trope that constantly recurs in subsequent chapters. Second, Cooke's consideration of the uncreative treatment of voice-over in his case studies provides a useful counterpoint to McMahon's consideration of the poetic treatment of the device in the essay film and points towards a later discussion of narration by Jamie Sexton.

The relationship between the music for documentary and fiction film continues with the next chapter. Here, John Corner explores the various forms of sonic engagement initiated in recent feature documentaries, arguing that despite some initial similarities to the fiction film soundscape, music in the cinematic documentary has the ability to navigate boundaries between aesthetics and knowledge. At the same time, he argues, music also possesses the unique ability to enter into the argument of the film. Focusing on the ways in which documentary music engages with viewer consciousness, Corner offers an analysis of James Marsh's *Man on Wire* (2008), Ari Folman's *Waltz with Bashir* (2008) and Charles Ferguson's *Inside Job* (2010).

K.J. Donnelly takes a different approach to the documentary form. Comparing the original, orchestral music for Robert Flaherty's fictional documentary, *Man of Aran* (1934), with a new score by English indie band, British Sea Power (2009), he demonstrates the ways in which a change in soundworld can not only influence the reception of a film, but, through a process of 'masking' can also problematise documentary as an object of historical value. New scores such as this, he argues, can contemporise a film in order to enhance its accessibility to a modern audience; but they also run the risk of creating a rupture between diegesis and 'real world' as the disconnect between sound and vision can dramatically age the images.

Sexton runs with the idea of indie culture in his chapter, in which he explores the ways in which fan-based media and YouTube have contributed to an expansion of musical material in American indie music documentaries. Referring to the expanded range of available archival material (which can include amateur found footage and fan footage), he points out a rejection of voice-over narration, which can create the feel of objectivity and distance, for a more subjective approach; and the embrace of hybrid technologies to form an inconsistent style particularly applicable to the variety of modern platforms on which such documentaries can be viewed.

Marion Leonard and Rob Strachan take our attention back to the very nature of audiovisual, nonfiction aesthetics in the first of two essays that build on Birdsall's ideas to consider the ways in which real-world sounds can aspire to the condition of musical soundtrack. Here, the authors consider films that tread the stylistic and aesthetic boundaries between documentary and European art film. Through close analysis of two poetic landscape documentaries, *sleep furiously* (Gideon Koppel, 2008) and *Silence* (Pat Collins, 2010), Leonard and Strachan explore the ways in which ambient soundscape is highlighted through volume and changing audio qualities to such an extent that film goers are encouraged to listen aesthetically. Such concentrated listening allows real-world, ambient sound to become a signifier of emotional and thematic intent in a way similar to a nondiegetic score.

Like Leonard and Strachan and McMahon, Selmin Kara and Alanna Thain consider the ways in which visual perception can be complicated or undermined through sound. Referring to the unusual sound design in *Leviathan* (Lucien Castaing-Taylor and Véréna Paravel, 2012), an experimental documentary that also acts as a sonic ethnographic study of the deep-sea fishing industry, the authors return to our maritime theme, exploring how the placement of small cameras and microphones in unusual locations results in a multi-sensory confusion that draws attention from the images and places it instead on the other senses. This initiates, argue the authors, a disconnect between hearing and listening, as well as between listening and perception.

To finish off, Anahid Kassabian draws out the main themes woven through these chapters, before outlining some new directions in recent forms of documentary audiovisuality. Her consideration of the use of sound and music in viral videos and video blogs shows how new media further problematise the audio and visual boundaries between fact and fiction.

In these chapters, then, are many divergent themes. The essays can either be read as a historical narrative that runs from the earliest forms of documentary filmmaking to the most recent varieties of new media, or they can be experienced in complementary groups; city films (Birdsall, McMahon); seascapes (Cooke, Kara and Thain, Donnelly); histories of early documentary sound (Birdsall, Deaville, Hubbert, Cohen); the relationship between voice-over and music (McMahon, Cooke, Sexton); ruminations on rural life (Donnelly, Leonard and Strachan); and contemporary forms of nonfiction filmmaking (Corner, Sexton, Kassabian).

Notes

1 Bill Nichols, *Representing Reality: Issues and Concepts in Documentary* (Indiana: Indiana University Press, 1991), 12.
2 Nichols, *Introduction to Documentary* (Indiana: Indiana University Press, 2010), xiii.
3 Albert Maysles quoted in *Capturing Reality: The Art of Documentary* (Pepita Ferrari, 2008), 1.00'.
4 Rakesh Sharma quoted in ibid., 55'.
5 Nichols, 'The Voice of Documentary', in *Film Quarterly*, 36:3 (1983), 20.
6 Stan Neuman quoted in *Capturing Reality*, 1'19".
7 Michel Brault quoted in ibid., 1'19".
8 Werner Herzog, 'Minnesota Declaration', at http://wernerherzog.com/main/52.html (accessed 1 September 2013).
9 Agnes Varda quoted in Claudia Gorbman, 'Finding a Voice: Varda's Early Travelogues', in *Substance: A Review of Theory and Literary Criticism*, 41:2 (2012), 56.
10 Errol Morris quoted in *Capturing Reality*, 33'30".
11 John Grierson quoted in Nichols, *Introduction to Documentary*, 6; Nichols, 13.
12 Nichols, ibid., 13.
13 Michael Renov, 'Introduction: The Truth About Non-Fiction', in *Theorizing Documentary*, ed. Renov (New York and London: Routledge, 1993), 2–3, 21.
14 Paul Arthur, 'Jargons of Authenticity (Three American Moments)', in *Theorizing Documentary*, 108.
15 Renov, 'Towards a Poetics of Documentary', in *Theorising Documentary*, 21.

16 See, for example, Ruby Rich, 'Documentary Disciplines: An Introduction', in *Cinema Journal*, 46:1 (2006), 110.

17 Werner Herzog's first point states that 'by dint of declaration the so-called *Cinema verité* is devoid of *verité*. It reaches a merely superficial truth, the truth of accountants': Herzog and Paul Cronin (ed.), *Herzog on Herzog* (London: Faber and Faber, 2002), 238, 239.

18 Herzog and Cronin, *Herzog on Herzog*, 301.

19 Herzog quoted in Dave Davies, 'Filmmaker Herzog's "Grizzly" Tale of Life and Death', on *National Public Radio* (13 January 2006), at http://www.npr.org/templates/story/story.php?storyId=4774946 (accessed 7 February 2010).

20 Joshua Oppenheimer, 'Background', at http://theactofkilling.com/background/ (accessed 10 February 2014).

21 Ibid.

22 Nichols, *Representing Reality*, 21.

23 David Raskin quoted in Robynn J. Stilwell, 'Breaking Sound Barriers: Bigelow's Soundscapes from *The Loveless* to *Blue Steel*', in *The Cinema of Kathryn Bigelow: Hollywood Transgressor*, ed. Deborah Jermyn and Sean Redmond (London: Wallflower Press, 2003), 55.

24 Patricio Guzmán quoted in *Capturing Reality*, 1'01".

25 Kim Longinotto quoted in ibid., 1'01".

26 Jeffrey Ruoff, 'Conventions of Sound in Documentary', in *Cinema Journal*, 32:3 (1993), 27.

27 The documentary film scores by Thomson and Copland are some of the only to have received scholarly attention. See for example, Neil Lerner, 'Aaron Copland, Norman Rockwell, and the "Four Freedoms": The Office of War Information's Vision and Sound in *The Cummington Story* (1945)', in *Copland and His World*, ed. Carol J. Oja and Judith Tick (Princeton and Oxford: Princeton University Press, 2005), 351–377; Lerner, 'Damming Virgil Thomson's Music for *The River*', in *Collecting Visible Evidence*, ed. Jane M. Gaines and Michael Renov (Minneapolis: University of Minnesota Press, 1999), 103–15; Lerner, *The Classical Documentary Score in American Films of Persuasion: Contexts and Case Studies, 1936–1945* (Unpublished PhD thesis: Duke University, 1997); and Claudia Widgery, *The Kinetic and Temporal Interaction of Music and Film: Three Documentaries of 1930s America* (Unpublished PhD Thesis: University of Maryland, 1990).

28 Gail Kubik, 'Music in Documentary Films' (1945), in *The Hollywood Film Music Reader*, ed. Mervyn Cooke (Oxford: Oxford University Press, 2010), 149.

29 Ibid., 148.

30 John Corner, 'Sounds Real: Music and Documentary', in *Popular Music*, 21:3 (2002), 362.

31 Nichols, *Representing Reality*, 19.

32 Corner, 'Sounds Real', 362.

33 Box office figures at http://www.boxofficemojo.com/genres/chart/?id=documentary.htm (accessed 1 September, 2013).

34 Oppenheimer, 'Background'.

35 Morris quoted in *Capturing Reality*, 40'.

36 Ibid., 108'.

37 Ibid., 120'.

38 Kevin Macdonald quoted in *Capturing Reality*, 108'.

Chapter 1

Resounding City Films
Vertov, Ruttmann and Early Experiments with Documentary Sound Aesthetics

Carolyn Birdsall

The concepts of the 'document' and 'documentary' as associated with evidence are linked to both the historical rise of media of mechanical reproduction (photography, phonography, cinema) and the professional field of history in the nineteenth century.[1] This simultaneous development gave rise to notions of knowledge acquisition by observing palpable traces of the past, as enabled by historical documentation (written or otherwise). In early cinema, a preoccupation with street scenes allowed the film camera to open up new ways in which to understand social life. Indeed, both documentary photography and film have subsequently been understood as developing a *visual* language able to comment on the modern city and its inhabitants.[2] More specifically, the silent 'city films' of the 1920s have been revisited in recent scholarship as a case in point for both formal experimentation and social commentary on urban modernity, often with the aid of (dialectical) montage. The most well-known European examples of this transnational genre include short city films, such as Alberto Cavalcanti's *Rien que les heures* (1926) and Jean Vigo's *Á Propos de Nice* (1930) and the feature-length films of Walther Ruttmann (*Berlin: Sinfonie der Großstadt*, 1927) and Dziga Vertov (*Man with a Movie Camera*, 1929).

This chapter revisits the genre of the city film and investigates how the representation of urban sound was approached by directors like Cavalcanti, Ruttmann and Vertov between the mid-1920s and mid-1930s. The analysis will pay close attention to the 'symphony' motif developed in silent city films, a motif used as an analogy for filmic structure, formal experimentation or as a metaphor for the social body. During the 1920s, as Kurt London has observed, European films increasingly adopted a symphonic structure, with the dramatic action usually running according to the following sequence: Introduction – Main and subsidiary theme – Development – Recapitulation – Coda.[3] Along with the symphony, notions of melody and rhythm were drawn on as metaphors for experiments in cinematic style and action, from the work of Soviet directors like Sergei Eisenstein to the visual experiments of figures like Hans Richter and Viking Eggeling. This essay examines the different ways in which the 'symphony' metaphor was adopted across silent and sound film and situates its relevance in a medial awareness heightened by the significant crossovers of radio and film experimentation during the 1920s.[4] While audiovisual experimentation is at

the forefront of this investigation, close attention will also be paid to the technological, political and aesthetic concerns governing early sound documentary
practice.

In recent scholarship, there has been an effort to reincorporate the city film
genre into the broader history of cinema. Keith Beattie, for instance, has suggested that more recognition be given to the centrality of visual language and to
this genre's links to early cinematic forms of display and tricks. This represents an
effort to reevaluate the city film from outside of traditional accounts of documentary history, which have tended to emphasise content and information over form
and poetic expression.[5]

While this intervention is a welcome challenge to the dominant focus
on the serious aspects in documentary, dubbed by theorist Bill Nichols as
the 'discourses of sobriety', Beattie's approach nevertheless significantly
downplays the role of sound within the nonfiction tradition, from silent film
onwards.[6] Beattie's account is consistent with the broader field of documentary studies, in which theoretical debates have traditionally focused on the
indexical qualities of the film image. Since the 1990s, however, a growing
number of scholars have begun to give more attention to the role of sound
within documentary film. Apart from camerawork, it has been argued, two
of the most important documentary codes consist of commentary/voice and
authentication through sound/music.[7] Such scholarship has drawn attention
to the importance of sound in establishing the rhetoric of documentary and
its claims to 'truth', as well as contributing to the techniques of nonfiction
dramatisation.

Despite such important groundwork, however, existing studies on nonfiction film sound have focused on relatively narrow fields of investigation and
only rarely elaborate on the portrayal of modern cities and their inhabitants. In
what follows, the fundamental oppositions that emerged in early documentary
practice will be examined in relation to the urban as a crucial site for thinking
through 'real sound' in the late 1920s and early 1930s. This chapter focuses in
particular on the distinctions that arose between outdoor and studio recording techniques; synchronous and montage editing; and between the themes
of labour and leisure. The first section will outline several examples – in the
work of Dziga Vertov, Joris Ivens and John Grierson's GPO Film Unit – that
illustrate such tensions and oppositions in early documentary sound practice.
The analyses will show how attempts to distinguish between fact and fiction
reveal the politics of representing urban sound, often evidenced by the positioning of spoken voice, scored music and sound effects/ambient noise within
the sound design.[8] Such broader developments in documentary sound practice will form the basis of a closer investigation of German filmmaker Walter
Ruttmann, best-known for his development of rhythmic montage in *Die Sinfonie der Großstadt*. Ruttmann's later city films of the 1930s will provide a case
in point for considering shifts in both the representation of urban modernity
and documentary sound aesthetics within the production context of National
Socialist-era cinema.[9]

Experiments in Documentary Sound

Compared to the introduction of synchronous sound in the feature film, documentary audiovisuality was slow to emerge; despite several early attempts at newsreel synchronisation for Fox Movietone in 1927 (as evidenced in James Deaville's chapter), most newsreels did not switch to sound until 1932 or later and even then tended to rely on stock music and studio voice-overs, rather than on location sound recordings. When it did appear, the synchronisation of music and voice with the documentary image led to widespread worry – particularly amongst the modernist avant-garde – that it would interfere with cinema's modernist project, and silent documentary film continued until at least the 1960s. In what follows, I will dwell on three concerns – outdoor recording (of original source sounds), montage editing and a thematic stress on workers' labour – which are bound up with political investments in the documentary representation of urban sound. I will focus on the work of Vertov, Ivens and members of Grierson's GPO Film Unit, all of whom have been described as the first filmmakers to fully explore the possibility of soundscape composition within documentary.[10]

Prior to the 1920s, the ability to document urban sound in European cities was prevented due to the technological difficulty of making wax disc recordings outdoors and the primary use of the gramophone for speech and music studio recordings. In the 1910s, Vertov, inspired by Futurist responses to urban and mechanical noise, began to create sound poetry by using a phonograph with recording and playback functions. In 1916, as part of this 'Laboratory of Hearing', the artist experimented with the various tonalities of a waterfall and a lumber mill, although he was ultimately disappointed by the limitations of phonographic recording at this time.[11]

In the following decade, Vertov was involved in the theorisation and practice of Cinema-Eye, a broader project intended to develop cinema as a dynamic art form in response to and for Soviet society in the wake of revolution. In the many statements and texts by Vertov in this period, he continually asserts the necessity for a radical approach to filmmaking, in order to educate the masses and generate political consciousness. Intrinsic to the Cinema Eye method, as initially developed for newsreels, was the recording of real events, often with a hidden camera, which would subsequently be reorganised through the technique of montage editing.

With footage taken over a period of several years, Vertov's city film experiment, Man with a Movie Camera, is commonly cited in terms of its innovative visual organisation, use of optical effects and heightened medium awareness. And yet this silent feature-length film, which depicts a multitude of urban settings spanning from morning until night, was originally conceived as a sound film.[12] Vertov had already predicted the potential of sound media both theoretically, in his article 'From Kino-Eye to Radio-Eye' (1926) and practically, in the film Radio Kino Pravda (1925), which provided visual versions of sonic events, such as radio waves. In a statement about Man with a

Movie Camera in early 1929, the filmmaker also spoke about the 'Radio Eye' (*Radioglaz*), an idea related to his desire to radically dispense with artificial or staged cinema and radio programming.[13]

In addition to its morning-to-night structure, *Man with a Movie Camera* foregrounds its own construction, with the film's production from camera and lab processing to editing and cinema screening offered as a central thread. This self-reflexive awareness extends to sequences of imagined sound and media connectivity. The film's opening scene introduces the cameraman, followed by shots of a cinema, as projectionist, lighting technician and audience members prepare to view a film. In terms of imagined sound, the film displays the ringing of a bell and close ups as a conductor and pit orchestra prepare to perform to the film. In terms of imagined sound, an exemplary scene takes place halfway through the film, when alarm bells are shown ringing for both ambulance and fire crews, who drive rapidly through urban traffic. Shortly after this fast-paced sequence, which includes shots of the filmmaker documenting the action, a montage sequence increases the speed, with work activity (factory, mining, offices) interspersed with women rapidly patching connections on a telephone switchboard. These sequences allude to noisy sounds in the metropolis, the multiple movements of machines and workers' labour and the connectivity of subjects through modern transmission media. The final 10 minutes of the film depict a former church, now the Lenin's Workers' Club, where radio amateurs are gathered. Here, too, the imagined sounds of piano accordion, sound effects, singing and dancing are visualised through superimpositions on a radio loud-speaker and black background (figure 1.1). This sequence, which also depicts listeners' reactions to the radio sounds, is followed by a final resolution to the film, which foregrounds the cinema audience's point of view and their reactions to the montage sequences, closing with the superimposed image of the camera lens over the cameraman's eye.

In his proposal for the film, dated 1928, Vertov provided the subtitle 'A Visual Symphony', describing his 'non-acted' film as an experiment in visual language that dispensed with intertitles, script and theatrical conventions like acting and sets.[14] He was later incensed that the German press perceived *Man with a Movie Camera* as a film that was made after Ruttmann's Berlin film, which had used the symphony concept to govern its five-act structure.[15] One key difference is that Vertov's film disrupts the usual temporal ordering of the city symphony, allowing for film material to be reused in other timeframes and with its footage drawn from multiple Soviet cities. Vertov argued for the pioneering role of Soviet documentary and its preexisting use of the symphony motif:

> The majority of kino-eye films were constructed as a symphony of labor, as a symphony of the whole Soviet land, or as a symphony of a particular city. In addition, the action in these films frequently developed from early morning to evening. Thus in Part One of *Kinoglaz* ... a city awakens and comes to life. And in *Forward, Soviet!* a day gradually

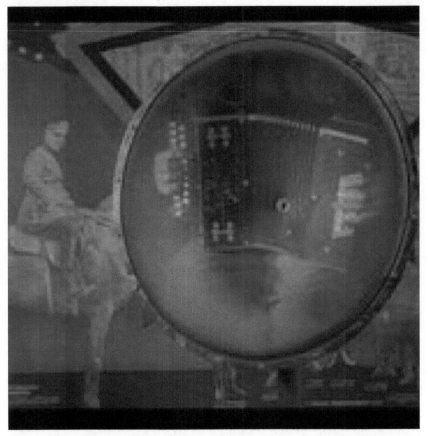

Figure 1.1 The sound of an accordion is imagined through its superimposition onto a loudspeaker. Still from *Man with a Movie Camera* (Dziga Vertov, 1929).

develops into evening and concludes at midnight. [...] Ruttmann's recent experiment should therefore be regarded as the result of years of kino-eye's pressure through work and statements, on those working in abstract film.[16]

Vertov's comments suggest that the Soviet investment in the symphony for early cinema experiments had already established its own variant of the city film, in which montage editing was used to reveal the multitude of everyday minutiae that together made up a coherent whole. The symphony metaphor was also drawn upon in early 1920s Soviet culture as a way in which to incorporate industrial sounds into music composition. This is evidenced by avant-garde composer Arseny Avraamov's 'Symphony of the Factory Sirens' (1922), which was staged as a large-scale public performance comprising a sound machine with whistles, factory sirens, military artillery and numerous vehicles as orchestral instruments.

In Russia, sound film production was delayed until around 1930 as inventors such as Pavel Tager (Moscow) and Alexander Shorin (St. Petersburg) sought to develop homegrown alternatives to European and American synchronisation systems.[17] Before these alternatives were available, however, filmmakers Eisenstein, Vsevolod Pudovkin and Grigori Alexandrov released their 'Statement on Sound' in August 1928.[18] The statement is best known for its renewed emphasis on montage and the proposed technique of asynchrony as a means of treating image and sound as separate elements. Although they had not themselves seen a sound film, the directors predicted that synchronised sound would result in a regression in film aesthetics by reverting to bourgeois drama and literary traditions. Nonetheless, the statement can be understood as a cautious acceptance of sound synch systems, albeit with a strong concern that the push for synchronisation by the international film industry could constrain the universal visual language developed in filmic practice and its appeal to international audiences.

Vertov shared some of these concerns about the development of sound conventions in American and British cinema, which emphasised clear spoken dialogue and background music.[19] In terms of technology, too, the filmmaker observed a number of challenges inherent in the transition to synchronised sound, such as the problem of outdoor recording and the development of sound montage editing. Despite delays in mobile microphone recording technology, Vertov countered assertions by critics like Ippolit Sokolov, who argued that natural or outdoor sounds were too noisy to be 'audiogenic' and that, as a result, sound film production must remain restricted to a soundproof studio.[20]

While numerous obstacles remained to production, then, Vertov was resolute about recording the real source of a sound, rather than its approximation as sound effect or studio recording. He remained convinced, however, that the resulting sound montage should not provide a 'simple synchrony', but rather a 'complex interaction of sound with image'.[21] Produced by Soviet film studio Ukrainfilm (formerly VUFKU), *Enthusiasm: Symphony of the Donbas* (released in 1931) documents industrial and agricultural progress at a key site in the Soviet Five Year Plan (1928–1932) for economic development: the Donbas region in the Ukraine. This period was marked by increased centralised control over Soviet cinema and with it direct attacks on Vertov, who refused to adhere to the increasing emphasis on socialist realism in the early 1930s.[22]

A year before filming began, Vertov focused on the sound concept, conceiving the film as a musical symphony. Working in close collaboration with composer Nikolai Timofeev in late 1929, a musical score was established that incorporated a range of noises; along with radio voice and diegetic musical performance, some noise samples were reworked in post-production according to a montage concept.

The symphony referred to in the film's title can be found in the structure of overture plus four movements (*allegro, moderato, allegro vivace, andante cantabile*). The overture presents a historical narrative, whereby the features of the past (the church, Tsarist rule) are cued by discordant church bells and choir sounds, along with the location recordings of alcoholics in public places. The revolutionary break leading to a Soviet present is indicated with the Internationale as well as locational recordings of whistles, industrial noise, marching music and cheering communist crowds. In a perceptive essay, Olga Bulgakowa points out that:

> Vertov used principles of program music in *Enthusiasm*, but he substituted noises for the melodies ... By the end of the film, march music has pushed out the noises altogether; the abstract qualities of the non-referential sounds have been replaced by music that is perceived as 'pictorial' in relation to the noises. Vertov's symphony thus moves from abstract to diegetic sound, from noise to music.[23]

Indeed, the second and third movements show volunteers arriving for work in the Donbas coal mines and iron works, with the soundtrack incorporating wind and brass instrumentation, along with the sounds of machines, hammers, engines and sirens. In the final part, coal and metal are transported away, while a 'Day of Industrialisation' celebration is held to mark the arrival of grain and thus the success of the Five Year Program.

As noted above, Vertov had previously used the cameraman to foreground cinema technology and the visual act of filmmaking. In *Enthusiasm*, the technological basis of sound is highlighted in the film in the form of a woman with 'radio-ears' (headphones), who appears in the opening scenes. Subsequently, a sonic form of self-referentiality occurs, with a radio announcement appearing: 'Attention, attention, Radio Leningrad speaking. RW3 RW3 Wavelength 1000 broadcasting the march The Last Sunday from the film Symphony of the Donbas'. For the remainder of the film, wireless alerts explain or motivate the action, while also suggesting the importance of radio and loudspeaker connectivity within the Soviet project, with the Internationale reinforcing the idea of being united in song. Similar to Vertov's earlier shots of the cameraman, here, recording technicians are shown holding mobile microphones.

It was only after several months of filming in the Donbas in late 1929 that Vertov returned to Russia for training in Alexander Shorin's recording system. Following a number of indoor and outdoor experiments, Vertov 'filmed' outdoor urban sounds in mid-1930, which were later edited and screened in a St. Petersburg cinema as an audio track without images.[24] The development of a documentary form of sound in *Enthusiasm* was initially hampered not only by technological limitations, but also by the changing social-political norms concerned with cinema aesthetics in Soviet Russia. Recording industrial sounds in a remote location was challenging, as the crew were unable to process and hear their recordings on site; it was only after the shoot that they discovered that some recordings had been lost due to the overly loud frequencies of industrial equipment. Nonetheless, Vertov argued that *Enthusiasm* was a pioneering example of a documentary soundscape created from on-location sounds:

> The final, decisive month of our sound shooting took place in a setting of din and clanging, amidst fire and iron, among factory workshops vibrating from the sound. Penetrating into mines deep beneath the earth

and shooting from the roofs of speeding trains, we abolished, once and for all, the fixity of sound equipment and *for the first time in history* recorded, in documentary fashion, the basic sounds of an industrial region (the sound of mines, factories, trains etc.).[25]

In one sense, Vertov's documentary is similar to the other Russian early sound films, such as *The Plan of the Great Works* (Abram Room, 1930), which all thematise industrial construction and development. Nonetheless, the loud volume formed part of the negative response to *Enthusiasm* in the Russian reviews, which panned the film for its failure to provide an obvious political perspective. The film clearly offered praise for Soviet reconstruction, yet it was released at a time of increased preference for socialist realism and criticism of Vertov's formal experimentation.

Similar to Vertov, the left-wing Dutch filmmaker Ivens articulated a similar engagement with documentary – based on formal experimentation and social-political commentary – in opposition to 'acted' films. For Ivens, earlier commissions from businesses like Philips were necessary, paradoxically, in order to make films outside of the constraints of the commercial film industry. The industrial film, *Philips Radio* (1931, 36 mins) documents the company's production process, starting with radio receiver and transmitter lamps, radio transmission and laboratory research, before moving to the assembly line and a final poetic segment demonstrating the completed loudspeakers. Although he initially conceived *Philips Radio* as a silent film, Ivens realised the 'symphonic' potential of the Philips work environment several months into production:

> Beautiful material for a sound film. Inhuman symphonies of tinkling glass combined in all kinds of strange, chime-like chords. Low, dull, explosive sounds like faraway timpanic beats, and in between, the voice of a warehouse manager, who bellows through the loudspeaker.[26]

With composer Lou Lichtveld, Ivens investigated the possibilities for adding sound to create a soundtrack that was entirely synched in post-production. The resulting film, with the title *Symphonie industrielle* in France, has a predominance of scored orchestration for several string and brass instruments. Along with several silent scenes and the occasional spoken passage, the post-synched soundtrack included sound effects for industrial machines, ovens, whistles, sirens, typewriters, clocks and other everyday sounds of the factory. Sharing the avant-garde suspicion of synchronised dialogue, Ivens significantly downplayed voice in favour of industrial noises and an illustrative musical score. In keeping with the filmmaker's commitment to leftist politics, this sound film experiment draws attention to both the rhythms of workers and their industrial machines.

Ivens expanded his engagement with industrial sounds in *Komsomol: Song of Heroes, Youth Speaks* (1933, 50 mins), commissioned by the Russian-German film studio Mezhrabpom-Film. Produced during the Five-Year Plan, the film documents a project where young communist league members (*Komsomol*) and workers set out on a difficult project to construct blast furnaces and towns in the remote Ural mountains. What is significant about the film's preparation as an audio-visual text is the director's close collaboration with German composer Hanns Eisler from the beginning of filming. During the shoot, Eisler acted as a 'musical reporter' by recording various industrial noises and folk songs on location.[27] The resulting soundtrack has a rhythmic arrangement of noises – drills, hammers, whistles, engines and explosions – in combination with occasional voices, post-synch sound effects and musical score.

While there is no formal spoken commentary in the film, intertitles at the beginning comment on newsreel images of communist youths under attack by police in German cities, with the dedication 'To you, Komsomol of the West, on the front lines of class struggle'. In addition, the background to the construction project is explained through an animated map, with voices with radio transmission quality from Moscow, Stalingrad and Lugarsk each explaining that metal and iron ore are needed across the Soviet Union. As before, radio is considered a crucial communications device and, in Ivens' view, this sequence raises questions that the remainder of the filmic action provides answers to.[28] Unlike Vertov's score for *Enthusiasm*, this soundtrack does not make use of the Internationale; however it does engage in similar sonic symbolism by establishing a break between rural past and industrial present. The first scene at the Ural Mountains, for instance, foregrounds a nomad playing a reed recorder, which is interrupted by loud explosions and a goods train passing by, with an intertitle emphasising that '300 million tonnes of high grade ore will be contributed to the Soviet construction'. As for Eisler's 'Ballad of Magnitogorsk' theme, recorded during post-production in Moscow, the exuberant lyrics and brass instrumentation stress the political imperative of the film; it features at the opening and triumphant closing of the film, as well as during a crucial scene where a young local shepherd registers for the project and later when the Komsomols positively evaluate their progress. While the film engages in occasional poetic montage sequences, its unambiguous use of song and political message seems to indicate Ivens' tenuous position as a non-Soviet director within the context of socialist realism production.

The previous examples reflect a desire to record real sounds drawn from the filmed environment, rather than use those that were staged or reenacted in a studio setting. In the context of British filmmaking, John Grierson also asserted the creative potential of documentary sound with microphone recording:

> [T]he microphone, like the camera, can do better things rather than merely reproduce, and that at the cutting bench and the re-recording bench as many new possibilities open out before sound film as once opened out before the cutting bench of silence. [...] The documentary film will do pioneer work for cinema if it emancipates the microphone from the studio and demonstrates at the cutting and re-recording benches how many more dramatic uses can be made of sound than the studios realise.[29]

Prior to 1934, Grierson had not devoted much attention to the advent of sound, with his silent documentaries usually receiving a soundtrack by their distributors. As the head of the GPO Film Unit from 1933 onwards, Grierson took a more proactive approach to sound, inviting the avant-garde filmmaker Alberto Cavalcanti to join the unit and instruct its members.[30] Within the institutional framework of the state-funded GPO Film Unit, there are several examples of experimentation with nonsynchronous uses of sound. *Pett and Pott: A Fairy Story in the Suburbs* (1934), for instance, is representative of Cavalcanti's contribution to the unit and the new possibilities enabled by mobile sound recording equipment from 1934.

Grierson attributed to film sound the potential for providing atmosphere or dramatic tension. However, he also noted a fundamental lack of semantic precision in sound and gave examples of engine noise or ship whistles that could produce unintended connotations or spatial signatures when detached from their origins. Building on this semantic mobility, Grierson gestures towards the importance of the poetic within documentary: '[R]ealist documentary, with its streets and cities and slums and markets and exchanges and factories, has given itself the job of making poetry where no poet has gone before it'.[31] In terms of sound aesthetics, Grierson ultimately settled on a concept of complementariness between the image and sound and a renewed commitment to narrative and dramatic structure, which he perceived as lacking in the experimental films of Vertov and Ruttmann.[32]

Cavalcanti, too, was eventually criticised by Grierson and several others for being too experimental and fantastical. As Charles Drazin points out, such criticisms were unjust, particularly since Cavalcanti's *Rien que les heures* (1926) was one of the first nonfiction films to give a portrait of urban life in Paris:

> Cavalcanti followed the social agenda of the Soviet film-makers in taking ordinary people as his subject-matter, but also emulated them in feeling free to move between a fictional and a documentary approach ... At the GPO, building on the tradition of the Soviet cinema, he sought to encourage a creative flexibility that saw no fundamental distinction between the two.[33]

These disputes attest to the ideological investment in the representation of urban sounds. As James Mansell has observed, modernity is depicted 'as a rhythmic force in GPO films, but GPO film-makers were at odds about British workers' relationship to the global dance of industrial capitalism'.[34] While noise was sometimes pursued as a source of creative energy, then, it appeared that Grierson preferred this noise to be subsumed or defused within a consistent audiovisual rhythm (or societal order).

Even following the establishment of the 'direct address' style in war-era documentaries, we can observe in Humphrey Jennings' film with Stewart McAllister *Listen to Britain* (1942, 18 mins) both the possibility for public instruction and poetic lyricism. The original treatment, entitled 'The Tin Hat Concerto', draws on the symphony motif; in this case across various sites in Britain from early evening to the following afternoon. Similar to the early city symphonies, the film depicts a range of scenes that are constituted as parts of a greater whole during wartime, bridging social stratifications (miners and factory workers to the Queen), geographical distance and musical taste (light, dance and functional tunes to Mozart and British music). Sound recordist Ken Cameron also emphasised this connection in a later account, arguing that the visuals were supplementary to sound in this 'symphonic conception of all the sounds heard in everyday wartime Britain'.[35] While the film has no intertitles or voice-over narration, it uses text and radio announcers to cue contextual information about time and place.

The opening scene sets up a contrast between farm crops blowing in the wind and the imposition of war, with planes heard overhead and military personnel monitoring the sky. This scene is overlaid with the beeping sounds of radio transmission and a BBC news intro, which form a bridge to urban scenes. In a subsequent scene, the sounds and image of Big Ben are used to symbolise London as a resilient centre of empire, with images of a control centre and a sound montage of 'London calling' in multiple languages to various world regions. Radio transmission is used here as a symbol for technological modernity, but also for the networked unity of nation, empire and the war effort. Elsewhere, radio narration occurs with an overlay of 'Calling all workers' by Eric Coates, presenter of the daytime programme *Music While You Work*. This popular music accompanies the sounds and images of factory machines with workers singing along, suggesting the possibility of cheerful music to rhythmically organise work production.

In the final scenes of the film, the climactic resolution of an orchestral lunchtime concert is drowned out by the increasing volume of industrial production as tanks come off the production lines. Whirring and banging industrial sounds are initially presented alone, before being interspersed with sequences depicting a military parade with marching band, tanks and cheering crowds. Finally, factory sounds and images are musicalised with the final flourish of a choir singing the patriotic lyrics to 'Rule Britannia!'. This lyric is repeated with the concluding images of the smoking chimneys of factory rooftops, the same farm crops blowing in the wind and images from a British plane looking down over the country.

While music has subsequently been eschewed by many documentary practitioners, John Corner affirms its potential in *Listen to Britain* for 'providing us with the time to look properly, giving us a framework in which to gaze and to think'.[36] Jennings and McAllister demonstrate the reassuring qualities of musical and broadcast sound during wartime, by showing how the activities of listening, playing and singing along to music could reinforce resolve and collectivity. Disturbing sounds like sirens and explosions are absent, with the potential disturbance of plane engines reincorporated within the sound design as a reassuring sign of air force protection. Industrial noises are featured, but are soon overlaid by or incorporated into musical sound and are thus positioned as a central device for narrative commentary.

Comparison of the working practices of Vertov, Ivens and Grierson's GPO Film Unit clearly reveals the points of debate underlying the emergent practice of documentary sound design, particularly for those filmmakers seeking to achieve a symphonic staging of the real. The oppositions identified in the analyses above – particularly between outdoor and studio recording; and synchronous and montage editing – reflected political agendas bound up with cinematic representations of the urban as a metaphor for the social. To some extent, the experimental explorations into documentary sound were relatively short-lived, as they were supplanted by direct-address style with 'voice of God' commentary in Europe and North America from the mid-1930s onwards, a trend that can be seen in films such as *Housing Problems* (Arthur Elton/ E.H. Anstey, 1935), *The River* (Pare Lorentz, 1937) and, after 1939, wartime propaganda films like Frank Capra's *Why We Fight* (1942–1945). As Bill Nichols explains, 'collage, sound, and documentary became tamed, placed at the service of sponsors'.[37] In other words, industrial film commissions were sometimes seen as offering a viable space for experiments, as in the case of Ivens, whereas state-sponsored filmmaking was increasingly governed by restrictions and censorship. Against the backdrop of this shift, the following analysis will return to the urban as a key site for investigations of documentary sound and its saliency as a metaphor for society and social power. I will examine the work of Ruttmann as an illustrative case for the (often ambivalent) treatment of documentary sound and urban subject matter across the late 1920s and 1930s.

Urban Sound in Ruttmann's City Films

Ruttmann's *Sinfonie der Großstadt* was conceived as a formal study of temporal rhythms in the urban metropolis, from early morning until late evening. Its 'symphonic' structure conforms to London's outline by organising the day into five main temporal rhythms, or sections. The various rhythms of the day reflect Ruttmann's conviction that modernity is a break with the past and speeds up temporality, most notably through media technologies and the rapid dissemination of information. The modern metropolis, in turn, is constructed in the film as an unfolding series of present moments, which are positioned in relation to both cyclical routines and the linearity of industrial work time, cued in the film via several shots of clock faces in public and work settings. The natural rhythms of the sunrise to sunset structure suggest some respite from the rhythms of technological modernity; in fact, maintaining both elements has been read as evidence of an unresolved tension and 'intense ambivalence about modernity' in the Berlin film.[38]

While often classified as a silent film, Ruttmann worked closely with composer Edmund Meisel during production, conceiving the film as a collaborative experiment in depicting the polyphony of urban rhythms. The extent of the collaboration is demonstrated by Ruttmann's (re)editing of certain sequences according to musical principles in order to fit with the five-act structure and musical intensity of the score. Meisel's film-specific composition (*Geräuschmusik*) for a full orchestra and (futurist-style) sound effect machines has since been lost; instead, a rediscovered version for two pianos plus assorted percussion is the basis for present-day reconstructions. While the image track often alludes to the imagined sounds of urban life (organ grinders, newsboys, traffic police, skirmishes and demonstrations), the musical score also includes humouristic references or commentary on the onscreen action (figure 1.2). One illustration is the muted trumpet 'wah wah' effect that is used when a cinema screen reveals a close up of Charlie Chaplin's shuffling feet; combinations of symphonic music with dissonant sequences are also used to distinguish between bourgeois entertainment culture and the destitute on the margins of the city.

Figure 1.2 A Berlin newspaper seller is imagined calling out to potential customers. Still from *Berlin: Sinfonie der Großstadt* (Walther Ruttmann, 1927).

In preparation for the film, which would address 'the city dwellers and their environment', Meisel actively listened to the noisy sounds of the city and sought to feed this experience into the musical score.[39] Some of these noises included tram bells, car horns, night-time track work and factory sounds, which were approximated with instruments (horns, tubas, cymbals) as well as anvils, iron rods, metal sheets and car horns. The use of recognisable sound effects and patterns, then, was designed to prompt the audience's acoustic recognition of their own urban experience. In fact, Meisel requested that these sounds be heightened during screenings: 'In the moments when a total impression is absolutely necessary, parts of the orchestra will be positioned around the auditorium'.[40] This use of surround sound in the cinema precisely suggests the staging of the multidirectional urban soundscape.

Meisel's concept, moreover, contributed to Ruttmann's creative rendering of daily life in the city, which was produced just prior to the reorganisation of cinema spaces with 'wired' sound. During the first two decades of film exhibition, as Ian Macpherson points out, cinemas coexisted with the noisy public spaces of modern urban life.[41] The rise of large cinema palaces in the 1920s and the introduction of synchronised sound were part of the process by which the cinema was cordoned off from the soundscape around it. The notion of both the sound recording studio and cinema as cut off from the social environment – as 'tombs' or 'coffins' – is precisely the condition to which Vertov reacted in the production of *Enthusiasm*. Meisel's employment of noise instruments and a surround-sound orchestra in this context might also be seen in terms of difficulties in amplification within these large cinemas prior to the introduction of loudspeaker systems in the late 1920s.

Before collaborating with Ruttmann, Meisel had worked with key proponents of montage and counterpoint, including Eisenstein. The tradition of audiovisual counterpoint, as Caryl Flinn has remarked, 'upholds that music should be used in contrast to the image and should try to dispel any illusion of unity. In so doing, music would then expose – and exploit – cinema's basic heterogeneity, not conceal or deny it as under parallelism'.[42] Despite their opposition to audiovisual parallelism, advocates of counterpoint, such as Eisenstein and Eisler, still endorsed a concept of cinematic rhythm based on certain correspondences between visuals and composed score.[43] Eisler opposed film music that was 'a mere duplication, ineffective and uneconomical': yet he did concede that image and sound, 'however indirectly or even antithetically, must correspond to each other'.[44] Correspondingly, Meisel's score for *Sinfonie der Großstadt* was not completely contrapuntal, since he also operated on the principle that the melody should be motivated by the film's narrative content.[45] Although the musical score did not play a completely independent role, however, it still represented an important contribution to the intensification of movement and rhythm in order to reflect Meisel's attempt to evoke the atmosphere of urban soundscapes.

As pointed out above, there was considerable suspicion about the threats posed by synchronised sound film around 1927, particularly amongst filmmakers pursuing a 'pure' visual language. Ruttmann, however, clearly asserted the creative potential of sound film in his 1928 article 'Kopfnotiz über den Funk-Tonfilm'. Following recent technological developments, he argued, the most pressing issue at hand was how to create an 'aesthetic of the sound film'. The director stressed that sound film had the ability to stage an interaction between listening and viewing in cinema through a process of 'optical-acoustic counterpoint, by playing visible and audible movements against each other'. Ruttmann's article, moreover, invoked a radiophonic model when discussing the 'Funk-Tonfilm' (radio-sound film), a connection which had already been drawn by Vertov in his film writings and practice in the 1920s.[46]

Ruttmann's comments on the exchange between radio and film were made shortly before the premiere of his film experiment, Deutscher Rundfunk (1928), which was promoted both as a sound film (Tonfilm) and a radio play (Hörspiel). This advertising film, commissioned by the Reichs-Rundfunk-Gesellschaft and Tri-Ergon Musik, was presented at the annual German Radio Exhibition in August 1928.[47] During its production, in July 1928, Germany's radio stations were visited by cameramen, who filmed radio broadcasts, city streets and industrial workplaces. Meisel was proposed as the composer for the project and collaborated with Ruttmann to create a blend of field recordings, composed music and sound effects.[48] While both commented on their interest in counterpoint for this project, the archival evidence suggests that this work did not have a contrapuntal organisation, since its purpose was to demonstrate the novelty of synchronised sounds and image. Nonetheless, the film, which is no longer available, highlighted the exchange between radio and film media and their respective industries in the transition period. It adopted the repeated motif of 'Achtung, achtung' to emphasise Berlin as the centre of a broadcasting network, for instance, the epicentre from which radio sound waves emanated and reached out to German and international listeners via the Deutsche Welle station.[49]

The spatial dimensions of sound were explored, to some degree, by Ruttmann's subsequent commission, the first German feature-length sound film, Melodie der Welt (1929), although only a few uses of original location recording were possible in its compilation of scenes from around the world.[50] Following Deutscher Rundfunk and Melodie der Welt, Ruttmann worked on another commission – Weekend (1930) – for the Reichs-Rundfunk-Gesellschaft, Berlin Funkstunde and Triergon Musik AG. Weekend used sound-on-film techniques to create a sonic narrative of weekend routines, doubling as a radio play and a 'blind' film presented in a darkened cinema space. The piece loosely follows a couple as they enjoy a Sunday outing before returning to work on Monday morning. Ruttmann's attempt to create a sound-based narrative allows for a dramatisation of the ubiquitous aspects of daily soundscape, such as footsteps, conversations and whistling, along with the sounds of cash registers, street bands, streetcars and birds. Weekend has sometimes been described in terms of the aestheticisation of urban noise and its organisation within a narrative rhythm, as an experiment to provide a soundtrack that would correspond to Ruttmann's 1927 Berlin film.

With this in mind, I will conclude with the example of Ruttmann's commissioned city film, Kleiner Film einer großen Stadt ... der Stadt Düsseldorf am Rhein (1935), which has a score by composer Wolfgang Zeller. The production of this film in the context of National Socialist rule after 1933 invites consideration

of the extent to which Ruttmann's earlier interest in (documentary) sound aesthetics and rhythmic plurality were reoriented in this period.

When interviewed in 1935, Ruttmann described the film as a 'symphonic
impression of Düsseldorf'. Later in the same interview, the director reinforces
his own role in mediating the essence of the city, noting that:

> For me Düsseldorf is a special concept: a concept that I have viewed,
> palpably sensed, compiled, experienced. I have [created] a special urban
> perspective of this city [....] In this film, Düsseldorf speaks for itself.[51]

Even though Ruttmann emphasises the rhythmic composition of the film narrative, his statement implies that the visual and auditory composition would
synthesise various aspects of Düsseldorf into a 'total' rhythmic concept.

Thus, even though Ruttmann here invokes the symphony metaphor again,
his work is primarily understood (or at least discussed) in visual terms: the filmmaker is praised for his eye and for visually mediating the rhythm and experience of the city for the audience. Ruttmann, however, continued to stress that
Düsseldorf would 'speak' for itself via an integrated audiovisual rhythm.

Closer examination of the musical score by Zeller indicates two main
themes. The first is a light string and wind instrumentation, often offset by
harp and other string glissandos, which is usually used for idyllic scenes such as
flower fields, the Rhine and the parks, gardens and lakes of the city. The second
theme is a melodic brass line with upward rising tuba notes, which is used to
cue signs of industrial modernity, such as steamships, modern train stations and
high-rises and a short sequence foregrounding the repetitive movements of factory machinery and an iron foundry. Other minor themes include brass marching music, used twice for images of carnival parades and street processions,
and a solemn brass instrumentation deployed for one scene that foregrounds a
chronological narrative of Düsseldorf's 'great men' by scanning over images of
gravestones and busts.

Only two short sequences make use of diegetic sound during the opening
and closing scenes, featuring carnival and St Martin's Day respectively. In the
opening sequence, the diegetic voice of a carnival washtub speaker proclaims
that the crowds should be merry. The viewer is then placed amongst the gathered Düsseldorfers, providing a point-of-view from within the ritual expression of community. However, we do not hear the noisy cheers of the carnival
crowds. Instead, the newsreel-style sequences are accompanied by light instrumental music. Despite the absence of diegetic sound in many other scenes, the
film immediately recuperates any sense of alienation by emphasising the city as
a communal space. The final scene of the film follows a visual transition between
bright liquid iron ore, a montage of bright advertising signs for large Düsseldorf businesses and a superimposition onto paper lanterns, which cues in the
St Martin's Day children's procession. The diegetic sounds of children singing are
heard first, before groups with lanterns are seen walking through the city under
the supervision of police and adults. Unlike the frantic nightlife scenes and jazz

music in the final act of the Berlin film, here, diegetic sound contributes to a sentimental understanding of the city at night. The film concludes with a brass fanfare flourish as the children wait for a gift of sweets from the city's mayor, who is positioned as a benevolent authority figure and representative guardian of the city.

Given Ruttmann's active interest in the possibilities of sound montage and counterpoint in representing the urban during the 1920s, his symphony principle was partially revised during National Socialism. While his earlier work sometimes tended towards an aestheticised urban, there was nonetheless a concerted effort to incorporate a range of tonalities derived from the everyday city soundscape. In contrast to the contrapuntal effects of *Sinfonie der Großstadt*, Ruttmann's film about Düsseldorf only uses instrumental music as *Untermalung* (illustration). In other words, music takes on a supportive or 'connective' (*verbindende*) function, as one reviewer described Werner Schütze's score.[52] This 'connective' function implies that music should not complicate or interfere with the visual narrative organisation: instead, it should allow the image track to assert a direct experience of the city. This marks a difference from the use of music and sound in *Sinfonie der Großstadt* to foreground the modern experience of fragmentation, distraction, sensorial stimulation and modern subjectivity.

Kleiner Film still shares certain trademarks with Ruttmann's earlier style in that it alludes to the micro and macro rhythms constituted by everyday life and major events in the city. Each vignette presents a different path of movement or theme of activity in the city, and the film interweaves various temporal and spatial planes. The narrative is temporally framed by events across a whole year: it begins with the carnival season opening around January and spans to St Martin's Day in November. These traditional customs, repeated each year, suggest both a cyclical rhythm and a sense of permanence under Nazism. Yet there are no asynchronous rhythms to disrupt this portrayal of Düsseldorf, such as the street disturbances and social divides alluded to in *Sinfonie der Großstadt*. Working within the institutional framework of the part-government owned UFA (Universum Film AG: cultural and advertising section), Ruttmann's 1930s films thus offer insight into how aspects of avant-garde film aesthetics were reworked into film production under National Socialism. Derek Hillard, for instance, notes that Ruttmann appropriated scenes from *Sinfonie der Großstadt* for his later film *Blut und Boden* (1933). According to him, a sequence from the earlier film about the theme of money:

> displays the anxieties that persist in an urban setting without visually resolving them. *Blut und Boden* uses this very same footage to construct modernity and the big city as a space of decadence, economic ruin, and the potential threat that unchecked urbanity and racial downfall pose for the German people.[53]

In other words, Ruttmann's film – made at the outset of the Third Reich – reorients an earlier ambivalence about the modern metropolis in order to reflect National Socialist anti-urban discourse.[54] By 1935, when Ruttmann began a series of city films about Stuttgart and Düsseldorf, there was a general move to reinvest the city under National Socialism as a unified, conflict-free space, also evidenced by the role of sound as merely supportive in suppressing the earlier tensions within documentary sound practice.

Indeed, the stress on narrative congruity implies that there should be no ambiguity in the presentation of the city. The reluctance to reveal ambivalence or anxiety about the city is reflected in the fact that *Sinfonie der Großstadt* was rarely shown after 1933. Film critics in the 1940s noted that Ruttmann's Berlin film had 'no plot' (*keine Spielhandlung*). While this same phrase had been employed as a positive attribute in the film's promotional material in 1927, the supposed lack of a clear plot and intertitles was a cause for criticism during the National Socialist era.[55] Nonetheless, the filmmaker continued to draw on his earlier symphony concept, which foregrounded audiovisual rhythm. The resulting tension that emerges in Ruttmann's Düsseldorf film is one between visual movement and stasis. On the one hand, the status of *Kleiner Film* as (tourist) promotion required the camera to linger long enough to allow the city's architectural, historical and cultural icons to be visually registered. On the other hand, Ruttmann maintained certain characteristics of his earlier visual transitions and fluid camerawork, which is suggestive of the argument that National Socialism sought to assimilate the avant-garde project of a visual cinematic language.[56]

Set against broader developments of the late 1920s and 1930s, the shift in Ruttmann's documentary sound practice is consistent with the trend towards a state-sponsored documentary style across Europe and North America, resulting in films identified by Nichols that encourage ritual participation:

> Like newspapers and radio before it, cinema contributed a powerful rhetorical voice to the needs of the modern state. The modern state had to find ways to enact popular, compelling representations of the state's policies and programs. Such enactments engage its members in ritual, participatory acts of citizenship. Documentary film practice became one such form of ritual participation.[57]

As a product of (local) government-sponsored advertising, *Kleiner Film* tried to offer something for everyone, particularly for potential tourists. Yet the overall emphasis of the film is on a coherent synthesis of the city's rhythm or essence, based on historical continuity, spatial control and a unified community (*Volk*). My discussion has drawn on Ruttmann to show the ways in which experimental uses of documentary sound for meditations on the modern metropolis were reworked according to ideological projections onto the city as a site of historical tradition, social harmony and tourist promotion. Ruttmann's use of music as illustration reflects the prevailing aesthetic of a commentative score where industrial sounds are alluded to but no longer incorporated into poetic experiments in montage. The status of sound as supportive illustration, in this case, is underpinned by the idea that neither music nor voice-over should complicate or interfere with the visual narrative organisation.

Notes

1 Philip Rosen, 'Document and Documentary: On the Persistence of Historical Concepts', in *Theorizing Documentary*, ed. Michael Renov (New York: Routledge, 1993), 58–89.
2 Guntram Vogt, *Die Stadt im Kino: Deutsche Spielfilme, 1900–2000* (Marburg: Schüren, 2001).
3 Kurt London, *Film Music* (London: Faber, 1936), 71–72.
4 Douglas Kahn, *Noise, Water, Meat: A History of Sound in the Arts* (Cambridge and London: MIT Press, 1999), 98, 123–156.
5 Keith Beattie, *Documentary Display: Re-Viewing Nonfiction Film and Video* (London: Wallflower, 2008), 9–31.
6 Bill Nichols, *Introduction to Documentary* (Bloomington: University of Indiana Press, 2001), 39.
7 See, for instance, Manfred Hattendorf, *Dokumentarfilm und Authentizität: Ästhetik und Pragmatik einer Gattung* (Konstanz: UVK, 1999); Jeffrey Ruoff, 'Conventions of Sound in Documentary', in *Cinema Journal*, 32:3 (1993), 24–40; John Corner, 'Sounds Real: Music and Documentary', in *Popular Music*, 21:3 (2002), 357–366.
8 For a recent comparative account of urban soundscape representation in feature film in the 1930s, 1950s and 1970s, see Jasper Aalbers, 'Echoes of the City: Staging the Urban Soundscape in Fiction Film' (Unpublished PhD Thesis: University of Maastricht, 2013).
9 An earlier version of this essay was published as 'Die Orchestrierung urbaner Akustik: dokumentarische Form, akustische Medien und die Modern Stadt', in *Ton: Texte zur Akustik im Dokumentarfilm*, ed. Volko Kamensky and Julian Rohrhuber (Berlin: Vorwerk 8, 2013), 76–97. This work expands on my initial reflections on Ruttmann's oeuvre in *Nazi Soundscapes: Sound, Technology and Urban Space in Germany, 1933–1945* (Amsterdam: Amsterdam University Press, 2012).
10 Michael Chanan, *The Politics of Documentary* (London: BFI, 2007), 116, 125.
11 Kahn, 'Introduction: Histories of Sound Once Removed', in *Wireless Imagination: Sound, Radio, and the Avant-Garde*, ed. Kahn and Gregory Whitehead (Cambridge and London: MIT Press, 1994), 1–29; Erika Brady, *A Spiral Way: How the Phonograph Changed Ethnography* (Jackson, MS: University Press of Mississippi, 1999).
12 Soviet composer Konstantin Listov is sometimes credited as having written the original score for Vertov's film, but no information is available on this score, which is presumed to be lost.
13 See Vertov, 'Kinopravda' i 'Radiopravda' (1925), cited in Vlada Petric, 'Dziga Vertov as Theorist', in *Cinema Journal*, 18:1 (1978), 32.
14 Vertov, 'The Man with a Movie Camera (A Visual Symphony)' (19 March 1928), reprinted in *Kino-Eye: The Writings of Dziga Vertov*, ed. Annette Michelson, trans. Kevin O'Brien (Berkeley: University of California Press, 1984), 283–289.
15 In Vertov's 1929 critique of the Berlin press, he stressed the influence of Soviet montage on German filmmakers working in abstract film, which included Hans Richter and Ruttmann. Indeed, Ruttmann's decision to abandon abstract films has been credited to his viewing of surrealist works by René Claire and Ferdinand Léger that deployed real photographic imagery, as well as the impact of Eisenstein's montage in *Battleship Potemkin* (1925). See Vertov, 'Letter from Berlin' (1929), reprinted in Michelson, *Kino-Eye*, 101–102.
16 Ibid.
17 The Russian sound-on-film systems were developed by Pavel Tager (Moscow) and Alexander Shorin (St. Petersburg).
18 See reprint in *Close Up, 1927–1933: Cinema and Modernism*, ed. James Donald, Anne Friedberg and Laura Marcus (Princeton, NJ: Princeton University Press, 1998), 83–84.
19 Lucy Fischer, '*Enthusiasm*: From Kino-Eye to Radio-Eye', in *Film Quarterly*, 31:2 (1977/1978), 27, 32.

20 See Ippolit Sokolov, 'The Possibilities of Sound Cinema', in Kino 45 (1929), cited in Michelson, Kino-Eye, 112–113.
21 Vertov, 'Let's Discuss Ukrainfilm's First Sound Film: Symphony of the Donbas' (The Author on his Film), reprinted from the newspaper Sovetskoe iskusstvo (Soviet Art), February 27, 1931, cited in ibid., 111.
22 For the growing attacks on the Ukrainian VUFKU film studio during the late 1920s and its reorganisation as Ukrainfilm (as a branch of the centrally-organised Soiuz-kino), see Bohdan Y. Nebesio, 'Competition from Ukraine: VUFKU and the Soviet Film Industry in the 1920s', in Historical Journal of Film, Radio and Television, 29:2 (2009), 159–180.
23 Oksana Bulgakowa, 'The Ear Against the Eye: Vertov's Symphony', in Monatshefte, 98:2 (2006), 234.
24 See review by D. Rfailovich (26 April 1930), quoted in ibid., 223.
25 Vertov, 'Let's Discuss Ukrainfilm's First Sound Film', cited in Kino Eye, 106.
26 'For thirty metres of film', in De Telegraaf (25 December 1930), cited in Karel Dibbets, 'High-Tech Avant-garde: Philips Radio', in Joris Ivens and the Documentary Context, ed. Kees Bakker (Amsterdam: Amsterdam University Press, 1999), 77.
27 Eisler, 'Hochofenmusik', manuscript quoted in Claude Brunel, 'Music and Soundtrack in Joris Ivens's Films', in ibid., 200.
28 Ivens, 'On the Method of the Documentary Film – in Particular the Film Komsomol (1932)', in ibid., 233.
29 Grierson, 'The Creative Use of Sound' (1934), reprinted in Grierson on Documentary, ed. Forsyth Hardy (London: Faber and Faber 1966), 158, 163. For more on the development of documentary sound techniques within 1920s radio, see my own essay, 'Sonic Artefacts: Reality Codes of Urbanity in Early German Radio Documentary', in Soundscapes of the Urban Past, ed. Karin Bijsterveld (Bielefeld: Transcript Verlag, 2913a), 129–168.
30 For a more detailed account of Cavalcanti's participation in British documentary, see The Projection of Britain: A History of the GPO Film Unit, ed. Scott Anthony and James G. Mansell (London: BFI, 2011).
31 Quoted in Corner, The Art of Record: A Critical Introduction to Documentary (Manchester: Manchester University Press, 1996), 13.
32 Grierson, 'The Creative Use of Sound', 159.
33 Charles Drazin, 'Alberto Cavalcanti: Lessons in Fusion at the GPO Film Unit', in The Projection of Britain, 47.
34 Mansell, 'Rhythm, Modernity and the Politics of Sound', in ibid., 162.
35 Ken Cameron, Sound and the Documentary Film (London: Isaac Pitman, 1947), 42.
36 Corner, 'Sounds Real', 365.
37 Nichols, 'Documentary and the Coming of Sound', in Documentary Box (1995), at http://www.yidff.jp/docbox/6/box6-1-e.html (accessed December 10, 2013).
38 See, for example, Derek Hillard, 'Walter Ruttmann's Janus-faced View of Modernity: The Ambivalence of Description in Berlin. Die Sinfonie der Großstadt', in Monatshefte, 96:1 (2004), 91–92.
39 See, for instance, Edmund Meisel, 'Wie schreibt man Filmmusik?', in Licht-Bild-Bühne (July 4), 1927; Meisel, 'Edmund Meisel über seine BERLIN-Musik', in Film-Kurier (September 20), 1927.
40 'Für die Momente, in denen der Totalitätseindruck unbedingt erforderlich ist, werden Teile des Orchesters in den Zuschauerraum postiert' (Meisel (1927b).
41 Ian Macpherson, 'The Electric Ear: Early Film Sound Technology and Acoustic Spaces – From a Box of Insects to a Tomb of Make-Believe', in The New Soundtrack, 1:1 (2011), 39.
42 Flinn, Strains of Utopia: Gender, Nostalgia, and Hollywood Film Music (Princeton: Princeton University Press 1992), 46–47.

43 For the specific differences between Eisenstein and Eisler's understanding of image-sound relations, and for a reorientation in the definition of counterpoint, see Nicholas Cook, *Analysing Musical Multimedia* (Oxford: Clarendon, 1998), 57–65, 113–121.

44 Theodor W. Adorno and Eisler, *Composing for Films* (London: Athlone, 1994), 3, 47.

45 Adrianus van Domburg, *Walter Ruttmann en het beginsel* (Purmerend: Muusses, 1956), 52.

46 Ruttmann, 'Kopfnotiz über den Funk-Tonfilm', in *Film-Kurier* (August 11, 1928).

47 For the significant exchange between the film, music and electroacoustic industries in the sound transition years, with the concentration of patent ownership by the Tobis conglomerate, see Wolfgang Mühl-Benninghaus, *Das Ringen um den Tonfilm: Strategien der Elektro- und der Filmindustrie in den 20er und 30er Jahren* (Düsseldorf: Droste, 1999), 81–205.

48 For the production context and critical reception of *Deutscher Rundfunk*, see Fiona Ford, 'The Film Music of Edmund Meisel (1894–1930)', (Unpublished PhD thesis: University of Nottingham, 2011), 219–223.

49 The script is reprinted in the censorship report no. 19946, Berlin Film-Prüfstelle, 30 August 1928.

50 For an elaboration on the imagination of global sounds in this film, which are positioned within the frame of a travel film, see Birdsall, 'Sound Aesthetics and the Global Imagination in German Media Culture around 1930', in *Sounds of Modern History: Auditory Cultures in 19th and 20th Century Europe*, ed. Daniel Morat (New York: Berghahn, 2014), 256-277.

51 Ruttmann, 'Kleiner Film einer großen Stadt: Ein Gespräch mit Walter Ruttmann', in *Film-Kurier* (August 28, 1935).

52 Reviewer quoted in 'Weltaufführung in Düsseldorf: Kleiner Film einer grossen Stadt', in *Film-Kurier* (November 19, 1935).

53 Hillard, 'Walter Ruttmann's Janus-faced View of Modernity', 92.

54 It should be noted that this very ambivalence was one of the causes for criticism of *Sinfonie der Großstadt*. Grierson, for instance, writing in the 1930s, argued that the city symphony films were potentially politically dangerous. This reflects Grierson's social utilitarian model for 'documentary', with voice-over increasingly attributed a key role in educating the audience. See Grierson, 'The Symphony Film I', in *Cinema Quarterly* (1933), 138, reprinted in *Grierson on Documentary*, 157–63.

55 'Rhythmus der Grossstadt: Zu Liebeneiners Berlin-Film' (August 18, 1942), quoted in Vogt, *Die Stadt im Kino*, 362; 'Berlin. Die Sinfonie der Großstadt', Special Issue of *Illustrierter Film-Kurier* (1927), 658.

56 The partial continuation of the earlier 'New Objectivity' style has led to suggestions that filmmakers like Ruttmann and Riefenstahl participated in a revised modernism or 'Nazi Sachlichkeit.' See Brigitte Peuckert, *The Material Image: Art and the Real in Film* (Stanford: Stanford University Press, 2007), 49; Barry A. Fulks, 'Walter Ruttmann, The Avant-Garde Film, and Nazi Modernism', in *Film and History*, 14:2 (1984), 26–46.

57 Nichols, 'Documentary Film and the Modernist Avant-Garde', in *Critical Inquiry*, 27:4 (2001), 604.

Chapter 2

Sounding the World
The Role of Music and Sound in Early 'Talking' Newsreels

James Deaville

> The newsreel brings to a modern world a truer picture of itself, and of its
> people, than any other agency heretofore known to mankind.
>
> Stephen T. Early, Press Secretary to Franklin Delano Roosevelt[1]

With his 'News on the March' segment from the beginning of *Citizen Kane*
(1941), Orson Welles may have satirised the highly successful *The March of Time*
broadcast news series, which appeared first on radio (beginning in 1931) and
then in theatrical newsreel format (beginning in 1935), yet he arguably also paid
homage to the newsreel programme as a media format. As Jonathan Stuart Setliff
postulates, 'in order to structure the newsreel account of Kane's life, career and
death ... Welles imitates the form and structure of the most prominent newsreel
of the day'.[2] The director used the same type of logo and lettering, the same narration and the same style of non-stop, highly descriptive orchestral music.

Despite Welles' recognition of the importance of the newsreel for American
culture of his time – indeed, it was instrumental in promoting the war effort
during the Second World War – little research has been undertaken into the
historical role and significance of the cinematic medium. One monograph study
exists, *The American Newsreel: A Complete History, 1911–1967* by Raymond
Fielding, which, although exceptionally thorough in its command of primary
sources and documentation, harbours biases that skew the coverage.[3] Fielding
regards the introduction of sound to the newsreel as an impoverishment of the
medium, so he devotes only ten pages to the conversion and proportionately
little space to the newsreel after that development, despite its tenacity well
into the era of television news reporting. Other literature has documented the
newsreel's function in specific political contexts, in particular during World
War II, yet none has managed to extend Fielding's comprehensive approach.[4]

The importance and popularity of the newsreel certainly belie its scholarly
neglect. As Fielding observes:

> By the mid-1920s ... between 85 and 90 per cent of the eighteen thousand
> theaters in the United States exhibited one of the six newsreels then avail-
> able to a weekly audience numbering in excess of forty million people.

By 1946 the *Fox International Movietone Newsreel* was regularly exhibited in forty-seven foreign countries and in more than a dozen languages. At that time its worldwide audience was estimated at a staggering two hundred million a week.[5]

If the disciplines of film, media and communication studies have neglected the newsreel, musicological research and film music studies have yet to find it in any serious manner. Here, again, the researcher encounters a scattering of essays that look at the propagandistic practices of wartime newsreels, drawing upon their musical components, as well as studies of historical musical performances that are documented by newsreels.[6] Neil Lerner's PhD thesis about scores for documentary films from 1936 to 1945, for instance, includes a section about the history and types of music used to accompany newsreel of the silent era, but does not trace its development into the sound era, independent from documentary film.[7] And yet it was during the early sound era that the newsreel unleashed the music and sounds of the world upon theatre-goers, creating an experience as if, as one commentator remarked, 'you weren't sitting in a theatre at all.'[8]

Arguably, the defining moment for the sound newsreel was the interview with Charles Lindbergh on May 20, 1927, on the eve of his departure for France.[9] The tremendous popularity of this early talking news item helped establish the importance and secure the success of the new sound technology. The speaking Lindbergh has become iconic in the diverse studies of film's conversion to sound format, not least because it predates the release of *The Jazz Singer* (1927), and its popularity – in combination with the enormity of Lindbergh's achievement – reflects the public's willingness and even eagerness to embrace sound-on-film technology.

Contra Fielding, I would argue that the sound component represents a deepening and broadening enhancement of the theatrical newsreel experience, as commentators of the day observed and theatrical statistics testify. That producers of the early sound newsreels would fetishise those markers of its progress – diegetic sound and music – stands to reason, considering the novelty and popularity of the new sound-on-film technology. What is surprising, however, is just how much of the newsreel soundscape was taken up by music in performance, which vied with the speaking voice and diegetic sounds, such as crowd and street noises, for the public's attention.

This essay cannot hope to engage in a comprehensive study of music in the sound newsreel, but it can provide an introduction to the topic and present an idea of what Americans were seeing and hearing about the world and its musical practices for the first time during the late 1920s. This was a crucial time for the newsreel, since the emergent sound-on-film technologies would shape the cinematic experience of the news for the next forty years. The following study will focus on the Fox Movietone newsreels, which, due to their pioneering adoption of sound technologies to the newsreel, led the field during the first years of sound (1927–1929).

Early History

The newsreel itself dates back to before the First World War. Even though 'actualities' and news films could be viewed already in the 1890s – after all, the Lumière Brothers' films presented the events, people and technologies of the day – Fielding sets 1911 as the terminus post quem for the newsreel. The format that existed until its ultimate demise in the United States in 1967 – British Movietone News released newsreels until 1979 – involved multiple news and entertainment stories brought together into a program of about 10 minutes total and shown on a weekly or biweekly basis. In regular cinemas, they were placed before feature films, but there also existed newsreel theatres where audiences could quickly catch up with the news of the day.

The leading newsreel production companies during the silent era in the United States included Pathé (with French, British and American versions), Hearst, Universal and Fox (the latter with the silent Fox News Service beginning in 1919). Film exhibitors had a choice of providers, with a competition between six production companies in 1928, each company able to support about 100 cameramen across the globe in the race to provide the most current product of sights and sounds.[10] Writing in 1933, Howard T. Lewis described what he termed the 'intense competition' in the newsreel market, with a result that 'some theaters purchase more than one newsreel service and edit them by making up a composite newsreel ... of their own'.[11]

The typical silent newsreel featured a mix of 'hard' news and entertainment. The absence of accompanying sound meant that the emphasis was on visually alluring, self-explanatory stories, which placed a narrative burden on the accompanying music in the theatre (and there were cues specifically written for news stories). The photoplay anthologies that provided music for the silent films in the theatres were also put to use for the newsreels: Fielding cites Volume 2 of the *Sam Fox Moving Picture Music Catalogue* of 1914 as featuring composition subjects that found their way onto motion picture screens in the newsreels of that day:

Part 1—European Army Maneuvers
Part 2—Funeral March
Part 3—Paris Fashions
Part 4—Aeroplane or Regatta Races ...[12]

Samuel L. 'Roxy' Rothapfel, manager of a number of leading movie palaces during the 1920s, took special care over the music for his newsreel presentations:

For the Topical Special, or as it is best known, the "Weekly," we play absolutely according to the scenes used, the national airs of different countries and little bits of marches and waltzes that will fit the scene ... We pay a good deal of attention to this portion of our program and I attribute the wonderful successes of our Topical Review to the musical accompaniment.[13]

Standard film-music literature from the early 1920s likewise devotes space to music for the newsreel. As Lerner notes, both George Benyon's *Musical Presentation of Motion Pictures* (1921) and Ernö Rapée's *Encyclopedia of Music for Pictures* (1925) include discussion of appropriate musical cues for newsreels. These authors both suggested that, while normal principles for photoplay music apply to the news, the style there should differentiate itself from that for narrative film. Thus Benyon concerned himself with maintaining a certain dignity in the music selected to accompany 'the real', whereas Rapée addressed the issue of decorum specifically with regard to the overuse of marches and the careful selection of patriotic tunes for Presidential representations.[14]

This concern with music exponentially increased in the years after 1926, as the newsreel entered the sound era. The so-called Vitaphone Shorts, dating from 1926 to 1931, illustrate the ways in which music was fetishised in the drive to demonstrate and exploit the new technologies.[15] Neither newsreels nor examples of sound-on-film technology (the Warner Brothers Vitaphone sound system relied on the synchronisation of a phonograph recording to a projector), the shorts nevertheless did present the cinematic audience with the types of speaking, singing and playing subjects that were so prevalent in the earliest 'talking' newsreels. The first short features (1927) ranged in subject from pianist Harold Bauer playing Chopin to banjo player Rex Schepp and the black gospel group Utica Jubilee Singers, with over 1000 short films released through 1931. While the sound newsreels would also strongly favour musical performances, they were customarily heavily edited and reduced in length – in contrast, the Vitaphone Shorts presented full performances as allowed by the technology.

In terms of a competing sound technology, inventors Theodore Case and Eric Sponable (with the aid of radio and film pioneer Lee de Forest) had been collaborating since 1922 on perfecting a sound-on-film system, which William Fox purchased on July 23, 1926 and which led him to create the Fox Movietone Corporation in that same year.[16] The silent Fox News Service became Fox Movietone News, and with the Lindbergh footage in 1927, the era of the sound newsreel was essentially launched. The tremendous success of the Lindbergh coverage, which featured a single pan shot of the take-off with sounds of the crowd and plane, ensured the preeminence of the company that also presented the return ceremonies on July 12 of that year, in a talking newsreel of 10 minutes. The speeches of President Coolidge and Lindbergh had an electrifying impact upon theatrical audiences, drawing 'praise from audiences and exhibitors alike'.[17] According to one contemporary commentator, 'at various high points of the Coolidge address and the Lindbergh reply, the applause of the audience was so terrific that the reproduction of the sound was drowned'.[18] Fielding assesses this newsreel's powerful impact as the result of its 'presence, immediacy, and an obviously unmanipulated reality'.[19]

The date of the 'first' sound newsreel is the subject of debate: on April 30, 1927, the Roxy Theater in New York screened a short scene of West Point cadets in a musical drill and parade with a speech by the commanding officer; a full sound newsreel aired in the Roxy Theater later that year, on October 28 (subjects: Niagara Falls, trains, the Army-Yale football game and a rodeo in New York); and the first national theatrical newsreel release occurred with Fox Movietone Newsreel Number One on December 3 (the Vatican choir, the dynamiting of a bridge and an Army-Navy game).[20]

Fox exclusively maintained the field for the first years and the business was lucrative: its newsreel activity earned the company $100,000 per week.[21] By May of 1930, four of the Big Five studios – Fox, RKO, MGM and Paramount – as well as Pathé were issuing sound newsreels (Warner Brothers never became involved, perhaps because of its investment in the Vitaphone technology, which disappeared after 1931). However, Fox remained the largest, able to provide its own material while the other companies had to rely 'upon an exchange with foreign newsreels to fill out their weekly releases'.[22]

The guiding spirit behind Fox's early pre-eminence in newsreels was Winfield R. Sheehan, the studio's vice-president and general manager, who recognised how the addition of sound could give Fox the edge over Pathé and undertook a series of concrete steps that would ensure its introduction into the studio's newsreel product.[23] Sheehan's enthusiasm was not shared by everyone at Fox, however: the director of Fox News, Truman Talley, expressed a more cautious attitude when he noted how 'whenever anything occurs that can be photographed which will be more interesting and entertaining when accompanied by sound we will spare no effort to see that it is done'.[24] Sheehan's stated policy was to station camera and sound crews around the world, in order to capture important events and 'world figures in action and sound', which he accomplished with a fleet of 40 Movietone trucks. By late 1928, Fox moved to a twice-a-week all-sound newsreel exhibition schedule, further expanded to four releases per week in 1929.

It should be noted at this point that, despite Fox's leading role in the sound newsreel, there was no assurance that a given release was heard and seen in every theatre. Exhibitors had a choice of news product, and the transition to sound took place over time. Not all cinemas were properly equipped for Movietone, especially in the beginning (1927–1928), so their earliest sound newsreels (as of December, 1927) may have enjoyed national distribution, but that provides no assurance of actual widespread consumption.

The potential and actual popularity of the incorporation of sound into the newsreel is hard to overestimate. At a Movietone demonstration in April of 1927, Karl Hoblitzelle, President of Interstate Amusement theaters, signed up on the spot with the following justification: 'One of the great problems which the progressive exhibitor has to face is how he can increase his patronage. I believe that Movietone, especially the plans for its extensive use in Fox News, will have a definite effect in that direction'.[25] Sheehan's vision was to establish 30,000 Movietone installations worldwide by 1930 and indeed, by the end of 1927, 150 were already in place with 100 on back order and installations in 1928 targeted at the rate of two per day.[26] Fox took further control over the Movietone releases by establishing its own newsreel theater on Times Square, which exclusively exhibited its new sound subjects.

The earliest sound newsreels were designed to take full advantage of the new technology and not only in subject matter. As film historian Donald Crafton observes, 'the first sound newsreels were constructed to foreground the impression of being-there-ness. Their outdoor settings recorded with omnidirectional microphones created transportive pictures and placed the viewer-listener "in" the Yale Bowl or brought Lindbergh "inside" the local theater for his speech'.[27] For example, theatre owner Samuel Rothapfel reported how a newsreel item on the Army-Yale football game on November 1, 1927, caused the patrons of the Roxy Theater (at 50th and 7th) to 'burst into a frenzy of cheering and for the moment you weren't sitting in a theater at all, but in the bowl at New Haven. It wasn't just a picture, but the game itself'.[28] To make sure that these auditory benefits of the Fox product were not lost on the theatre visitors, the company created a logo that read 'Fox Movietone News. It speaks for itself'. Indeed, the promotion surrounding a number of the studio's 1927 newsreel releases stressed the audience's ability to hear the moving images, such as the *New York Times* campaign for a speech by Benito Mussolini, which—beginning on September 19, 1927—read as follows: 'See and Hear "The Man of the Hour" His Excellency Benito Mussolini, Premier of Italy. He speaks to you and lives before your eyes on the Movietone!'[29] In June of 1928, Chicago exhibitors Marks Brothers initiated what they called the 'see and hear' campaign for their Movietone news product – as their publicity director J.J. Hess remarked, 'Movietone News is actually news of the world, and … it presents both the scene and the sounds of the news event. The "see and hear" factor was literally pounded into the patron'.[30]

Music

It should be of little surprise that music would occupy 'front row centre' in this fetishisation of sound, which can be observed in the three subjects of the first edited and nationally distributed Fox newsreel, from December 4, 1927: 1) A review at West Point featuring the Academy's marching band; 2) the Vatican Choir singing at the Tomb of the Unknown Soldier; and 3) the demolition of the Conowingo Bridge in Maryland.[31] If these items do not strike the news consumer of later times as particularly worthy of presentation, they do reflect a shift in news reporting towards a softer, more tabloid style, which interestingly parallels the television news scene of the 1980s, as the increasing reliance upon music contributed to the escalating adoption of high-concept entertainment values.[32] They also all feature onscreen music-making or – in the case of the bridge demolition – arresting sound.

This move toward entertainment was not unwelcome to the theatre-going public and to exhibitors, whose interest in building audience through sound technology bore out the prediction of Hoblitzelle. What it meant practically was a tendency toward set-up scenes and staged events, for which musical performance was well suited. However, as is well known, sound and music possess at the same time the ability to give reality and presence to the moving image: to mask the artificiality of a given scene.[33] When the images started coming in from outside of New York City, i.e. from the rest of the world, music helped create a sense of authenticity among audiences, by suggesting that they were seeing and hearing the world as it was. Moreover, these were the days before sound editing: a Fox insider reported in *Film Daily* of September 1, 1929 that 'except for the musical accompaniment used with titles, there has never been an attempt made to score a Fox Movietone subject ... The natural sounds are transferred from the film track to discs for theaters thus equipped and no effort is made to doctor it'.[34] This professed fealty to the real, natural and aesthetic notwithstanding, the news in sound was anything but a factual window on the world, aided and abetted by music, as will become apparent.

This is not to say that sound newsreels lacked hard news items, whether historical events, political speeches, or natural disasters. However, in every case sound was front and centre, eventually replacing the intertitle dialogue cards that were sole sources of onscreen information in the newsreel of the silent era. During the period of transition to widespread newsreel narration in the early 1930s, subjects nevertheless still relied upon title cards and intertitles to set-up and frame the news stories.[35]

A sampling of footage from and for the early sound subjects by Fox Movietone (1927–1929) will help to demonstrate the studio's dedication to presenting the auralities made possible through the new technology. The primary public collection for Fox Movietone newsreels exists at the University of South Carolina, a donation by Twentieth-Century Fox Film Corporation in 1980 that amounts to 2000 hours of 'edited stories, complete newsreels, and associated outtakes from the silent Fox News and sound Fox Movietone News Library' from 1919 to 1934 and 1942 to 1944.[36] For the years after 1927, the USC collection consists of substantial unedited sound footage, more than perhaps suggested by the library's own description, yet a good portion of it appears to have been ultimately used in theatrical newsreels and those serve as the primary subjects for closer consideration below.[37] At the same time, the longer outtakes and unedited video material for music-specific subjects (as well as edited footage) represent valuable documentary sources in and of themselves, recording events, performances and practices from the late 1920s that might otherwise be lost to posterity.

For the purposes of this introduction to the sights and sounds of the world through Movietone newsreels, it is perhaps most useful to provide an overview of the types and treatments of subjects that prominently feature music and sound. We could organise the sound 'fetishisation' of the early newsreel into three categories of aurality: talking celebrities, soundscapes and musical performances. Only rarely did sound take a leading role in the reporting of a regular news item, but it did occur on October 24, 1929, when Prince Umberto II of Italy visited Brussels to lay a wreath at the tomb of the unknown Belgian soldier.

An anti-Mussolini activist fired one shot at the king-in-waiting and missed him, but the cameras and microphones were there, capturing this remarkable 'auricular' moment. The stationary camera and microphone that created the Movietone footage of the assassination attempt presents an interesting moment of auditory chaos that later sound editing would have removed: a band is playing off-screen, then we hear the shot (off-screen as well) and ensuing screams from onlookers/onlisteners while the band continues with its routine, the ensemble clearly unaware of the unfolding drama.

With regard to collecting newsworthy personalities, Sheehan and Talley made a concerted effort to record the most recognisable and notorious, so that beyond Lindbergh, they were able to record for example Benito Mussolini, George Bernard Shaw, King George V of England, King Alonso XIII of Spain, Sir Arthur Conan Doyle and John D. Rockefeller, all of whom added to the exotic draw of the talking newsreel in its first years. Jack Connolly produced these interviews, which took him and his camera and sound crew to Europe for over two years.[38]

The first foreign dignitary recorded in sound was Benito Mussolini, who was filmed on May 6, 1927, before the Lindbergh coverage, even though it first aired on September 23.[39] The media buff Mussolini directly addressed the American people, after which he allegedly commented, 'Let me speak through [the newsreel] in twenty cities in Italy once a week and I need no other power'.[40] George Bernard Shaw's 'interview' on June 25, 1928 is remarkable for its wit and satire, and this exclusive talking appearance in North America in the Globe Theater of New York was 'an immense success and it was the talk of the lobby both at intermission and after the show'.[41]

The early fascination with sounds of the world, natural and man-made, revealed itself in the most varied contexts. Anything that was sound-worthy, whether crowd scenes at important occurrences, natural disasters, sporting events, even animals and bridge demolitions, found its way onto the Movietone newsreel, with the noise of warfare to follow by the end of the 1920s. For example, the sounds of skaters in Central Park provided opportunity for one of these non-narrative, purely sound-based items within the first month of regular newsreel release (the edited item, captioned 'Children enjoy first skating of year in Central Park, New York City', dates from December, 1927).[42] The camera and microphone capture the ambient sounds from the skating surface, largely the voices, whistles, cries of children at play (there is no substantial or recognisable narrative and no musical features).

Musical performances comprise the third auditory category prominently featured in the early sound newsreel. The addition of sound enabled the crews to film longer musical sequences without worrying about the loss of audience interest, so that musicians on the most diverse instruments (incapable of reproduction by theatre musicians) could deliver performances of several minutes for the newsreels. Thus the static visual quality of an accordion trio playing at a park in Camden, New Jersey (November, 1927) is more than compensated by the linking of performance gestures with recognisable musical sounds.[43]

As a significant feature of the American music scene, bands—whether associated with the military, ceremonial or sporting events—became popular musical
features of the sound newsreel.[44] These bands belonged to American culture of
the time and were eminently suited for sound film, as ensembles that projected
well for the microphone while conveying a sense of dignity and national pride.
Marching bands populated the newsreels of the silent era, but with the addition
of sound it was possible to use a fixed camera and microphone to record stationary events.[45] For example, a comparison of the silent footage for the parade
at the opening of the Ashley River Memorial Bridge, May 6, 1926, with the
Movietone subject 'Army Band Plays at National War College', December 10,
1927, reveals how much the music adds to the scene: the 1927 film may lack
visual appeal, but it contributes the sound of the National Anthem (among
other music) to the diegesis as well as the narration of band director William J.
Stannard, who welcomes the Movietone audience.[46]

Sound newsreel subjects with popular dance music and jazz were as numer-
ous as band performances and here African-Americans appeared on theatri-
cal screens, although their footage also ended up on the cutting-room floor.
Perhaps the most significant of the exhibited 'talking' subjects featured the
Jenkins Orphanage Band from Charleston, South Carolina, performing on
November 22, 1928, which makes for an interesting comparison with the
silent outtakes from Fox News Story B2703, May 22, 1926, with the Jenkins
Orphanage Band accompanying dancer Bee Jackson (figure 2.1). While both are

Figure 2.1 Fox Movietone News Story 1–507: Jenkins Orphanage Band, Charleston,
South Carolina, 11/22/1928.

staged at the same spot in front of the orphanage, the silent footage focuses on the feet and body of Jackson, while the sound film intercuts between the full ensemble, clusters of performers and dancers, creating a dynamic experience of sound and image. As Daniel Eagan observes, the existing material for the footage from 1928 reveals the complexity of shooting and recording sound, involving ten separate shots of the dancers alone.[47] The orphanage itself was a leading 'incubator' for early jazz, which invests the Movietone document with particular cultural value, whereby it was added to the American National Film Registry in 2003.[48]

One or more Movietone camera and sound crews seem to have made a tour from Virginia to South Carolina in late November 1928, gathering performances by African-American musicians that were staged in settings that enhanced their authenticity, so newsreel consumers had the sense that they 'were there' as the music was being made. Thus the performances of the Jenkins Orphanage Band (November 22) and the Hampton Institute Glee Club (singing the Nathaniel Dett arrangement of the spiritual 'Let Us Cheer the Weary Traveler' on November 19) took place in front of the institutions respectively in Charleston, South Carolina and Hampton, Virginia.[49] Another Hampton Glee Club a cappella presentation by its male members was recorded the same day (and place) by the Movietone cameras and microphones, whereby we see and hear a polished ensemble singing 'From the Shadows through the Moonlight', with interesting details in the vocal timbres and dynamics.[50] At the same time, Carl Scott (ukelele) and Eddie Thomas (washboard) sung and played 'Today' and 'My Old Home' at a location in Richmond, Virginia that could pass for the homestead of the artists (November 21, 1928).[51]

Other American musical traditions found vision and voice on the Movietone screens of the country. Thus fiddler Bascom Lamar Lunsford and friends on banjos and guitar performed 'Doggett Gap' on the porch of an Asheville, North Carolina homestead on October 7, 1928, for the news story 'Mountaineer Minstrels' (figure 2.2).[52] The Movietone crew recorded a kazoo chorus from New York P.S. 130 on February 24, 1928, with pupils performing 'My Blue Heaven', 'Me and My Shadow' and 'Swanee River'.[53] And the newsreel captured San Francisco's Dick Hunter, the 'Caruso of the Ferries', singing to his passengers on September 21, 1928.[54] These sites for the sounds may not have been exotic, but they brought unique or rare musical performances to an audience that desired to see and hear the 'realities' of their world – however staged they may have been – as an integral part of the cinema experience.

Unfortunately, racialised discourses in general found amplification when image and music coincided in soft news stories that featured staged musical performances. On one occasion in late 1928, African-American children were portrayed singing the spiritual 'Nobody Knows the Trouble I've Seen' while picking cotton in a field near Memphis.[55] African-American banjo player 'Uncle' John Scruggs was featured in a staged performance of 'Little Log Cabin Round the Lane' in front of a dilapidated home, where chickens ran free (inside and outside) and children danced to his picking.[56] Such musical newsreel items may

Figure 2.2 Fox Movietone News Story 1–390: Mountaineer Minstrels, Asheville, North Carolina, 10/07/1928.

represent set-up performances for the cameras and microphones, thus raising the question of authenticity, yet they are also historical performances that document the abilities and styles of individuals and ensembles and provide insights into what American cinema-goers were consuming as indigenous culture.

As Fox's camera and sound crews spread across the globe during 1928, the sights and sounds of the larger world found their way into American film theatres. At the end of 1928, Movietone had its camera and sound crew Frederick Brutt and Larry Ellis 'document' life in Palestine and Egypt with street scenes and exotic musical performances. Thus they filmed a staged desert scene on December 28, 1928, where whirling dervishes went through their motions with the accompaniment of exotic, yet traditional instruments: the lack of explanation for these 'inscrutable' practices tended to confirm preconceptions of the Middle East already ingrained within the imagination of Americans, delectating the Orientalist eye and ear.[57]

In the fetishisation of sound, however, sometimes the camera and sound crew simply let the film roll to capture a novel soundscape, such as Brutt and Ellis did on the streets of Bethlehem on Christmas Day, 1928.[58] This edited subject features a title with a short musical accompaniment that narrates a story of its own in twelve seconds. The script reads as follows: 'HERE IS WHERE CHRIST WAS BORN. The sights and sounds of Bethlehem today are not quite what they were 1929 years ago'. Over this we hear strings and harp, presenting a hymn-like tune on the tonic, then on the mediant (for slight tension) and back to the tonic for a satisfying close. In combination with the words and just prior to the street soundscape (that includes animal sounds and speech in Arabic), however, the music has the effect of elevating Christianity in a civilised triumph over the Islamic world of Palestine.

Among the most interesting Movietone newsreel subjects from the Middle East was the Palestine Police Band of Jerusalem playing excerpts from *The Vagabond King* under the direction of composer Rudolf Friml himself.[59] Brutt and Ellis documented this staged performance on December 26, 1928, which – according to the Jewish Telegraphic Agency – was the 'first talking film made in Palestine'.[60] Recorded in front of the Citadel of Jerusalem, the stationary band was first conducted by its leader Aubrey Silver, with Friml then picking up the baton for a medley of excerpts from his operetta. The subject's prurient exoticism, considering its Middle Eastern location, its 'Orientalised' band members and the presence of the celebrity musician, would undoubtedly have appealed to North American cinema audiences.[61] The multiple outtakes reveal above all the visible discomfort of conductors and ensemble with the task of making an audiovisual recording, a fairly common response among speakers and musicians to the new aurality of film.[62]

A final musical item from the first year of Movietone newsreels seems to create a narrative for the introduction of sound to the news. In a subject from November 9, 1927, the audience sees (and hears) a 'Giant Victrola on [the] roof of one of the Victor Buildings ... Camden, New Jersey', according to the Movietone dope sheet.[63] The cabinet opens and the Sousa march 'Fairest of the Fair' (undoubtedly added in editing) resounds, at which point the viewer becomes aware of a woman waving from inside the door of the gigantic speaker. The opening of the cabinet and concurrent release of music could be read as symbolising the arrival of the sound era in the newsreel, while the waving woman not only gives us an idea of scale, but also invites us into the sound experience.

That experience in the context of newsreels would last until 1967 in the United States.[64] As sound newsreels established themselves in the early 1930s, we find nondiegetic music beginning to underscore news items, albeit rather crudely at first, as tunes (often recognisable) that would accompany certain actions, like the Universal Newsreel subject about Pacific Armada maneuvers from February 4, 1932.[65] All of World War II replayed itself on the film screens of North America, with appropriate music of menace and jubilation. It stands to reason that the war's aurality would find an eager audience among cinemagoers, who could see and hear its progress in their local theatre. That the same style of music would accompany the Universal Newsreel coverage of the Vietnam War from the mid- to late-1960s is astonishing, considering that at the same time, television newscasting did not feature music in any significant way.[66]

This study suggests the impact that the introduction and fetishisation of sound-on-film had for the theatre-going public of America, and how the newsreel's newly acquired aurality in the late 1920s contributed to and yet also reaffirmed American perceptions of the world. That music played a major role in this 'sounding of the world' confirms what news providers would rediscover in the 1980s: that it is a crucial component in the selling of news and, ultimately, in the shaping of public opinion.

Notes

1 'The Newsreels' script for Broadcast, October 15, 1954; cited in Betty Houchin Winfield, *FDR and the News Media* (Urbana, Illinois: University of Illinois Press, 1990), 116. I gratefully acknowledge the assistance of the staff at the Fox Movietone News collection at the University of South Carolina. Other newsreel collections include the Universal Newsreels, which are available online through the Internet Archive and the Hearst Metrotone Archive at UCLA. I thank Agnes Malkinson for her generous assistance in the preparation of this article.

2 Jonathan Stuart Setliff, 'The March of Time and the American Century' (Unpublished PhD Thesis: University of Maryland, 2007), 25.

3 Raymond Fielding, *The American Newsreel: A Complete History, 1911–1967*, 2nd ed. (Jefferson, North Carolina: McFarland, 2006).

4 See, for example, *Yesterday's News. The British Cinema Newsreel Reader*, ed. Luke McKernan (London: British Universities Film & Video Council, 2002); Roger Smither, 'Welt im Film: Anglo-American Newsreel Policy', in *The Political Re-education of Germany & her Allies after World War II*, ed. Nicholas Pronay and Keith Wilson (Totowa, New Jersey: Barnes & Noble Books, 1985), 151–172; Howard Smith, 'The BBC Television Newsreel and the Korean War', in *Historical Journal of Film, Radio and Television*, 8:3 (1988), 227–252; and Brett Bowles, 'German Newsreel Propaganda in France, 1940–1944', in *Historical Journal of Film, Radio and Television*, 24:1 (2004), 45–67.

5 Fielding, *The American Newsreel*, 81, 121.

6 Among others, see Catherine Chamblee, 'The Juxtaposition of Visual and Musical Elements in Nazi Films (1933–1945)', in *Music Research Forum*, 18 (2003), 2–28; Barbara Boisits, Peter Stachel and Heidemarie Uhl, 'Mythos Staatsvertrag – Mythos Musik: Die Staatsvertrags-Reportagen der Austria Wochenschau als musikalischer Gedächtnisort', in *Österreichische Musikzeitschrift*, 604 (April, 2005), 4–11; John Winn, *The Beatles' Recorded Legacy* (Sharon, Vermont: Multiplus Books, 2003); and Marlaine Glicksman, 'Citizen Artist: On Shostakovich and the Soviets', in *Film Comment*, 24:6 (November-December, 1988), 50–51. Newsreel sound footage is used in other research contexts, although primarily as raw material for the documentation of performances and practices and not for discussion of the original contexts.

7 Neil Lerner, 'The Classical Documentary Score in American Films of Persuasion: Contexts and Case Studies, 1936–1945' (Unpublished PhD Thesis: Duke University, 1997), 42–49.

8 Donald Crafton, *The Talkies: American Cinema's Transition to Sound, 1926–1931* (Berkeley, California: University of California Press, 1997), 98.

9 Fielding, *The American Newsreel*, 102–106.

10 The dearth of academic study of exhibition practices among cinema chains and individual theatres has made it difficult if not impossible to determine which newsreels were screened at a given location on a given date.

11 Howard T. Lewis, *The Motion Picture Industry* (New York: D. van Nostrand, 1933), 134.

12 Fielding, *The American Newsreel*, 81.

13 S.L. Rothapfel, 'Dramatizing Music for the Pictures', in *Reel Life* (September 5, 1914), 23.

14 Lerner, 'The Classical Documentary Score in American Films of Persuasion', 46–48.

15 About Vitaphone shorts, see above all William Shaman, 'The Operatic Vitaphone Shorts', in *ARSC Journal*, 22:1 (Spring 1991), 35–94; Roy Liebman, *Vitaphone Films: A Catalogue of the Features and Shorts*, 2nd ed. (Jefferson, North Carolina: McFarland, 2010); and Edwin Bradley, *The First Hollywood Sound Shorts, 1926–1931* (Jefferson, North Carolina: McFarland, 2005).

16 Fielding, *The American Newsreel*, 102.
17 Aubrey Solomon, *The Fox Film Corporation, 1915–1935: A History and Filmography* (Jefferson, North Carolina: McFarland, 2011), 101.
18 Cited in Solomon, ibid.
19 Ibid., 103.
20 The second 'official' Movietone newsreel followed one week later on December 10.
21 Will Hays, *See and Hear: A Brief History of the Motion Picture and the Development of Sound* (New York: Motion Picture Producers and Distributors of America, 1929), 54.
22 Fielding, *The American Newsreel*, 113.
23 Crafton, *The Talkies*, 96.
24 Ibid.
25 Solomon, *The Fox Film Corporation, 1915–1935*, 101.
26 Crafton, *The Talkies*, 98.
27 Ibid., 100.
28 Ibid., 98.
29 Cited in Janet Bergstrom, 'Murnau, Movietone and Mussolini', in *Film History*, 17 (2005), 187.
30 J. J. Hess quoted in 'Marks Bros. Open "See and Hear" News with Big Campaign', in *Exhibitors Herald and Moving Picture World*, 34 (June 16, 1928), 48.
31 'A History of the Newsreel', in *Fox Movietone News*, at http://archive.is/0xAVE (accessed January 24, 2014).
32 See James Deaville, 'The Changing Sounds of War: Television News Music from the War in Vietnam to the Persian Gulf', in *Music, Politics, and Violence*, ed. Susan Fast and Kip Pegley (Middletown, Connecticut: Wesleyan University Press, 2012), 104–126.
33 See, for example, Ron Rodman, 'John Williams's Music to *Lost in Space*: The Monumental, the Profound, and the Hyperbolic', in *Music in Science Fiction Television: Tuned to the Future*, ed. Kevin J. Donnelly and Philip Hayward (New York: Routledge, 2013), 48.
34 Solomon, *The Fox Film Corporation, 1915–1935*, 102.
35 Examples of the use of titles and intertitles in the time of transition to sound include the newsreel subjects 'Gandhi Welcomed Back to India by Followers', Fox Movietone, December 28, 1931, at http://www.youtube.com/watch?v=lXDDildSE_o; and 'Pacific Conquered!', Paramount Sound News [October, 1931], at http://www.youtube.com/watch?v=2SEGPyB-LBg (accessed January 24, 2014).
36 'Fox Movietone News Collection', Moving Image Research Collections, University of South Carolina Libraries, at http://library.sc.edu/mirc/list.html?cat=6 (accessed January 24, 2014).
37 Given the fragmentary nature of the documentation for early newsreels, it is difficult to ascertain the extent to which footage was actually used in the final product unless an edited version exists. A meritorious yet time-consuming and labour-intensive project would involve creating a chronological listing of known newsreel releases for any given studio.
38 Fielding, *The American Newsreel*, 106.
39 Bergstrom notes that a Movietone crew was sent to Italy specifically to interview Mussolini and the Pope; 'Murnau, Movietone and Mussolini', 192.
40 Crafton, *The Talkies*, 96.
41 Bradley, *The First Hollywood Sound Shorts, 1926–1931*, 85; Peter Vischer, 'Shaw Movietone Steals the Show at Premier of "The Red Dance"', in *Exhibitors Herald and Moving Picture World*, 34 (June 30, 1928), 22.
42 MVTN 0-86; Moving Images Research Collection, University of South Carolina Libraries. Unless indicated otherwise, all Fox News and MVTN newsreels indicated below are preserved in that collection.

43 MVTN 0-90, dated November 9, 1927.
44 Thus Movietone's very first newsreel sound subject, from April 30, 1927, was the aforementioned scene of a musical drill and parade by West Point cadets.
45 For example, compare the silent footage for the parade at the opening of the Ashley River Memorial Bridge, May 6, 1926 (Fox News Story B, B2733–B2734), with the Movietone subject 'Army Band Plays at National War College', December 10, 1927 (MVTN 0–28).
46 Fox News Story B, B2733–B2734; MVTN 0–28.
47 The close-ups of the dancers were filmed without sound; the music was added in the editing process. Daniel Eagan, 'Fox Movietone News: Jenkins Orphanage Band', in *America's Film Legacy: The Authoritative Guide to the Landmark Movies in the National Film Registry* (New York: Continuum, 2010), 153–155.
48 Paul Cimbala, 'Review of John Chilton, *A Jazz Nursery: The Story of Jenkins' Orphanage Bands* (1980)', in *South Carolina Historical Magazine*, 82 (1981), 174–175.
49 The spiritual's melody appeared in Nathanael Dett's *Religious Folk Songs of the Negro as Sung at the Hampton Institute* (Hampton, Virginia: Hampton Institute Press, 1927).
50 MVTN 1–491.
51 The Movietone title card reads 'This Dixie Artist Plays Clean Jazz. Richmond dusky extracts music from washboard and other odd utensils', MVTN 1–600.
52 MVTN 1–390.
53 MVTN 0–338.
54 MVTN 1–141.
55 November 23, 1928, MVTN 1-509. The footage begins with the children in a choir formation in a field and then they proceed to pick the cotton while still singing, which positions this subject apart from the traditional static camera and microphone for ensembles and thereby suggests a dramatisation.
56 The footage was recorded in Powhatan County, Virginia, on November 8, 1928, MVTN 1–486.
57 MVTN 2–49.
58 MVTN 2–54 A–C.
59 MVTN 2–68 A–B.
60 Reference cited in http://www.filmography.co.il/articles/93-1928,-1929,-1930.html (accessed January 24, 2014).
61 The band consisted of Jewish musicians from various parts of the world. See Sylva M. Gelber, *No Balm in Gilead: A Personal Retrospective of Mandate Days in Palestine* (Ottawa: Carleton University Press, 1989), 122–123.
62 Perhaps the most notorious example of this unease is seen and heard in the awkward presentation of actor John Miljan, for the trailer to *The Jazz Singer* (1927).
63 MVTN 0–90. As explained by the curators of the Movietone Collection at the University of South Carolina, 'each roll of [newsreel] film was accompanied by a "dope sheet." Dope sheets contained information from the camera crews to help newsreel editors understand the contents of the film ["dope", by the way, was slang for "information"]'; 'The Movietone News Dope Sheets: The War Years', at http://library.sc.edu/digital/collections/movietoneabout.html (accessed January 24, 2014).
64 Universal Newsreels, the last cinematic news producer in the United States, ceased operations in 1967, while Fox Movietone released its last newsreel in 1963.
65 Here the music of the newsreel story represents a continuation of the martial-sounding music that accompanied the titles: 'Pacific Armada', Universal Newspaper Newsreel, February 4, 1932, at https://archive.org/details/1932-02-04_Pacific_Armada (accessed January 24, 2014).
66 Deaville, 'The Changing Sounds of War'.

Chapter 3

Race, War, Music and The Problem of One Tenth of Our Nation (1940)

Julie Hubbert

As many film historians have observed, nonfiction filmmaking blossomed in the U.S. between 1930–1945, producing some of the most iconic American documentaries including *The Plow That Broke The Plains* (Pare Lorentz, 1936), *The River* (Lorentz, 1937), *The City* (Willard Van Dyke and Ralph Steiner, 1939) and *Valley Town* (Van Dyke, 1940). Until recently, our understanding of the films of this period has been fairly uniform, varying in scope and detail but not in general philosophical outlook. In their broader historical overviews, for instance, Richard M. Barsam and Erik Barnouw both describe most of the films made in this country before World War II as springing from a generally leftist political agenda.[1] William Alexander and Russell Campbell describe that ideology as more specifically Marxist and radical at times, but their histories, while more narrowly focused and detailed in the number of films and filmmakers they consider, draw conclusions that are fundamentally the same and equally monolithic.[2] According to these authors, early American documentary films were primarily political and primarily leftist.

As study of the period has developed in recent years and expanded to consider a much greater range of nonfiction filmmaking, however, a more nuanced picture of the period has emerged. Facilitated greatly by archival projects such as the 'orphan film' movement, which has identified and made visible a much greater range of material for study, our view of the period has become much less monolithic. Amongst the important scholarly volumes to have emerged from this development are Rick Prelinger's *The Field Guide to Sponsored Filmmaking* and the essay collection *Learning With the Lights Off: Educational Film in the United States*, two studies that have helped to redefine nonfiction filmmaking during this period as not just generically documentary, or politically radical, but as covering a diverse range of genres and springing from an equally wide range of philosophical motivations.[3] For Prelinger in particular, the period is rich not just with a few dozen feature-length documentaries, but with a host of films conceived, financed and made, or 'sponsored', by an array of institutions and industries. His terminological redefinition and recategorisation of the period to include genres once considered ephemeral, such as commercials, training films, corporate reports, political campaign films, public service announcements, educational and experimental films, as well as documentaries, has facilitated not just a more detailed understanding of filmmaking, but also a more nuanced understanding of sponsorship.

The rediscovery of *One Tenth of Our Nation* (Film Associates, 1940), a feature-length, institutionally-sponsored film of the period long thought lost, contributes significantly to this newly-expanded landscape. It gives special emphasis to an observation previously only hinted at: that nonfiction filmmaking in the U.S. expanded both philosophically and organisationally in the years immediately preceding the outbreak of the war in Europe. As this film reveals, the war played a significant role in making leftist ideology less compelling and in making moderate ideological approaches, like the British documentary model, more attractive and practical. The degree to which the growing war in Europe in 1939 and 1940 affected the content of this film can clearly be seen, particularly in the more 'democratic' depiction of race.

One Tenth of Our Nation also contributes significantly to our understanding of the role music played in American documentary films. This topic has not been neglected, but to date it too has been treated as monolithic, especially among film scholars who understand most of these scores as having been designed simply 'to appeal to nationalistic sensibilities'.[4] Recently, music historians Neil Lerner and Elizabeth B. Crist have challenged this assumption by showing how the American sound of these scores was also nuanced by references to race, ethnicity and geography, but in general their perspective, as with other music historians, has been composer-centric.[5] As one of the only films of the period to overtly consider the problems of race in America, *One Tenth* quite understandably complicates and deepens this history. In 1940, as the war in Europe escalated, discussions of America's identity as a 'democratic' nation brought new scrutiny and discomfort to questions of oppression and racism at home. This new climate complicated the making of the film, its script especially. But it also problematised the construction and reception of the score. Composer Roy Harris brought with him a long and outspoken discussion of what constitutes 'authentic' American music. For decades, his music had been defined by its Western Frontier spirit and its white ethnography. As his film work on this and other scores that same year reveals, by the 1940s, the characterstics of race and geography were not only becoming less desirable; they were also becoming more difficult to define. Harris' score provides a unique look not just at a forgotten film score, one that played an important role in the new sponsored film, but also at the very complex and problematising role that race was playing in the definition of American music before WWII.

The British Invasion and American Documentary Filmmaking, 1938–42

The political foundation of institutional documentary filmmaking in the U.S. has been well documented. The earliest organisation, The Worker's Film and Photo League, established in 1930, had strong ties to leftist and communist organisations. Its members were primarily activists who saw film as a way to expose the social injustices of the capitalist system and the Great Depression. Critical of the newsreel as capitalist propaganda and inspired by examples of labour activism in other countries, members of the WFPL looked to German and Soviet films by Sergei Eisenstein, Dziga Vertov, Alexander Doveshenko, Fritz Lang and Walther Ruttmann in particular for political strategies, ideological guidance and filmmaking techniques. Without a consistent source of funding, and hampered by a largely untrained membership and ad hoc exhibition methods, however, the WFPL produced only a handful of films before disbanding in 1934.

Several splinter groups quickly sprang up to carry on the work of socially-conscious filmmaking, however. One of the most successful was founded by former WFPL members Ralph Steiner, Leo Hurwitz, Paul Strand and Irving Lerner, who joined well-known photographers Paul Strand and Willard Van Dyke to form a new cooperative called Nykino. Renamed Frontier Films a short time later, most of the group's efforts focused on filming political events abroad, including the Spanish Civil War and the rise of communism in China. Members of Frontier also helped to make two celebrated domestic films; *The Plow That Broke the Plains* and *The River*, mentioned above. Both were directed by newcomer Pare Lorentz and funded by the U.S. government.[6] But because many saw them as socialist propaganda for Franklin D. Roosevelt's New Deal, they did little to expand nonfiction filmmaking in the U.S. away from its leftist core.[7]

When Steiner and Van Dyke left Frontier Films in 1937 to form their own company, American Documentary Films, they were motivated by a need for a more consistent stream of income and a growing dissatisfaction with Marxist ideology.[8] They were also inspired by a new model of nonfiction filmmaking that was emerging in England, a more observational approach pioneered by filmmaker John Grierson, who aimed to produce films of greater national public interest. Like many of his generation, Grierson had also been influenced by Soviet filmmaking and Marxist philosophy. Less ideologically-minded, however, Grierson saw film as a tool not just for propaganda purposes, but also for public good. 'Convinced that film was a medium of education and persuasion', Barsam observes, 'Grierson devoted his missionary enthusiasm and energy to the task of convincing others that film could and should be used to further social progress'.[9] Grierson also developed a unique method of encouraging both government entities and private institutions to finance his films. At the same time that Frontier Films was struggling to make a handful of films about foreign causes, Grierson and colleagues like Robert Flaherty, Basil Wright, Paul Rotha and Brazilian-born Alberto Cavalcanti, with the help of government entities like the Empire Marketing Board and the General Post Office, were producing an impressive number of documentary films about domestic issues and industries within the U.K. Very few of these films had been screened in the U.S. before 1937, however, when Iris Barry, the curator of the newly-established Film Library at New York City's Museum of Modern Art (MoMA), acquired many of them for the museum's collection.[10] For the first time, American filmmakers saw

British documentaries like *Housing Problems* (Edgar Anstey and Arthur Elton, 1935), *Granton Trawler* (Anstey and Grierson, 1934), *Enough to Eat?* (Anstey, 1936), *Night Mail* (Harry Watt and Wright, 1936), *Eastern Valley* (Donald Alexander and Rotha, 1937) and *Children at School* (Wright, 1937).

British filmmakers also travelled to the U.S. to share ideas. In the autumn of 1937, for instance, Rotha began a six-month fellowship at MoMA's Film Library, ostensibly to work on a documentary about the history of film. Instead, Rotha frequently lectured at screenings of the documentaries, promoting their uniquely British style and philosophy.[11] He also became acquainted with American documentary filmmakers and their films but was generally dismissive of them. For Rotha, Lorentz's films were too 'poetic' and Frontier's films were simply newsreels 'for showing to trade unions and Labour groups'.[12] According to him, the U.S. had no identifiable 'school' of thought and no unified commitment to unbiased and rigorous documentation.[13] He did, however, find some encouragement in American filmmakers, notably in Steiner and Van Dyke, who were both interested in pursuing the British approach.[14] Rotha also advised philanthropists, like the Rockefeller Foundation, to become more involved in socially-conscious filmmaking. Although his proposal to educate American filmmakers in British techniques through the establishment of 'experimental units' made up of both American and British filmmakers never materialised, Rotha was nevertheless successful in influencing the Rockefeller Foundation to establish an American Film Center in 1938, using the British Film Centre as its model.

The Making of *One Tenth*: American Documentary Film on the Eve of War

Steiner and Van Dyke were not the only filmmakers interested in pursuing the British idea of a more moderate and productive path. Between 1938 and 1942 especially, many film production companies sprang up with similar goals.[15] Most were small, staffed by former Nykino or Frontier Film members, and short-lived like Film Associations, Inc., a production company established in New York City in March, 1940. Not surprisingly, the company was comprised of former 'radical' filmmakers including Henwar Rodakiewicz and Theodore Lawrence, both of whom had worked with Van Dyke and Steiner on *The City*, and Irving Reis, who had worked with Joris Ivens on the soundtrack for the famed documentary *The Spanish Earth* (1937). The practice of rounding out a new company's letterhead with celebrities was not unusual, but to have the celebrities be exclusively British was.[16] Film Associates listed famed novelist Aldous Huxley and Gerald Heard, a popular British intellectual and commentator for the BBC at the time, as founding members. Both had recently emigrated to the U.S. in 1937.[17] A third Brit, Felix Greene, cousin of novelist Graham Greene, was a mentee of Heard's; but he was also well known in his own right, having started a new style of 'social action' radio programmes for the BBC in 1934, much in the vein of Grierson's documentary film work.[18] Greene's weekly program for the BBC, 'Time to Spare', dealt with pressing social concerns like unemployment, social inequality and poverty among the working classes and was so effective that the British government tried to have it cancelled. Instead the BBC reassigned Greene in 1935, making him the company's first foreign correspondent in America. Greene, a committed pacifist, gave up this position in 1940 shortly after England declared war on Germany. Stranded in the U.S. and looking for new employment possibilities, he joined Film Associates. His left-minded politics and his experience with the British documentary techniques made him a perfect addition to the Film Associates team.

In the course of its short life, Film Associates appears to have considered only four films for development, with only one, *One Tenth*, actually being made. The idea for the film originated with Claude A. Barnett, a Chicago-based entrepreneur and founder of the Associated Negro Press. Inspired by the planning of the Negro Exposition, which was to take place in Chicago from July to September 1940, Barnett approached the Rockefeller Foundation's General Education Board (GEB) on February 27 of that year with a request for funding to make 'a picture dramatising the progress of the Negro in 75 years [since Emancipation] dealing with education, agriculture, industries and cultural contributions in the arts'.[19] After agreeing to finance the film, the GEB asked Donald Slesinger, director of the newly-established American Film Center, to oversee the production, which they hoped would be not just for viewing at the Negro Exposition, but for national theatrical distribution as well. With a finished product needed in just six months, pre-production work began immediately. By mid-March, an advisory committee had been assembled consisting of prominent black educators, including Dr. Channing Tobias, National Council of YMCAs; Dr. Charles Johnson, Fisk University; Dr. Rufus Clement, President of Atlanta University; Dr. F.D. Patterson, Tuskegee Institute; Claude Barnett; and Dr. Arthur Wright, president of the Southern Education Foundation.[20] In mid-April, after Film Associates had been secured to make the film, a profusion of articles appeared in major urban newspapers from Chicago to Pittsburgh, Philadelphia, New York and Atlanta, announcing the film's production and celebrating it as 'the first educational picture ever prepared with Negroes as its subject'.[21]

Very early in the process, Slesinger drafted a scenario for the film, a five-page outline entitled 'A Film on Negro Education,' a sketch that included suggestions for content and production.[22] Slesinger outlined scenes of Negro education and depictions of Negro contributions to the sciences (doctors, nurses) and the arts (philosophy, poetry, writers, dramatists and opera singers, including Marion Anderson). Images of Jim Crow laws were to be contrasted with passages from The Constitution and major contributions of the National Association for the Advancement of Colored People (N.A.A.C.P.) were to be highlighted. No final shooting script for the film appears to have survived, but a longer 'treatment' made two months later by Film Associates, retitled 'One-Tenth of A (sic) Nation' does. Inspired by several weeks in the South, scouting locations and shooting initial footage, the new treatment proposed significant changes to Slesinger's original scenario, including trimming the depictions of more affluent urban families and shots of secondary and higher education, while cutting out mention of the Jeannes Teachers and celebrations of black achievement in the arts and culture altogether. Anticipating resistance to this new outline, the filmmakers drafted an accompanying 10-page memorandum justifying the film's new focus on poverty, lack of education and social inequality. The memorandum begins with an observation that informs the film's new title and choice of direction: 'One American in every ten is Negro' and 'four-fifths of the Negro population lives in the South and three-quarters of these live by agricultural work'.[23]

Not everyone on the advisory committee was comfortable with these changes. The new emphasis on the plight of Southern Negroes was particularly troubling to Patterson and Barnett. In the hopes of producing a more positive film, they asked that coverage of the Jeannes Teachers be reinstated and that the cameramen for Film Associates consult with recommended local contacts.[24] Although their suggestions were largely ignored, Greene assured them that a more balanced overview would be forthcoming. One feature of the film that everyone could agree on at every stage of the planning, however, was that as much of the film as possible should be made by African-Americans. In his initial scenario and in letters to Barnett, Slesinger writes on several occasions that 'Negro writers, musicians, and film makers should be used as much as possible in developing the story and making the film'.[25] The later Film Associates' treatment also recommends 'that a Negro narrator and composer for the musical score be found'.[26]

With the script drafted, first shooting began in early June at Atlanta University, Tuskegee Institute and Meharry Medical College, as well as at rural sites in Tennessee, Alabama, Mississippi and Georgia.[27] While most of the filming took place as planned, the film crew did encounter some difficulty when shooting outside of Memphis, Tennessee. For the main shoot, Rodakiewicz had hired two additional cameramen: Robert Morris, a recent college grad, and veteran cameraman Roger Barlow, who had also worked on *The City* and had just finished shooting scenes for *Valley Town*.[28] As Barlow, Morris and Rodakiewicz were gathering footage in an African-American community on the outskirts of Memphis, they were arrested and jailed for three days. Their actions had stirred the suspicions of Memphis Chief of Police, Will Lee, who arrested the cameramen on the suspicion of being 'fifth columnists'; that is, disloyal Americans spying on the U.S. in preparation for a fascist invasion.[29] Fueled by worries that the war raging in Europe could at any moment erupt in the U.S., the police were deeply suspicious of the filmmakers' need to film gas storage tanks and the Harahan Bridge, a major bridge spanning the Mississippi, both of which were close to the Negro community they were filming.

The revelation that the cameramen were not spies but communists making a film about social justice and racial equality for Negroes in the South did nothing to speed their release. When their detention dragged on for a second day, Rockefeller Foundation attorneys consulted with the FBI and Greene threatened to bring in the British Embassy. In the end, it was the young Morris' connections that proved the most useful: his uncle, Newbold Morris, the powerful president of the New York City Council and descendant of Robert Morris, the great patriot and signer of the Declaration of Independence, secured their release. Although the crew proceeded without incident after Memphis, the event nonetheless revealed just how complex the issue of race was becoming in pre-war America and also how out of place the lingering Marxist sympathies of Film Associates were becoming.

The Score of *One Tenth*—American Music on the Eve of War

With the filming complete by the end of June, post-production work on the film began in earnest in early July. The desire to use Negro artists and musicians was addressed only in part. Film Associates hired Maurice Ellis, a young Negro actor recently featured in Orson Welles' famed all-black production of Macbeth, *'Voodoo' Macbeth* (1936), for New York's Federal Theater Project.[30] The quest to hire a black composer to score the film, however, never materialised. This was not from a lack of choice: just as there were black actors of national or regional prominence to draw on, there were several black composers of distinction who would have been suitable for the job. Because of his prominence in the early 1930s as a composer of race music and his current experience scoring motion pictures for several Hollywood studios, William Grant Still, for instance, would have been a good candidate.[31] And yet there is no evidence that Film Associates ever contacted or considered him for the commission. Perhaps they were aware that he was unavailable. On June 25, as post-production work on the film was beginning, Still had an important new choral-orchestral work premiered in New York City at the Lewisohn Stadium Concert Series. Despite the high profile nature of the occasion – over 13,000 people attended including celebrity guests like Eleanor Roosevelt – Still was not present at the performance.[32]

In addition to finding him unavailable, the filmmakers at Film Associates may have also found Still an unattractive possibility. The new piece he had just completed was a massive, racially-charged work for orchestra, soloists and double chorus (one black, one white) entitled *And They Lynched Him On A Tree* (1940). The text, by poet Katherine Garrison Chapin, depicts several aspects of the gruesome act of lynching. The mood of the work was so dark that the premiere's conductor, Artur Rodziński from the Cleveland Philharmonic, refused to perform unless it was rewritten. As Chapin tells Still in a correspondence the two exchanged at the end of their collaboration, it wasn't the violence of the subject that worried Rodziński, but its anti-American sentiment: 'I see Dr. R's point', she wrote, 'that the world situation being so dark and America the only place of hope, we don't want to add something darker to it'.[33] After the two made significant changes to the work, the premiere did go forward and was celebrated in the press.[34] As this incident reveals, though, as the war in Europe accelerated in 1940, the discussion of sensitive racial issues was not just difficult or depressing, but almost immediately perceived as anti-democratic and anti-American.

This recent, racially troubled event may have disqualified Still for the job of scoring *One Tenth*, an equally troubled film. Just as we can only surmise why Still was not commissioned to compose the score, however, we can also only guess at why Harris was. Only one letter between Harris and Film Associates is known to survive. Dated July 17, 1940, it contains nothing beyond basic production information. The score was to be 'of a maximum duration of 30' and [use] a limit of 10 players'. Additionally, it was to be completed by August 1, 1940, which gave Harris only a very short two weeks to complete his work.[35]

In many ways, and certainly on the surface, Harris was a very odd choice to score a film about Negro education in the South. He was not African-American, nor was he a film composer. Unlike Aaron Copland, Marc Blitzstein, Virgil Thomson, Hans Eisler and other concert hall composers living in the New York area at the time, Harris had never before scored a film. As the American Film Center's press release for the finished film suggests, however, these disqualifications were dwarfed by a more important virtue: fame. 'Excellent music', it said, was being provided by 'one of America's most competent composers in the field'.[36] In fact, by early 1940 Harris was at the peak of his popularity, enjoying a reputation as one of America's most important concert hall composers. 'No composer', Barbara Zuck observes, 'was more American, nor did the music of any other American composer—even Aaron Copland's—receive the acclaim of Harris's symphonic works'.[37]

As Beth Levy has pointed out, however, Harris' fame at this point rested almost entirely on the accepted authenticity of two defining aspects of his biography. Harris was not just an American composer: more specifically, he was a white, Western one.[38] From the earliest reviews and biographical sketches, Harris set about accumulating a host of Frontier attributes. He was an Oklahoman born in a 'log-cabin'; a 'plainsman' whose melodic style resembled the awkward walk of a 'cowboy'.[39] By the early 1940s, these tropes were still being repeated unconsciously but now in the national press. In a review of Harris' Third Symphony in 1940, for instance, *Time* magazine, called him not just a 'home-grown' composer, but a 'spare, gangly twangy Oklahoman ... as independent as a Panhandle cowhand and as dryly American as the Dust Bowl where he spent his early childhood'.[40]

The addition of race to these geographical assertions began just as early. When compared to contemporaries Copland and Blitzstein in particular, critics identified Harris' music as not only Western, but also as white. For contemporary critic John Howard Tasker, for instance, Harris was the 'white hope of American music', a conclusion that was quickly echoed in the national press.[41] In his review of Harris' *Symphony 1933* (1933), *The New York Times* critic Olin Downs reported that many listeners 'see in him a present white hope of American music' and in *Time* magazine in 1935, Harris was a 'log-cabin' composer 'whom admirers regard as the strong White Hope of modern U.S. music'.[42]

Although Levy asserts that Harris attracted and cultivated this Frontier authenticity exclusively, several activities surrounding the scoring of *One Tenth* suggest that, in 1940 in particular, Harris was making a concerted attempt to alter and soften his reputation. His Symphony No. 4 (1939, revised 1942), the 'Folksong Symphony', included the expected Frontier motifs in the 'Western Cowboy' and 'Mountaineer Love Song' movements, while the movements entitled 'Johnny Comes Marching Home' and 'The Girl I Left Behind Me' fit comfortably within the tropes of a rural, white America. The sixth movement, the 'Negro Fantasy', however, required explanation. In what Levy rightly calls the symphony's 'companion piece', an essay entitled 'Folksong – American Big Business', published in November, 1940, Harris defended the use of Negro folksong in general, not by claiming racial and geographic proximity to it, but rather by erasing those features as a condition of their use.[43] When not simply quoted but abstracted down to their component parts – their irregular rhythms and intervals and idiomatic modal qualities – folksong provided the perfect raw material for composition. It was the most authentic material, in fact, for the kind of intrinsic, organic, 'autogenetic' melodic and formal processes that Harris had been pursuing. For those composers who have been 'deeply influenced by the finest, clearest, strongest feeling of our best songs', Harris observes, 'they will absorb and use the idioms of the music as naturally as the folks who unconsciously generated them. They will have learned that folksong is a native well-spring, an unlimited source of fresh material'.[44]

This emphasis on the autogenetic qualities of folksong was a pointed critique of not just one but two contemporary sources. It was a rejection of Schoenberg and Stravinsky and their foreign, European techniques that perpetually deconstructed themes into tiny motifs and repeated them. It was also a criticism of Copland and his inauthentic, quotational use of folksong, which Harris refers to in less veiled terms later in the essay when he observes that 'some city boys may take a short motor trip through our land and return to write the Song of the Prairies – others will be folk song authorities after reading in a public library for a few weeks'.[45] Even more significantly, however, the essay also provided the basis for asserting a new racial-neutral policy toward folksong.[46] In a clear reference to his experience with scoring *One Tenth* a few months before, Harris very democratically declared all folksong material for American composition, not just the 'Scotch-Irish ballads', the 'Spanish love songs', the French 'chants populaires' and the 'German chorales', but also the material resources of the South, the hypnotising 'voodoo rhythms and indigo moods of our black fellow-citizens, our one-tenth'.[47]

The 'Folksong Symphony' and its companion essay both suggest a changing identity for Harris, a loosening up of his exclusively Western and white reputation. One additional event in 1940 also did much to recast and complicate the reception of his work. Along with Still's *And They Lynched Him on a Tree*, several other new American works were also premiered at the Lewisohn Stadium concert on June 25. One was a new choral work by Harris, *Challenge, 1940* (1940), which featured parts of the Preamble of the U.S. Constitution as its text. Harris says he started the piece on June 10 in direct response to Italy's entrance into WWII as an ally of Nazi Germany, but he was also commissioned to write the piece by Rodzinski, who was looking for an appropriate counter-measure or foil for Still's anti-American 'lynching' ballad.[48] As historian Wayne Shirley concludes, based on the correspondence between Chapin and Rodzinski, 'when faced with a work that could be seen as anti-American, Rodzinski asked Harris for a flagwaver to balance Still's piece'.[49] And it worked. Not just Harris' *Challenge*, but all the works on the programme, including Still's troubling ballad, were heard 'in light of what was happening in Europe' to be an 'affirmation of American democracy'.[50] Although headlines that day carrying the news of France's surrender to Germany also helped, Harris' work succeeded in giving the whole programme a patriotic wash. The evening 'had democracy as its theme ... and the 13,000 in the audience ... responded as if the issues raised by this program must be the core of all thinking and feeling these days'.[51] When Film Associates approached Harris to score their sombre film about the plight of Negroes in the American South, then, they turned to a composer who had just rescued a similarly unpatriotic work, Still's 'lynching' ballad, from a similar fate. If Harris' uplifting, 'democratic' style could counterbalance Still's dark and disturbing choral work, then perhaps it could have the same ameliorating effect on their troubled Negro film.

Although Greene promised the advisory committee that Film Associates would produce a positive depiction of progress and achievement in the Negro community, the finished film fell well short of that. Of the film's 25 minute running time, the first 19 minutes are devoted to the problems of poverty, nutrition and education in rural African-American communities in the South. The opening narration, accompanied by images from rural landscapes, such as churches, homes and fields, recounts the history of migration, including the enforced migration of Africans to the U.S. through slavery: 'Today one American in every ten has skin that is dark', it concludes; 'one in every ten is a descendant of an African slave. We are America. We helped to build her. We helped to make her the richest country in the world'. After this prologue, the film shifts to observe and catalogue the problems of elementary education of Negroes in the rural South. Many of the issues presented are dire. Sharecropping is still prevalent, as are overcrowed, one-room schoolhouses, extreme poverty and hunger, as well as bad nutrition and hygiene. Only a brief 3-4 minute episode near the end shows the progress and achievements that the blacks were making in urban high schools, trade schools and colleges. In this part of the film, the narrator is replaced by the voice-overs of students themselves, who reveal their desires to become teachers and skilled labourers; even doctors and nurses. Their hopeful comments are short-lived, however, as the film quickly returns to the opening images and observations of prejudice and neglect, this time sharpened by references to war and democracy. Over images of wilting cornfields and squalid one-room schoolhouses, the narrator observes that 'We in this country know our difference of race and colour will never be solved by using bombs and high explosive shells. We know there is a better way and thoughtful men must find it if we are to show the world our democracy can work without injustice'.

Like most films of the period, *One Tenth* was shot silent, with narration, voice-overs and music added during post-production. While the narration is sporadic, the score is heard for roughly 21 minutes of the 25-minute film, often playing under the narration. Two scores for the film survive, both for 10-piece chamber ensemble of two violins, viola, cello, flute, oboe, clarinet, bassoon, horn and piano.[52] Over the course the film, Harris' score performs a number of different functions. Harris strengthens changes in location or content with audible changes in instrumentation, tempo, rhythm and key in order to expertly articulate the structure of the film. The score also subtly negotiates the narration through volume and instrumentation.

In terms of musical content, the score is marked by quotations of two different kinds. As Dan Stehman points out, with only two weeks to complete his work, Harris understandably recycled parts of several pre-existing compositions, including his Third String Quartet (1937) and the Concerto for Piano, Clarinet and String Quartet (1927).[53] The rest of the score is newly composed and marked by quotation of a different kind. Harris makes use of 'De Trumpet Sound It In My Soul', one of the spirituals he had previously used in the 'Negro Fantasy' movement of the 'Folksong Symphony'. But here, he uses it even more abstractly. As transcribed in John A. and Alan Lomax's *American Ballads and*

Figure 3.1 'Moanin' or 'De Trumpet Sounds It In My Soul' from John A. and Alan Lomax's *American Ballads and Folk Songs* (1934).

Folk Songs (1934), the tune's structure and style make it a perfect candidate for Harris' autogenetic processes. Alternatively titled 'Moanin', the tune's simple three part form is explained by Lomax as a factor of its origins in 'backwoods congregations of the South ... [where] ministers would "line out" several phrases from the Bible, or perhaps, from Watt's hymnal, and the congregations would take them up and repeat them in a singsong fashion'.[54] The second phrase of the tune immediately varies and expands on the intervallic content and contour of the first phrase. The third phrase is also intervallic and delivers the rest of sparse text: 'De trumpet sounds it in my soul, I ain't got long to stay here'. The text makes the tune a good match for the sobering content of the film (figure 3.1).

In the first 19 minutes of the film, where the images dwell so heavily on poverty, hunger and disease, the references to the first phrase of the spiritual are fragmented, sporadic and often concealed within a dense, contrapuntal texture. A fragment is heard briefly in the clarinet and flute as children enter the Goodwin School, for instance (4:49–4:56), and again in the oboe when the narrator tells us that 'The South is poor; there is not much money and there is not much time; the crops are always growing and the fields are always pressing near' (7:12–7:25). It surfaces briefly again in the flute several minutes later (10:40) alongside images from the Bemis School where, despite progress, pictures of food are contrasted with images of hunger and the narrator observes that 'there is food, but only for some' (figure 3.2).

When the film shifts dramatically to images of progress (19:00), the score responds with a longer, more prominent statement of this first phrase of the

Figure 3.2 'The South is poor. There is not much money.' *One Tenth of Our Nation* (Film Associates, 1940): 7:14. Image courtesy of Rockefeller Archive Center.

spiritual. When well-groomed college campuses are shown, the tune is presented prominently in the violin. With the shift to an interior shot of a print shop (20:24), the tune is stated twice in each of the wind instruments (figure 3.3). This effusive presentation is repeated again verbatim near the end of the film (23:05), with one other statement heard in the string quartet (21:40) when we see and hear from aspiring nurses and doctors. In the same way that the struggle for the tune to be heard in the first two-thirds of the film mirrors the struggle to overcome poverty and hunger, the clarity of the tune during the later moments of the film gives them a kind of weight and resolve. With a melodic emphasis on the more hopeful and progressive images, Harris' simple and straightforward use of the spiritual seems calculated to diffuse some of the bleakness and despair depicted in the film. By using autogenetic processes rather than overt quotation, he renders the spiritual more American than Southern or black. As a result, the score can be heard to de-racialise the film, softening and 'democratising' its often stark and disturbing words and images.

Figure 3.3 'It will be tough to get a job when I am through college. There are not many jobs waiting for us in the printing trade. But maybe I'll have a machine of my own some day.' One Tenth of Our Nation, 20:44. Image courtesy of Rockefeller Archive Center.

Epilogue

When the film premiered on September 4, 1940, at the end of the Negro Exposition, it did so to general acclaim. Several newspapers heralded it as 'the first

great documentary film on Negro education'.[55] Many on the advisory committee and the General Education Board, however, were still troubled enough by
the lack of progress and achievement shown that initial plans to release the film
theatrically and nationally were put on hold.[56] Although the American Film
Center was given additional money to re-edit the film and add new footage, this
revised 1943 version was also shelved without release. Making a film about race,
it seems, was complicated not just before the war, but during it as well.

This observation is given even greater clarity on the only other occasion in
which the film was screened publically. A few months after its premiere at the
Negro Exposition, on January 12, 1941, an excerpt of *One Tenth* was featured
at a special League of Composers' concert at MoMA. Sponsored by the League,
the American Association of Documentary Film Producers and MoMA, the
concert also featured excerpts from five other documentary films 'with scores by
leading American composers', including *The Power and the Land* (Ivens, 1940,
with a score by Douglas Moore), *Roots in the Earth* (U.S. Department of Agriculture, 1940, with a score by Paul Bowles), *The City* (Copland), *The River*
(Thomson) and *Valley Town* (Blitzstein).

In his review of this concert, composer Henry Cowell called the event
'historic' for giving the new musical genre of the film score concert-hall
display.[57] The critical evaluation of Harris' score for the film, however, was
not as positive. Just as the proper depiction of Negroes consumed discussions
of the script, a similar battle over the proper sound for these images immediately emerged. For Cowell, it was Harris' choice of instrumentation that
was inauthentic: 'The sophisticated tonal weaving and the tone-quality of
the city-union string section', he notes, 'were very much out of place in the
cornfields'.[58]

Paul Bowles' review of the film in *Modern Music* was even more critical. He
too heard Harris' style as inappropriate for the rural imagery it was accompanying. Harris' score, he observes, 'isn't functional. It is complex, and it tends to be
descriptive rather than evocative ... it is essentially concert music ...'.[59] Being
too urban and academic was not Bowles' only criticism, however. The score's
studied avoidance of race music and its lack of overt quotation of folksong were
not only inauthentic, but patently racist. Instead of diffusing the racial problems of the film, Bowles observes, Harris' autogenetic style heightened them:

> I don't even reproach the composer with having chosen not to include one
> Negroism in his score. ... The film was made by Whites for Whites; it is
> without ethnographic overtones. And since it was only a sociological plea
> to the White population, its creators were esthetically free to use whatever
> idioms they thought most effective, provided that each element was com-
> pletely subservient to the discipline essential in a propaganda film.[60]

According to Bowles, then, the lack of quotation didn't make Harris' score
more authentic, American, or democratic: it made it more white. While not
entirely accurate, Bowles' observations are instructive for what they reveal

about the discussion of race and national identity in music in the pre-war period. For Harris, the stripping away of ethnicity, race and geography made folksong more American; for Bowles, the concept of de-racialising music was not only inauthentic, it was impossible. Harris' autogenetic technique, when applied to folksong, was just as racially charged as quotation.

In a way that few other works of the period do, *One Tenth* allows us to see just how complex and complicated the business of race and national identity had become in the pre-war period, for both film and music. The growing war in Europe was forcing the nation as a whole to confront and redefine what it meant to be 'American'. If the U.S. was to be a beacon of hope to those oppressed by fascism and dictatorship abroad, it could not present itself as being 'democratic' without renegotiating its own racial history domestically. For the filmmakers of *One Tenth*, the long-standing opposition of 'plight or progress' became increasingly complex and unsustainable in the pre-war climate. For composers, the use of folksong, quoted or not, was also becoming increasingly complicated and problematic, which is perhaps why this film effectively disappeared in 1943. When faced with the problem of redefining a national identity as American and democratic, the question of race in film and music was becoming too difficult to ask, much less answer.

Notes

This article owes its existence to the tremendous generosity of my colleague Craig Kridel who rediscovered the film *One Tenth of Our Nation* in the Rockefeller Archive Center in 2009 and graciously shared it and a great deal of accompanying evidence with me. I am also grateful to several others for their research expertise and assistance, especially Erwin Levold, Senior Research Archivist at the Rockefeller Archive Center, and Renee James, former curator of the Roy Harris Collection of Musical Scores and Personal Papers at Cal-State, Los Angeles.

 1 Richard M. Barsam, *Nonfiction Film: A Critical History, Revised and Expanded* (Bloomington: Indiana University Press, 1992); and Erik Barnouw, *Documentary: A History of Non-Fiction Film, Revised Edition* (New York: Oxford University Press, 1983).
 2 William Alexander, *Film on the Left: American Documentary Film From 1931 to 1942* (Princeton: Princeton University Press, 1991); and Russell Campbell, *Cinema Strikes Back: Radical Filmmaking in the United States, 1930–1942* (Michigan: University of Michigan Press, 1982).
 3 Rick Prelinger, *The Field Guide to Sponsored Film* (San Francisco: National Film Preservation Foundation, 2006); and *Learning with the Lights Off: Educational Film in the United States*, ed. Devin Orgeron, Marsha Orgeron and Dan Streible (New York: Oxford University Press, 2012).
 4 See, for example, David Bordwell and Kristin Thompson, *Film Art: An Introduction* (New York: McGraw-Hill, 2006), 115.
 5 Neil Lerner, 'The Classical Documentary Score in American Films of Persuasion: Contexts and Case Studies, 1936–1945' (Unpublished PhD Thesis: Duke University, 1997); Elizabeth B. Crist, *Music for the Common Man: Aaron Copland During the Depression and War* (New York: Oxford University Press, 2005), 921–110.

6 The examination of these two films is exhaustive. See, for example, Alexander, *Film on the Left*, 113–43; Charles Wolfe, 'The Poetics and Politics of Nonfiction: Documentary Film', in *Grand Design: Hollywood as a Modern Business Enterprise, 1930-1939*, ed. Tino Balio (Berkeley: University of California Press, 1993), 364, 73; Barnouw, *Documentary*, 113–21; and Barsam, *Nonfiction Film*, 151–57.

7 Lorentz's film 'aroused passions and sparked controversy': Wolfe, 'Poetics and Politics of Nonfiction', 364–66. As Alexander observes, however, although painted a leftist because of his connections with FDR's administration, Lorentz himself was not a political radical. He had no sympathy with what he variously called 'the radical school of critics' and 'the Communist or camp-meeting critical school': *Film on the Left*, 97–112.

8 'It was at this point of departure', Alexander points out, that Steiner and Van Dyke 'came under the influence of British documentary movement (the most prominent and successful extant movement in documentary film) and thus entered the realm of the sponsored film': Alexander, *Film on the Left*, 243.

9 Barsam, *Nonfiction Film*, 80.

10 The exceptions were Rotha's *Face of Britian* (1936), which had been shown at the premiere of *The Plow That Broke the Plains*; and Wright's *Song of Ceylon* (1934), which had had a short run in New York City earlier in 1937: Alexander, *Film on the Left*, 243–44.

11 Paul Rotha, *Documentary Diary: An Informal History of the British Documentary Film, 1928–1939* (London: Secker & Warburg, 1973), 171–212. Rotha's visit was made possible by a grant from the Rockefeller Foundation through the General Education Board (GEB).

12 Rotha, *Documentary Diary*, 181–82.

13 Ibid., 184.

14 Ibid., 181.

15 Similar production companies included Raymond Rich Inc., Dial Films, Real Film Productions, Willard Pictures and others: Wolfe, 'Poetics and Politics of Nonfiction', 373–79.

16 Frontier Films, for instance, counted writers John Dos Passos, Lillian Hellman, Archibald MacLeish and Clifford Odets amongst its advisory board; Wolfe, 'Poetics and Politics of Nonfiction', 361–2.

17 Nicholas Murray, *Aldous Huxley: A Biography* (New York: St. Martin's Press, 2002), 252–54.

18 A detailed account of Felix's life and career, including his relationship with Peggy Bok, Rodakiewicz' wife, is given in Jeremy Lewis, *Shades of Greene: One Generation of an English Family* (London: Jonathan Cape, 2010), 115–121, 181–193.

19 See correspondence from Charles Barnett to Jackson Davis (February 27, 1940), in Folder 2145, Box 224, Series 1, GEB records, Rockefeller Archive Center.

20 See correspondence from Donald Slesinger to Jackson Davis (March 29, 1940), Folder 2145.

21 For example, 'Film on Race Education to be Made This Spring', in *Chicago Defender* (April 27, 1940), 17. See also articles 'Grants $15,000 for Movie on Race Education', in *The Philadelphia Tribune* (April 11, 1940), 17; 'Board Grants $15,000 for Education Film', in *Chicago Defender* (April 13, 1940), 9; 'Progress of Negro Education to be Subject of New Motion Picture', in *The Atlanta Daily World* (May 10, 1940), 1; 'Education is Subject of Race Films', in *Chicago Defender* (May 11, 1940), 8; 'Camera Work Stats on Education Film', in *New Journal and Guide* (June 1, 1940), 16; 'Begin Filming of Movie for Exposition; Race Advance to be Traced', in *New York Amsterdam News* (June 8, 1940), 5; and 'One Man's Dream Comes True', in *The Pittsburgh Courier* (June 15, 1940), 18.

22 Although undated, this scenario is stapled to Slesinger's letter to Jackson Davis (March 7, 1940), Folder 2145.

23 This 'treatment' with its accompanying memorandum entitled 'A Film on Negro Education', and additionally accompanied by a two page letter titled 'To the American Film Center and Members of the Advisory Committee', can be found in

the 'Theodore Lawrence Materials', Folder 8, Box 1 of the Vera Brodsky Lawrence Papers, Special Collections, New York Public Library for the Performing Arts.

24 Barnett to Slesinger (May 25) and Jackson Davis to Slesinger (May 27, 1940), Folder 2145.

25 Schlesinger to Barnett (March 7, 1940) and Barnett to Schlesinger (May 25, 1940), Folder 2146.

26 Letter dated May 17, 1940, 'To The American Film Center and Members of the Advisory Board' that accompanied the Film Associates' 'treatment.' See Vera Brodsky Lawrence Papers.

27 There is only one brief mention of the existence of a final script (with narration): Slesinger to Davis (July 26, 1940), Folder 2146. The information on shooting locations comes from newspapers articles: see 'Camera Work Stats on Educational Film', in New Journal and Guide (June 1, 1940), 16.

28 Alexander, Film on the Left, 259, 268; and Wolfe, 'Poetics and Politics of Nonfiction', 377.

29 '3 Photographers for Exposition are Jailed', in The Chicago Defender (June 29, 1940), 1.

30 Susan McCloskey, 'Shakespeare, Orson Welles, and the "Voodoo" MacBeth', in Shakespeare Quarterly, 36:4 (Winter, 1985), 406–416.

31 Catherine Parsons Smith, William Grant Still: A Study in Contradictions (Berkeley: University of California Press, 2000), 79–82.

32 Wayne Shirley suggests that Still refused to travel not just because of studio work that needed quick attention, but also because he had recently divorced and remarried and didn't want to leave his new wife and child; 'William Grant Still's Choral Ballad and They Lynched Him On a Tree', in American Music, 12:4 (Winter, 1994), 425–461.

33 Chapin quoted in Shirley, 'William Grant Still's Choral Ballad', 442–3.

34 See The New York Times (June 26, 1940), 27; The New Yorker, 16:21 (July 6, 1940), 43; Time Magazine, 36:2 (July 8, 1940), 46; and Eleanor Roosevelt, 'My Day', in Washington Daily News (June 26, 1940), 20.

35 A description of the letter is included in Dan Stehman's Roy Harris: A Bio-Bibliography (New York: Greenwood Press, 1991), 105–6.

36 'News from the American Film Center', (August 26, 1940), Folder 2147.

37 Barbara Zuck, A History of Musical Americanism (Ann Arbor, Michigan: University of Michigan Press), 227.

38 Beth Levy, Frontier Figures: American Music and the Mythology of the American West (California: University of California Press, 2012), 227–67. See also Levy's article, 'The White Hope of American Music: or, How Roy Harris Became Western', in American Music, 19:2 (Summer, 2001), 131–67.

39 Ibid., 227–45; and ibid., 32, 139–44.

40 Time Magazine (April 8, 1940), 45–6. Harris himself reinforced the 'cowboy' imagery: see his essay 'Folksong – American Big Business', in Contemporary Composers on Contemporary Music, ed. Elliott Schwartz and Barney Childs (New York: Holt, Rheinhart and Winston, 1967), 161.

41 Tasker quoted in Levy, 'The White Hope of American Music', 152.

42 Olin Downes, 'Harris Symphony Has Premiere Here', in The New York Times (February 3, 1934), 9; 'Log-Cabin Composer', in Time Magazine (November 11, 1935), 36–7.

43 Levy, Frontier Figures, 274.

44 Harris, 'Folksong—American Big Business', 164.

45 Dan Stehman, Roy Harris: An American Musical Pioneer (Woodbridge, Connecticut: Twayne Publishers, 1984), 25–29.

46 Ibid., 163.

47 Ibid., 162.
48 *Time Magazine* (July 8, 1940), 46; quoted in Shirley, 'William Grant Still's Choral Ballad', 446.
49 Ibid., 447.
50 Oscar Thompson, 'Novelties for the Stadium: Three Works That Deal With Theories or Issues of American Democracy', in *The New York Sun* (June 22, 1940), 16.
51 Howard Taubman, 'American Music Heard in Stadium', in *The New York Times* (June 26, 1940), 27. Rounding out the programme was Earl Robinson's 'Ballad for Americans' (sung by Paul Robeson), the 'Largo' movement from Dvorak's Symphony No. 9 and Weinberger's 'Variations and Fugue on Under the Spreading Chestnut Tree.'
52 A manuscript copy exists at the Roy Harris Collection of Musical Scores and Personal Papers at California State University, Los Angeles, in an uncatalogued box. A performance copy of the score also survives in the Edwin Fischer Collection at the Free Library in Philadelphia.
53 Stehman, *Roy Harris*, 106.
54 John A. Lomax and Alan Lomax, *American Ballads and Folk Songs* (New York: Macmillian, 1934), 579–80.
55 'Film on Negro Education Show at Race Progress Exposition Here', in *Chicago Defender* (September 7, 1940), 17; 'One Tenth of Our Nation Was Shown at Chi Exposition', in *New York Amsterdam News* (September 21, 1940), 11.
56 See, for instance, Charles Barnett to Jackson Davis (September 25, 1940); Robert A. Lambert to Davis (September 25, 1940); Albert R. Mann to Davis (September 26, 1940); Folder 2146.
57 Henry Cowell, 'The League's Evening of Films', in *Modern Music*, 18:3 (March / April, 1941), 176–78.
58 Ibid., 177.
59 Paul Bowles, 'On the Film Front', in *Modern Music*, 18:2 (January /February, 1941), 133–34.
60 Ibid., 134.

Chapter 4

Music, Science and Educational Film in Post-War Britain

Thomas F. Cohen

Critical and historical scholarship on the British Documentary Movement has tended to focus on a golden age of documentary production that began with John Grierson's *Drifters* (1929) and reached an apogee with the wartime films of Humphrey Jennings.[1] It is generally acknowledged that the quality of film product diminished considerably during the postwar period; until its demise in 1952, the Crown Film Unit—the successor to the General Post Office (GPO) film unit—continued to make a few fine films such as Jennings's *Cumberland Story* (1947), but they also churned out a good deal of prosaic work.[2] The absence of aesthetically worthy films has led to a critical consensus that, to borrow Ian Aitken's words, 'there was ... little possibility of producing innovative films of aesthetic quality' within the boundaries set by postwar government agencies.[3] Even if few postwar films can lay claim to artistic value, however, others hold interest as historical documents for musicologists as well as for film scholars.

Although the films I analyse below lie outside the canon of British documentary, they have value nonetheless as audiovisual artefacts that represent particular historical circumstances, yet they are in danger of being forgotten.[4] In particular, I want to exploit the *kairos*—the opportune moment—for looking at Muir Mathieson's *Instruments of the Orchestra* (1946) because 2013 marked the 100th anniversary of the birth of the film's composer, Benjamin Britten (b. 1913). The time is overdue for an assessment of Britten's role in the British Documentary Movement. My present purpose, however, is not to attempt a close formal analysis of Britten's musical contribution, *The Young Person's Guide to the Orchestra*. Rather, I want to investigate the meaning gleaned from the representations of musicians—the film features the London Symphony Orchestra—and conductor Malcolm Sargent on screen. The second film in my study, *Science in the Orchestra* (Alex Strasser, 1950), can boast neither a score by a well-known composer nor a revered *auteur* as director. It is the product of a team of journeymen, not the work of an individual director. Its value derives from the light it sheds on changing attitudes regarding the aims of public education during the postwar period in the UK.

The link between educational films and the broader institutional goals of postwar Britain is less obvious than it was during the pre-war and war years. Those films made under Grierson's tenure at the Empire Marketing Board (EMB) and the GPO had the imprimatur of official government agencies even as they occasionally diverged from the latter's purposes. Films made under the aegis of the Ministry of Information (MOI) during the first five years of the 1940s found their *raison d'etre* in contributing to the war effort. However, when the MOI was dissolved and the Central Office of Information (COI) established in 1946, the centripetal force generated by the mutual objective of Allied victory disappeared. The postwar government adopted a tepid attitude toward the Documentary Movement and the ascendant Labour Party strove to maintain distance from what might be perceived as partisan propaganda.[5] Nevertheless, a friendly if somewhat cooler relationship between the government and the documentary film units continued into early peacetime. In this essay, I build on this historical foundation to show how specific sounds and images in certain postwar educational films reflected the changing priorities of pedagogical institutions in regard to the arts and sciences. I examine two films produced not only to promote the musical arts among British schoolchildren, but also to prepare those students for a peacetime world increasingly governed by bureaucracy, technology and practical science.

As noted above, the war had provided the Documentary Movement with a clear purpose, whereas peacetime left the Crown Unit essentially rudderless. Private industry now employed either in-house companies—Shell Oil being the most successful of these—or hired independent companies such as Strand or Realist (the latter of which we will encounter below), to which many of Grierson's former associates had defected. The commercial studios resumed regular production after the war, and the increased competition for exhibition space, along with the influx of Hollywood imports, effectively banished documentary to the non-theatrical market in the UK. Such a state of affairs was not catastrophic, however, because the advent of affordable 16mm film and projection equipment allowed teachers to incorporate film into the classroom. In contrast, exhibitors of commercial venues were reluctant to alienate paying customers by programming unpopular documentaries. The characteristically formulaic approach of many such films may justify their lowly status when judged as entertainment or art and undoubtedly educational films have a reputation for boring audiences. Brian Winston even claims that spectators anticipate the 'Griersonian public education model' as a 'virtual guarantee of boredom', indicating that this model may be responsible for the marginalisation of documentary as a popular form.[6] However, commercial viability should not constitute the primary measure of a documentary film's worth. The editors of the recently published collection, *Learning with the Lights Off*, admonish neglectful film scholars for the educational film's marginal status in the critical literature. They observe that 'as long as debates about auteurs, aesthetics, popularity, and filmic enunciation dominated media studies, the highly formulaic, seemingly banal styles and structures of educational media, and the institutional nature of their use and exhibition, ensured their marginalisation'.[7] In any case, scholars should not privilege entertainment over informational or pedagogical value without a critical, contextual examination of the criterion of value.

Very likely, few students regarded educational films as immensely entertaining; nevertheless, it is important to historicise audience reception. Although such films may seem dull in contrast to today's music documentaries presented in 3D Imax with multi-channel digital sound, students of that time most likely found film screenings a welcome relief from school-day tedium. For example, British journalist Simon Heffer recalls the positively inspirational effect that *Instruments of the Orchestra* had on his six-year-old self attending a 'little school on the Essex marshes'.[8] The film's appeal, however, was not limited to captive audiences of schoolchildren. Mathieson reports, for instance, that MGM acquired the rights to distribute the film commercially as a short feature in the United States.[9] Despite its appeal for audiences of yesterday, its musical score aside, *Instruments of the Orchestra* today seems an entirely forgettable instructional film devoid of interest for the average filmgoer. However, the film reveals much about documentary's role in restoring social order in Britain immediately following the war. Despite its ostensible purpose of promoting the arts in education, the film actually functions to undermine the equality that educational reform strove for in this decade.

The 1940s saw the realisation of long-deferred changes in public education with the passing of the 1944 Education Act (the so-called 'Butler Act'). Although this important legislation did not issue prescriptions that directly affected the curriculum, it did call for the reorganisation of secondary school education in England and Wales into a tripartite system, instituted compulsory education for children of ages 5 through 15 and provided students with free milk for nourishment. However, the McNair report (1944), which influenced the Act, stressed the importance of teaching music in public schools. The authors of the report bemoaned the lack of uniformity in music education in primary and secondary schools. They recommended vocal and instrumental training for students and also championed 'opportunities for all children to listen to good music well performed'. Focusing on the recruitment and training of educators, the report asserted the need for competent instructors who would 'furnish all children with healthy tastes, most children with simple vocal skill and many with instrumental practice'. Moreover, they maintained that 'the exceptionally gifted should be afforded suitable facilities and teaching up to any degree of proficiency'.[10]

Instruments of the Orchestra

In 1946, the Crown Film Unit commissioned Britten to compose the music for a short film intended to introduce young students to the symphony orchestra. Britten had previously written music for a couple of films associated with the Documentary Movement: *Coal Face* (Alberto Cavalcanti, 1935) and *Night Mail* (Harry Watt and Basil Wright, 1936). For his brief, 20-minute score for *Instruments*, Britten managed to feature each individual instrument, the various instrumental families (woodwind, strings, brass and percussion) and the entire ensemble.

He achieves this feat by reworking a theme borrowed from Henry Purcell's incidental music to Aphra Behn's *Abdelazar* (1695) into a piece known as *The Young Person's Guide to the Orchestra*. After an initial *tutti* statement of Purcell's revoiced Rondeau, the various orchestral sections take up the theme in turn. Britten then offers a series of variations in several keys and diverse tempos in order to demonstrate the characteristic tone colours of the instrumental families that comprise the orchestra. Following this analysis, the piece ends with a fugue played by the entire ensemble. Since its filmic debut, *The Young Person's Guide to the Orchestra* has become a popular piece of music in its own right, which continues to be regularly performed as a concert suite. Of course, independent listening produces a very different experience from watching Mathieson's film.

Apart from the musical score, *Instruments* makes few attempts to stimulate the senses, maintaining instead a tone of stuffy formality throughout. The film marks the directorial debut of Mathieson, who served as music supervisor for over a thousand movies, including many GPO/Crown Unit films. Despite the musical background of its director and its unusual focus on music, however, *Instruments* adopts a pedestrian approach on the whole. The action – such as it is – takes place in a single location: a soundstage at Pinewood Studios. The London Symphony Orchestra, composed almost entirely of dour-looking middle-aged men in dark suits and ties, provides little in the way of spectacle (figure 4.1). The uninspired *mise-en-scène* – with minimal lighting and an unadorned set – undermines the interesting black-and-white cinematography by Fred Gamage (who also shot Jennings's *Listen to Britain*, 1942). Aside from the music, the only sound is the commentary spoken by the conductor, delivered in a dry patrician dialect for an absent audience. In terms of sound design, gone are the progressive experiments that characterised *Coal Face* and other films made during Alberto Cavalcanti's tenure as GPO production chief. In the 1930s, the lack of technical resources at the EMB and GPO necessitated audiovisual experimentation, although the influence of the Soviet montage filmmakers also contributed to the preference for contrapuntal sound and image connections. Even after the acquisition of portable sound equipment, however, films continued to be shot silent with sound dubbed later in the studio. Some directors preferred this method of production, which promoted audiovisual asynchronisation – the 'magic word' according to filmmaker and historian Basil Wright.[11] Paul Rotha, for example, writes that 'synchronized sound and speech obtained simultaneously do not play a large part in [early] documentary production'.[12] Although the musical performance of *The Young Person's Guide* was recorded at Wembley Town Hall prior to the Pinewood shoot, in the final product all audiovisual elements are in sync. Of course, for a film such as this to function as a teaching tool, the sounds we hear must match the instruments we see, so that, when the conductor introduces the oboes, those instruments – and not the flutes – are the ones we observe playing. In educational films, fidelity to natural law usually trumps creative treatment of the subject.

Figure 4.1 The London Symphony Orchestra performs Benjamin Britten's *The Young Person's Guide to the Orchestra* in Muir Mathieson's *Instruments of the Orchestra* (1946).

Following the film's opening credits, the cacophony of the orchestra tuning up quickly fades to silence as the conductor enters and mounts the podium. Here, the film illustrates the power of a leader to impose order on and give purpose to a disparate group of individuals. The applause dies down and Sargent turns to address the camera (figure 4.2). In his introductory remarks, he promises to take this 'music box' apart for the spectator. These words cast the orchestra as a mechanical device whose several parts work together efficiently. Sargent demonstrates his power not only to take the machine apart, but also to reassemble it as he introduces the spectator to the individual instruments, the various sections and, finally, the entire ensemble. The overall effect of Sargent's commentary is not to illuminate spectators, but rather to intimidate them with his superior knowledge and command of this select fraternity. Note Sargent's patronising address to the viewer, 'Some of you have heard a symphony orchestra; many more of you have heard one on the radio'. The distinction between 'some' and 'many' exploits the perceived difference between the cultured elite and the philistine masses.[13] Sargent's remark establishes the social superiority of concertgoers over those whose means limit their access to serious music save for radio broadcasts.

Figure 4.2 Malcolm Sargent addresses the audience in *Instruments of the Orchestra.*

The choice of Sargent—Mathieson's former teacher—as the authoritative wellspring of musical knowledge in *Instruments* is logical yet somewhat controversial. A successful and popular conductor by the time of the film's production, Sargent had played a major role in creating the London Philharmonic and held the post of chief conductor of the Royal Liverpool Philharmonic Orchestra from 1942–48. Something of a celebrity in the realm of 'serious' music, he had acquired the nickname 'Flash Harry', which may have referred less to his conducting style than to his sartorial affectations, which included his sporting a red carnation in his coat's lapel (a foible noticeable in the film). As a performer, Sargent exuded the aura of an aristocratic dandy and an aesthete, even though he came from a working-class family. Following certain views the conductor expressed disputing a musician's right to tenure in a 1936 interview in the *Daily Telegraph*, many members of the rank and file treated Sargent as *persona non grata*. According to his biographer, the conductor 'became almost overnight a hate[d] figure in the English musical world'. The controversy persisted so that 'even thirty years later there were players who would not speak to him'.[14]

In *Instruments*, Sargent's narration hardly presents the symphony orchestra as a progressive, democratic institution. The freshness of Britten's music seems at odds with the musty odour of the traditional social order that pervades the film. Explaining the structure of a fugue, Sargent praises the musicians' ability to play in concert, i.e., together: 'Each making his own individual sound, but blending together to make the noble music of the full symphony orchestra'. He thus acknowledges the value of individual achievement so long as it serves the col-lective effort to produce 'noble' ends. In other words, through concerted effort, the bourgeoisie can aspire to aristocratic art. To some degree, the bureaucracy required to fund and administer such a large ensemble ensures its traditional or even reactionary social character. Musicologist Christopher Small has described a typical symphony concert as 'an activity that earns complete approval from those authorities who provide and attempt to enforce the norms of our social and political lives'.[15] Reaffirming the status quo, Mathieson's movie issues a call to order after the pandemonium of war has ended.

During the war, class differences were downplayed in favour of national unity. Contrast *Instruments of the Orchestra* with Jennings's *Listen to Britain*, which also uses musical performances to achieve its ends: in this case, a call for civic harmony to persevere in the wake of Nazi attacks. The most famous sequence in *Listen to Britain* consists of a series of musical segments that culminate in a performance of a Mozart piano concerto at the National Gallery. A couple of shots show the Queen in attendance, sitting among soldiers and government workers. As Jim Leach notes, the mix of musical performances from both popu-lar and high culture sends a message that all strata of British society are pulling together.[16] This democratic message is undermined by the Queen's attendance at the concert featuring renowned pianist Myra Hess (later Dame Myra Hess), whose civilian garb sets her apart from her fellow musicians onstage, who all—conductor included—wear their military uniforms. These uniforms emphasise the solidarity between musicians and soldiers. A uniform serves to downplay differences among members of a group as it signifies that group's difference from others—especially, of course, from the enemy. In Jennings's film, various shots of non-military citizens carrying helmets also lessen the distinction between civilian and military dress.

Science in the Orchestra

Cinema can represent music making by depicting the motor activity of per-forming musicians, as in *Instruments of the Orchestra*. Alternatively, a film can attempt a technical analysis of the phenomenon of sound production from the viewpoint of acoustic science. *Science in the Orchestra*, produced by the Real-ist Film Unit, takes such an approach. This work comprises three short films, all directed by Alex Strasser: *Hearing the Music*, *Exploring the Instruments* and *Looking at Sounds*. Strasser's film is commonly regarded as a companion to its 1946 predecessor.[17] This genealogical connection makes more sense than com-paring *Instruments* to Mathieson's later film, *Steps of the Ballet* (1948). Certainly, the latter two films share significant personnel and a general approach to their subjects, but evidence suggests that *Science* was intended to complete the pre-vious film on music.[18] Between these two films, a shuffling of personnel has occurred, with Mathieson replacing Sargent as compere and conductor and Malcolm Arnold composing the music. According to Strasser, *Science* was in production for more than three years.[19] If his timeline is correct, then work on that film must have begun only a year or so after the release of *Instruments*. The question arises: why did the producers, the Central Office of Information, deem it necessary to supplement Mathieson's film so soon after its release? The inference is that the COI found something lacking in the earlier film. For them, this 'missing ingredient' was science.

In the late 1940s and early 1950s, those charged with the task of educational reform scarcely saw a pressing need for young musicians; rather, they perceived the imminent necessity for more scientists and technicians if Britain were to remain competitive in the postwar global economy. Wartime had revealed the importance of scientific technology for a well-prepared, modern military and civilian officials were now committed to harnessing this technology for peaceful ends. The following comment from MP and Nobel Prize winner John Orr sums up this new faith: 'Men of science have now given us the physical means of attaining the new world order which our poets and prophets have only seen in their visions'.[20] Orr's exaggerated confidence in the positive social effects of science aside, the realisation of this utopia would require a highly-educated workforce. As Jon Agar notes, 'a lack of scientific and engineering "manpower" was seen as a severe problem'.[21] The British school system was doing a poor job of identifying and nurturing potential scientists and technicians. The 1946 report *Scientific Manpower* (a.k.a. the Barlow Report), which called for doubling the number of scientists in Britain, lamented that 'only one in five of the boys and girls who have the intelligence equal to that of the best half of the university students actually reach the universities'.[22] To counter possible accusations of 'scientism' from critics concerned with securing the status of the humanities in education, the authors asserted that they did not advocate 'any attempt to meet the increased demand for scientists and technologists at the expense of students of other subjects'.[23] Of course, a documentary combining science and music would ideally satisfy both humanists and scientists.

Both films share the ostensible educational aim of fostering a greater appreciation for and deeper understanding of music. However, a shift of goals has transpired. *Instruments of the Orchestra* endeavours not only to teach music appreciation to a general audience, but also to inspire students who possess a proclivity, perhaps a genuine gift, for music as a vocation. In contrast, Strasser's film appears designed to recruit future scientists rather than to encourage budding musicians. *Science in the Orchestra* responds to its predecessor by presenting science as a more desirable vocation than musical performance.

The choice of director exemplifies the contrast between the two films. Mathieson was a musician by trade; he had been musical director on many commercial films as well as several documentaries produced by the EMB and the GPO. Strasser, on the other hand, was best known for making educational science films. Austrian born, he had worked for the UFA (Universum Film AG) in Germany as a cameraman before migrating to England in 1934. He is credited as photographer on Len Lye's *Birth of the Robot* (1935), which was made for Shell. In 1944, Strasser joined the Realist Film Unit, an independent outfit started by Grierson alumnus

Wright, where he worked as cinematographer on several documentaries before graduating to director. Strasser also authored several books on photography and film.

Conceived for pedagogical purposes, *Science* employs a plethora of visual effects to delight and instruct its young audiences. In his book *The Work of the Science Film Maker*, Strasser takes great pains to explain how he and his colleagues achieved the film's special effects. This involved the construction of various three-dimensional material models, which would provide a visual and haptic experience for spectators. Various educational episodes featuring these models were then projected onto a large screen mounted to the side of the orchestra. Some of these designs were ingenious. For example, to show the pitch range of the orchestra, the crew constructed a huge musical stave spanning bass and treble clefs. This transparent prop could be placed in front of the musicians, creating the effect of superimposition without involving expensive post-production work. Fifty-two light bulbs, representing the heads of notes, ran diagonally across the lines of this stave and, as the musicians sounded tones on their individual instruments, the corresponding 'note' on the stave lit up. According to Strasser, the goal of employing such models rather than resorting to animations was to achieve 'the impression of a lecture-concert taking place before a live audience'.[24] Thus, the entire presentation presents an illusory unity of time that characterises a 'live' performance.

Although I cannot cite any hard data regarding the film's popularity with British schoolchildren, I can assess the rhetorical effect of the film, which does an excellent job of communicating with young viewers. For a start, it acknowledges and represents its intended audience on screen, a tactic absent from *Instruments*. Whereas the latter depicts only professional musicians, *Science* features schoolchildren in the *mise-en-scène*. These pupils encourage viewers to identify with their on-screen counterparts and provide a model for the appropriate behavioural response in the classroom. For instance, one segment in *Exploring the Instruments* involves straightening out the tubing of a French horn to exaggerated length. The film then cuts to a group of children laughing. As Sergei Eisenstein claimed, film can manipulate spectators to mimic the action they see on screen and produce the intended emotional response.[25]

Not only do the films show groups of students; they also introduce various individual characters with unique personalities. For example, *Exploring the Instruments* features a young man named Peter who demonstrates the panpipes and the bugle. An older student, Peter presents a likeable 'older brother' persona. The best example of this empathic strategy, however, occurs in part three, *Looking at Sounds*, where we encounter Mr. Watkins, a good-natured and handsome young scientist. After an establishing shot of the orchestra, the camera pans right to introduce a neatly but casually dressed Watkins, who is accompanied by an assistant wearing a white lab coat. The location has shifted from the stage to the laboratory and our attention is averted from the serious-looking orchestra led by Mathieson to the cheerful Watkins and his futuristic machines. Strasser astutely employs Watkins to provide some comic relief. For instance, the next time Mathieson calls on Watkins, he is caught off-guard, sitting in a relaxed pose amongst his equipment, apparently lost in thought. Apparently, the scientist's inquisitive mind finds the musical proceedings less than engaging. Clearly, it is Watkins the scientist—not the musicians or the conductor—who represents the intended role model for students. For, whereas the orchestra members demonstrate their skills with traditional musical instruments, Watkins exhibits his mastery of modern technology.

It is Watkins, not Mathieson, who introduces the most fascinating 'instrument' of the segment: the audio-spectrometer.[26] In the staged experiment that follows, Watkins dazzles his audience with the transformative power of modern science. First, he uses the audio-spectrometer to render visible the waveforms produced by various instruments; then he manipulates the overtones of two wind instruments to make an oboe sound like a flute. To these impressive demonstrations, Mathieson registers awe, cautioning the audience, 'it's quite a technical business', while praising the mastery of the young acoustician, who 'can cut out any harmonics he likes'. Here, the audio-spectrometer thoroughly upstages oboe and flute, just as the brilliant technician outshines the (apparently) dull musician. For, while Watkins busily adjusts the technical apparatus, the clueless oboist obediently plays his instrument on cue from the confines of an isolated sound booth. At the experiment's conclusion, Mathieson jokes, 'I hope Mr Whitiker [the oboist] never finds out what we did to his oboe'. At this point, oddly, it is the orchestra that applauds, as if they too have been amazed and humbled by this demonstration.

Despite its rhetorical efficacy, the film tends to reduce the activity of making music to a cold technical abstraction. Science in the Orchestra succeeds in making science appear alluring, but it fails to do justice to musical performance as a social activity. It also fails to acknowledge that the arts of musical composition, orchestration and performance cannot be reduced to the science of acoustics. The film achieves its goal of promoting science and technology, but does it do so to the detriment of music? Science in the Orchestra exemplifies Grierson's notion of using the cinema as a pulpit, but to what purpose?[27]

Ironically, by focusing on the potential benefits of enhanced science education, the government failed to predict the important economic role that England's popular music industry would play in the 1960s. David Simonelli observes that 'by 1968, London's metropolitan record market was the largest producer in the world outside the United States with 100 million records grossing approximately £40 million'.[28] And if the British people remained in the thrall of Hollywood movies, the musical groups of the so-called 'British Invasion' conquered American radio in the 1960s. Of course, this upsurge of popular music owed virtually nothing to formal education. On the contrary, the Ministry of Education's dismissive attitude toward popular music is evident in the 1960 pamphlet entitled Music in Schools. This report cautions that mediums such as radio, records and film have 'brought the teacher new problems as well as new possibilities'.[29] Deploring the increasing influence of 'bad music' in the culture at large, the authors insist that 'young people often show a remarkable instinct for assimilating music of high quality when they are given sincere, able and patient help in making direct contact with it'.[30] Indeed, while the majority of popular films encouraged some young people to forsake traditional orchestral instruments in favour of electric guitars and drum kits, documentary film as an educational resource helped to sustain musical diversity in British culture by bringing art music into the classroom.

Notes

1 Paul Swann, *The British Documentary Film Movement 1926–1946* (Cambridge: Cambridge University Press, 1989). Swann notes: 'the work of Jennings and the feature length story-documentary films have been at the expense of neglecting the other films made by the independent units during the war' (163). I maintain that this bias extends beyond the war years.

2 Ian Aitken, *The Documentary Film Movement: An Anthology* (Edinburgh: Edinburgh University Press, 1998). Aitken lists several reasons for this decline, including the pressure on filmmakers to accommodate the tastes of timid and unimaginative civil servants.

3 Aitken, ibid., 56.

4 See Devin Orgeron, Marsha Orgeron and Dan Streible, *Learning with the Lights Off: Educational Film in the United States* (Oxford: Oxford University Press, 2012), 4.

5 See Aitken, *The Documentary Film Movement*, 55–56. See also Timothy Boon, *Films of Fact: A History of Science in Documentary Films and Television* (London: Wallflower Press, 2008). On the limited role of post-war documentary, Boon notes that, 'in the new polity the COI was not primarily concerned with purchasing filmmaker's expertise in anything but filmmaking' (171).

6 See Swann, *The British Documentary Movement*. See also Brian Winston, *Claiming the Real: The Griersonian Documentary and Its Legitimations* (London: BFI Publishing, 1995).

7 Orgeron et al., *Learning with the Lights Off*.

8 Simon Heffer, 'The Time is Ripe to Rediscover Benjamin Britten', in *The Telegraph* (26 December 2010), at http://www.telegraph.co.uk/comment/columnists/simonheffer/8222708/The-time-is-ripe-to-rediscover-Benjamin-Britten.html (accessed 10 February 2014).

9 Muir Mathieson, 'Music for Crown', in *Hollywood Quarterly*, 3:3 (Spring 1948), 325.

10 *Teachers and Youth Leaders* (McNair Report), Education in England, at http://www.educationengland.org.uk/documents/mcnair/mcnair1944.html (accessed 3 January 2013).

11 Basil Wright quoted in Elizabeth Sussex, *The Rise and Fall of British Documentary: The Story of the Film Movement Founded by John Grierson* (Berkeley: University of California Press, 1975), 12.

12 Paul Rotha, *Documentary Film* (London: Faber and Faber, 1952), 165.

13 See Pierre Bourdieu, *Distinction: A Social Critique of the Judgement of Taste*, trans. R. Nice (Cambridge, MA: Harvard University Press, 1984). As Bourdieu observes, 'nothing more clearly affirms one's "class," ... than one's tastes in music' (18).

14 Richard Aldous, *Tunes of Glory: The Life of Malcolm Sargent* (London: Hutchinson, 2001), 81.

15 Thorstein Veblen, *Theory of the Leisure Class* (New York: Random House, 1918). As Veblen observes, 'the generation which follows a season of war is apt to witness a rehabilitation of the element of status, both in its social life and in its scheme of devout observances and other symbolic or ceremonial forms' (373).

16 Jim Leach, 'The Poetics of Propaganda: Humphrey Jennings and *Listen to Britain*', in *Documenting the Documentary: Close Readings of Documentary Film and Video*, ed. Barry Keith Grant (Detroit, MI: Wayne State University Press, 1998), 166.

17 Alex Strasser, *The Work of the Science Filmmaker* (New York: Hastings House, 1972), 142.

18 The Kino release of Volume III of their 1992 video collection *The British Documentary Movement* erroneously ascribes the music in *Steps of the Ballet* to Britten when, in fact, it was composed by Arthur Benjamin.

19 Strasser, *Work of the Science Filmmaker*, 144.

20 Orr quoted in Boon, *Films of Fact*, 135.

21 John Agar, *Science and Spectacle: The Work of Jodrell Bank in Post-War British Culture* (Amsterdam: Harwood Academic Publishers, 1998), 18. See also Boon, *Films of Fact*.

22 'Scientific Manpower' (The Barlow Report), in *Educational Documents of England and Wales 1816–1967*, ed. Stuart Maclure (London: Mathuen, 1973), 231. The 1945 Percy Report (ibid.) is also of some importance regarding these issues, although it says little about primary and secondary education but focuses instead on the creation of technical colleges.

23 Ibid., 232.

24 Strasser, *Work of the Science Filmmaker*, 144.

25 Sergei Eisenstein, 'The Montage of Film Attractions' (1924), in *Selected Works Volume 2: A Theory of Montage*, ed. Michael Glenny and Richard Taylor (London: BFI Publishers, 1994), 39–58.

26 As Strasser admits, 'the whole action centred around an audio-spectrometer'; *Work of the Science Filmmaker*, 160. An audio spectrometer is an instrument that measures the intensities of frequencies that make up a complex sound wave.

27 John Grierson, *Grierson on Documentary*, ed. Forsyth Hardy (New York: Praeger, 1946), 36.

28 David Simonelli, *Working Class Heroes: Rock Music in British Society in the 1960s and 1970s* (Lanham: Lexington Books, 2013), 97.

29 Ministry of Education, *Music in Schools 2nd ed.*, Education in England, at http://www.educationengland.org.uk/documents/musicinschools/musicinschools.html (accessed 3 January, 2013), 10.

30 Ibid., 11.

Chapter 5

Reinventing the Documentary
The Early Essay Film Soundtracks of Chris Marker

Orlene Denice McMahon

In his book entitled *The Essay Film*, Timothy Corrigan defines the genre as 'practices that undo and redo film form, visual perspectives, public geographies, temporal organizations, and notions of truth and judgement within the complexity of experience'.[1] Although stimulating, Corrigan's definition and, by extension, the rest of his book, highlight a common practice in defining and investigating the essay film, which stresses a visual rather than *audiovisual* approach to the genre. By focusing on the 'visual perspectives', Corrigan is not alone in side-lining the 'audio perspectives' that are 'undo[ne]' and 'redo[ne]' by this innovative genre; the audio dimension, which is, as Nora M. Alter puts it, 'one of the most important and determining forces in this type of film, for it structures the montage, shapes meaning, establishes tone, and encourages flights of fantasy'.[2] In an attempt to promote a truly audiovisual approach to analysing the essay film genre, this chapter will focus on the role of music, sound effects and commentary—the essential components of the soundtrack—in the early essay films of one of the most relentless and innovative essayists of all time, Chris Marker. Indeed, Marker will be remembered for having intertwined cinematic, photographic and literary techniques for over half a century to create some of the most evocative cinematic works in the essay film genre, most famously *La jetée* (1962), *Le fond de l'air est rouge* (1977), *Sans soleil* (1983) and, more recently, *Chats perchés* (2004). By means of his multimedial boundary crossing, Marker managed to redefine both the meaning and the medium of documentary filmmaking.[3] Given his groundbreaking role in the essay film genre, how then does the soundtrack operate in the combinative architecture of Marker's documentary films? What is the relationship between music, commentary and image in his essay films? And how does it differ from the soundtracks of 'realist' documentaries? This chapter will explore these questions by listening to and analysing the audiovisual relationships at play in a range of Marker's less-known early essay films, including two short travelogue documentaries from the fifties—*Dimanche à Pékin* (1956) and *Lettre de Sibérie* (1958)—and two politically engaged essay films from the early sixties—*Description d'un combat* (1960) and *Cuba sí!* (1961).

Marker first came to prominence in Paris in the late 1940s, a time when aspirations for cultural and political renewal dominated the postwar zeitgeist. Combining his interest in literature, travel and politics, Marker became involved during this period with a group of affiliated ventures that included the journal *Esprit*, two new organisations dedicated to popular education and the dissemination of culture – 'Peuple et Travail' and 'Travail et Culture' – and the publishing house Editions de Seuil.[4] For the latter, the inveterate traveller Marker launched a series of books collectively entitled *Petite Planète*: each text used facts and figures to support subjective, personal and sometimes poetic impressions of a foreign country.[5] These books predate any of Marker's cinematic works, yet they introduce aspects that would inform all of his subsequent film work: the foreign country is viewed through images of eccentricity and contradiction; the texts are designed for a spectator who has never been there (thus, the 'image-témoin' or 'eye-witness' format); and a unique prosaic form of commentary replaces the usual flat and formal language of most guidebooks and informational documentaries.[6] In fact, as André Bazin put it in 1961, Marker remained primarily a writer making films:

> Chris Marker is of the new generation of writers who think that the time of the image has come, but who do not say that it is necessary to sacrifice to the image the power and virtue of a language which remains the special interpreter of the mind: understanding. What this means is that for Chris Marker the commentary of a film is not what is added to images that have already been pre-arranged and fixed, but rather it is almost the first and foremost element.[7]

For Marker, then, a film's soundtrack is not a supplement to the image but rather a prerequisite. Indeed, as shall be borne out through the film analyses to come, Marker's film essays highlight the powerful effect the soundtrack can have on our perception of the image. Moreover, Marker uses the soundtrack – and in particular the music and commentary – to develop a strong audiovisual critique of the ethic of objectivity put forward by 'realist' documentary forms.

Of course, in order to understand Marker's critique, it is important to situate his films in relation to the 'realist' documentary tradition, which is founded on the belief that the filmmaker can present reality objectively by showing things as they 'really' are. An example of this tradition is observational film, exemplified by American direct cinema, based on the principle of non-intrusion on the part of the filmmaker. As Jeffrey Ruoff puts it, 'observational filmmakers were not to intrude on the lives of their subjects, not to ask questions, conduct interviews or otherwise direct, stage, or influence the events for the camera; they were to be as flies on the wall'.[8] Likewise, direct cinema (pioneered by filmmaker Robert Drew) sought reality by photographing people without intruding, with the intention that their subjects would reveal what they really felt and were like when unselfconsciously relaxed or deeply involved in some activity.[9]

As we shall see, Marker ultimately critiques this ethic of the non-intrusive filmmaker for its lack of acknowledging what Tammy Stone terms the 'inevitability of subjectivity' intrinsic to documentary filmmaking:

> [...] it must be assumed that any film, be it fiction or documentary, is by necessity constructed; that inherent in the filmmaking process is the need to shape, select, and therefore create the finished film.[10]

Marker's essay films are perhaps closer then to another tradition of documentary filmmaking specific to France—*cinéma vérité*. Pioneered by ethnographer and filmmaker Jean Rouch in the 1950s, *cinéma vérité* denies the idea that a filmmaker can achieve objectivity or that the camera can be unobtrusive.[11] Hence, Rouch felt that filmmakers must have a strong attitude towards the subjects, even to the point of provocation. The result is that everything we see and hear in *cinéma vérité* films is occasioned by the making of the film—the camera acts as a stimulus to explain the *raison d'être* of life, as opposed to direct cinema's desire to 'let life reveal itself'.[12]

To understand the novelty of Marker's approach in terms of the soundtrack, it is also worth establishing the ways in which sound and music are used in the 'realist' documentary tradition. In his work on documentary film sound, for instance, Ruoff points out the differences in sonic aesthetic between nonfiction and fiction film. Focusing predominantly on synchronous sound observational films, he shows how specific norms, such as location-recorded sound, are used to represent 'reality', even when this affects the issue of clarity, whereas in fiction film, and more specifically in classical Hollywood cinema, the fidelity of sound is sacrificed in favour of the more narratively central dimension of intelligibility.[13] In fact, the lack of clarity on the soundtrack (the use of direct sound, for instance) and the rough unpolished texture of these documentaries became major stylistic traits employed to exaggerate the 'realism' portrayed through the lens. These filmmakers want to eliminate overt narrational devices like voice-over in favour of stories that begin *in medias res* and unfold seemingly without a narrator.[14] In so doing, they aim to conceal the elements of subjectivity inherent in their creation, instead promoting an illusion of objectivity. Avoiding the creative use of sound, these observational and direct cinema filmmakers endeavour to achieve a lucid representation of reality through intentionally inaudible speech, radically differing sound levels between scenes and by allowing microphones to accidentally appear in the image.[15]

It is these norms and conventions of documentary sound that Marker's early essay films flout by deliberately drawing attention to sound's creative impact on the images and our perception of them. Closer analysis of two of Marker's earliest travel films clearly demonstrates the ways in which the filmmaker plays with sonic conventions to parody and thus critique the notion of being able to film objectively. Both films are scored by French composer Pierre Barbaud (1911–1989) and appeared at the end of the fifties: *Dimanche à Pékin* (1956) and *Lettre de Sibérie* (1958).

Dimanche à Pékin

As Sarah Cooper explains, *Dimanche à Pékin* brings together themes of subjectivity, memory, film and time through a narrator who, from the vantage point of 1956, takes us from Paris to Peking (now Beijing) and back in time, through the entry point of a black and white still image.[16] Marker's film, one of the first accounts of Mao's China by a Western filmmaker, offers views of Beijing city life and glimpses of a China hitherto unknown to the West, snapshots set to a witty voice-over commentary that delights in the oddities and contradictions of Chinese society. What makes the film unique as a documentary, however, is the subjectivity of the voice-over, which draws us into the film through a childhood memory. This immediate intimacy created between the narrator and the audio-spectator is in stark contrast to the objective stance taken by the observational documentary and would become a hallmark of Marker's films to come.

In terms of music, Barbaud's score plays into Marker's unique documentary style by adopting techniques associated with classical Hollywood film music scoring, such as Mickey-Mousing, synchronisation and audiovisual parallelism, yet pushing them to the limit in order to highlight their very conventionalism, thus pointing out the role of sound, and particularly music, in the documentary. In line with this, Barbaud's score is divided into sequences (comprising a credits sequence and 11 following sections, marked 0 to 10), whereby the tone of each sequence fits perfectly with the thematic of the images, underscoring the action on screen to the point of overemphasis. When it comes to how the sequences interact, however, Marker intentionally sets up binaries between the alternating scenes, resulting in a constant oscillation of tone from one sequence to the next.

Although little is known about the collaborative relationship between Barbaud and Marker and how exactly they worked together, it is perhaps safe to say that given the nature of these films as travelogues, Barbaud most likely composed the music after shooting, therefore leaving it to be added to the film in postproduction along with the narration, which was either creatively woven into and around the score or vice versa. Written for flute, oboe, cor anglais, bass clarinet in B-flat, harpsichord, drums, viola and cello, the score's instrumentation resembles the small ensembles for which Barbaud's earliest film scores were composed, though the harpsichord here takes the place of his earlier preference for the ondes Martenot in films such as Alain Resnais' *Malfray* (1948) and Pierre Gout's *Les Petits mystères de Paris* (1949).

The clash of a gong is heard at the film's opening before the music takes up the form of a waltz, with the melody played on strings (viola and cello) and the rhythm provided by woodwind, harpsichord and drums. Barbaud's use of the harpsichord is especially interesting, since it is made to resemble the sound of an accordion, thus giving the music a distinctly French vibe. This is significant since the film begins in 1956 Paris and is narrated from the viewpoint of a French man, looking back on his time in Peking. By opening the waltz with the percussive sound of a gong, however, Barbaud imbues this introductory sequence with a sound from the East, thus musically bringing the two sides, East and West, together. This union is also visibly portrayed in the text of the credits, which is written in both French and Chinese. The ending of the opening credits on an interrupted cadence sets up an atmosphere of mystery, which is extended into the music of Sequence 0 by the sonority of successive arpeggiated harpsichord chords. A swift tilt shot upwards from an array of antiques and what appears to be Chinese memorabilia, accompanied by a lengthened arpeggiated chord synched with the sound of a triangle, brings the Eiffel Tower into full view, leaving us in no doubt as to the film's opening setting.

Once the harpsichord chords are replaced by a soft, woodwind melody in a major pentatonic scale, evocative of traditional Chinese folk music, the narrator explains:

> For thirty years in Paris, I had been dreaming about Peking without knowing it. In my imagination, I could still see an illustration from a book I had looked at in my childhood, without knowing exactly what it referred to. It was in fact a scene at the Gates of Peking, the avenue leading to the tombs of the Ming emperors. And one fine day, here I was. It's not very often that one can step into a picture belonging to one's childhood. Yet here I am on this Ming avenue [...]

By means of a dissolve, we are transported from the still photograph of Peking into the footage taken by the narrator on his visit to the city. Hence, Marker makes it clear from the outset that this is not a 'conventional documentary'. Rather, it is one openly connected to the narrator's personal interest in Peking. This openness on the part of the narrator/creator is highly unusual, as it serves to emphasise not only Marker's acknowledgement of the poetic, but also his embrace of the subjectivity inherent, but often concealed, in 'realist' documentary forms.

The first images we see of Peking and its temples, 'draped in mist', show early morning commuters on foot, on bicycles and a man pulling a cart, all accompanied by the previously-heard traditional folk pentatonic melody, played this time first on viola, then by cor anglais, cello and finally on flute. A shot of a moving train triggers a change in the tone of the music from one of serenity to one of frenzy, with the harpsichord providing a decidedly percussive rhythm, rather than its earlier melodic contour, demonstrating the instrument's sonic diversity in Barbaud's score. This blatant contrast in the music's tone perhaps suggests that there is more to this city and its inhabitants than the politeness the narrator has mentioned several times in his voice-over. Indeed, the alternation of tone from one sequence to the next is characteristic of Barbaud's score, with the odd-numbered sequences offering a gentle, bucolic tone and the even-numbered sequences (with the exception of the last one, sequence 10) providing a more frenzied and percussive tone.

Take for example the wholly percussive opening section of Sequence 2, written in 3/4 for gong, cymbal, a tambourine *sans timbre* and drum, which first accompanies the agile movements of a man doing exercise with a sword before moving onto two men engaging in Chinese boxing. This is preceded and followed by a gentle, four-note, stepped motif, which is played in various transposed keys by the different woodwind instruments and appears throughout the score, especially over images of children (see figure 5.1, top). As mentioned above, this alternation of tone from one sequence to the next, both in the images and in the soundtrack, continues throughout the film and is arguably linked to Marker's wish to uncover the dialectical nature of life in Peking. Not only does he contrast young and old, as well as the individual and the masses, he also sets out before us the age-old dichotomy of tradition versus modernity. In Sequence 4, for example, a shot of a moving steamroller is accompanied by a harpsichord providing rhythmic accompaniment to a high-pitched viola melody (see figure 5.1, middle). The constantly alternating time signature of the harpsichord's rhythm, from 5/8 to 3/4, links the scene to Sequence 2, perhaps because both accompany images of modernity (a train and steamroller) as opposed to the quiet sequences of tradition shown in the sections in-between.

Political life in Peking is also treated by Marker in Sequence 8, which shows footage from the celebration of the 'National Day of the People's Republic of China', accompanied by upbeat and percussive music written in a 4/4 rhythm appropriate to the marches we see performed on screen. The music gets especially loud and animated when we see a shot of Chairman Mao smiling and waving to the crowds, with a traditional Chinese melody, heard on flute, oboe and harpsichord, accompanying this historically-important footage of the Chinese leader (see figure 5.1, bottom). Moving back from the masses to the individual, Sequence 9 shows footage similar to that of the film's opening, with many close-up facial shots of the men, women and children of Peking, smiling and talking as they spend the afternoon at the city's zoo, accompanied by a soft, almost indecipherable, melody heard under the narrator's voice. Finally, Barbaud ends the film's score in Sequence 10 with a Chinese children's tune, which the narrator refers to as 'a little tune that will stay with me until the end of the afternoon'. The fugal melody in 4/4 is played first on oboe and then by viola, joined by the cor anglais, before becoming transformed and extended by the entire orchestra. The closing shots of the film and of this 'Sunday' in Peking are accompanied by slow, long notes heard sustained on woodwind and strings as we watch a family rowing on the serene lake at the Summer Palace. A tracking shot of the banks of the lake show us groups of families, enjoying the tranquil Sunday afternoon, and the narrator closes his voice-over on an enigmatic phrase about Peking: 'one wonders about both past and future'. Marker ends his film on this questioning tone, emphasising the overall sense of ambivalence with a final sustained, unresolved chord.

With hindsight, such a conclusion was a prescient decision by Marker. Only two years after the making of *Dimanche à Pékin*, Chairman Mao implemented the 'Great Leap Forward', resulting in the deaths of an estimated forty-five

Figure 5.1 Pierre Barbaud's score for *Dimanche à Pékin* (Chris Marker, 1956).
Top: Four-note Motif; Middle: Sequence 4, Steamroller, Alternating Time
Signature; Bottom: Chairman Mao Music; © Association Pierre Barbaud.

million people. Retrospectively then, the voice-over narration, the images and
the music reflect the volatility of Peking and China in general during these
years, resulting in a tone that was somewhat prophetic of the historical and
political events to come over the next few years. Barbaud's music, albeit often

Sequence	Music	Screen Grab
Credits	Sound of gong at opening evokes the East; ensuing waltz evokes France (the setting for the film's opening)	
0	Successive arpeggiated chords on harpsichord synched with camera movement upwards to see Eiffel Tower	
I	Soft melody in a major pentatonic scale on woodwind instruments; evocative of traditional Chinese folk music	
2	Percussive section in 3/4 time, written for gong, cymbal, tambourine *sans timbre* and drum	

(Continued)

3	Gentle, four-note, stepped motif, played in various transposed keys by the different woodwind instruments; appears throughout the score, especially over images of children	
4	Harpsichord provides rhythmic accompaniment (constantly alternating time signature from 5/8 to 3/4) to a high-pitched viola melody	
5	Oboe and horn play a repetitive melody	
6	Percussive sequence dominated by rhythmic drumming	

(Continued)

Sequence	Music	Screen Grab
7	Ethereal bell-like sound of a celesta combined with a melody on harpsichord; reminiscent of the gentle tunes played by music boxes	
8	Music is both upbeat and percussive; written in a 4/4 march rhythm	
9	Soft, almost indecipherable melody heard under the narrator's voice is based on the following flute motif: 	
10	Chinese children's tune; fugue in 4/4 – played first on oboe and then by viola; joined by the cor anglais and is hence transformed and extended by the orchestra	

Figure 5.2 Illustrated Analysis of *Dimanche à Pékin*.

conventional in its style and relation to the image, plays a distinctive role in conveying this tone. By adopting conventional film music techniques, Marker uses the constant changes in the music's style, rhythm and tone to truly underscore (to the point of overemphasis) the evolution that took place at this time, transforming traditional agrarian China into Mao's modern Communist China. This subversion of convention is perhaps brought to a more conspicuous level, however, in Marker's subsequent film.

Lettre de Sibérie (1958)

Made two years after *Dimanche à Pékin*, Marker's *Lettre de Sibérie* embodies a similar audiovisual approach. This time, however, Marker captures the diversity of Siberia, a land the narrator describes as 'somewhere between the Middle Ages and the twenty-first century ... between humiliation and happiness'. Characteristic of Marker's boundary-crossing aesthetic, the film transcends genres, moving from documentary to travelogue, animated cartoon to philosophical tract. As one reviewer has noted, the freshness and modernity of the film come from Marker's 'sympathetic ethnography', which was so much against the grain of the partisan American documentaries of the 1950s, in which the omniscient voice tells one 'how' to read each image.[17] Unlike the observational tradition mentioned above, these postwar partisan documentaries embraced the use of subjective voice-over commentary (which aptly came to be known as 'voice of God' narration) and often used it as a means of propaganda.[18]

Lettre de Sibérie in fact addresses and ultimately critiques the practice of propagandist agendas in documentaries. Moreover, Marker's critique is clearly articulated by means of the soundtrack by drawing our attention to the power of both the commentary and the music in persuading an audience of a certain point of view. In fact, one of the film's most insightful and perhaps most famous sequences highlights the powerful relationship between music, commentary and image by showing the same sequence of footage four times, each time with different commentary and different music. By doing so, Marker calls into question the very role of narration: is it something that simply joins together images to create a narrative flow or something that determines our reading of a film? Marker also employs Barbaud's music in innovative, often humourous, ways, which position *Lettre de Sibérie* as a quasi-spoof on the actual documentary process.

Whereas Marker chose a photograph to kick-start the narrator's reminiscence in *Dimanche à Pékin*, here he employs a letter from Siberia as a springboard into the film. The voice-over begins with the sentence, 'I am writing you this letter from a distant land; its name is Siberia', which is heard over snapshot images of Siberian landscape accompanied by what sounds like a traditional Siberian song, sung by a chorus of harmonious voices with no instrumental accompaniment. Like the opening of *Dimanche à Pékin* then, this introduction is highly personal in comparison to 'realist' documentaries, as the narrator's recollection once again establishes an expectation for a subjective, nonconformist nonfiction style.

In his score, Barbaud delineates his split orchestration marked as 'Formation A: flute, oboe, cor anglais, bassoon, piano, drums, strings (8, 3, 2, 1)' and 'Formation B: 2 oboes, trumpet, trombone, piano, drums, strings (4, 4, 3, 2, 1)', (figure 5.3). It is with the passing of a tram that we hear the music for the first

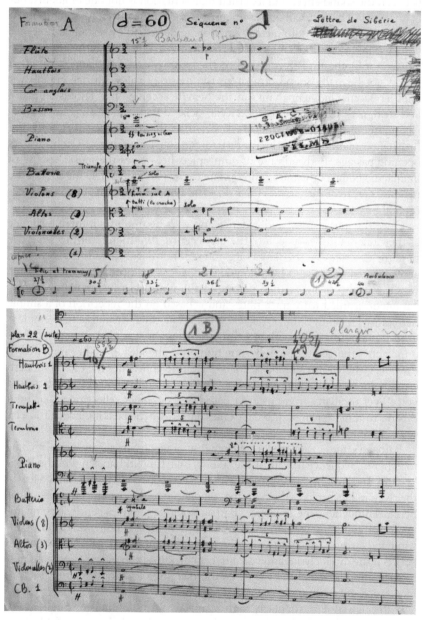

Figure 5.3 Pierre Barbaud's score for *Lettre de Sibérie* (Chris Marker, 1958).
Top: Orchestra A. Bottom: Orchestra B; © Association Pierre Barbaud.

time: tremolo chords on piano and violins in 3/2, introduced by a single note on the triangle, mimic the bell of the tram, thus creating a moment of audiovisual synchronicity, not between sound effects and image, but between music and image – a moment which Rick Altman terms 'iconic' in that the relationship between the sound effect and its visual representation is not one of fidelity, but of analogy.[19] The first half of this opening sequence is written for Orchestra A, comprised of a sparse solo melody on viola underscored by sustained notes on flute, violins and cellos. This sparsity is short-lived, however, as the first passage written for Orchestra B is triggered by the passing of an ambulance. Although we do not hear the sound of a siren, the music of this sequence creates yet another 'iconic' moment thanks to the heavily accented bass chords on piano and strings, which denote the gravity associated with the passing ambulance. The music of this section is much denser than that of Orchestra A, with the *ff* dynamic marking in stark contrast to the soft *p* marking of Orchestra A's opening passage. Barbaud's use of quintuplets here gives the music a sense of drama, the pomp of the music appropriate to the panoramic tracking shot of the majestic centre of the city of Angarsk, so far removed from the opening scenes of rural Siberia.

Once the music stops, mid-cadence and with no resolution, there is silence as the camera finishes its pan of the city's centre. We then return to what the narrator describes as the 'stone-age forest', the Taiga; a transition which is accompanied once again by a nondiegetic, vocal, traditional song. The song, which was also heard at the opening of the film, lacks instrumental accompaniment, is filled with grace notes and is based on the repetition of a simple harmonised melody. Similar to *Dimanche à Pékin*, then, the music here employs classical narrative film scoring techniques whereby it underscores the images on screen – the quiet, rural folk song reinforces the idea of tradition related to the Taiga whereas the pompous, energetic music underlines the idea of modern city life in Angarsk. Likewise, the rhythm, tone and volume of the narrator's voice-over oscillates from a slowly-paced, serene, quiet reflection about rural Siberia to a more agitated, louder enunciation when speaking about the city of Angarsk.

Barbaud's music and the traditional singing of Siberia eventually come together in Sequence 3. Whilst the soloist, Ella Timourkhan, sings of the River Lena in Russian, the camera, mounted on a boat, shows us a panoramic view of the river and its banks as the narrator compares it to the river he knows best, the Seine. Throughout the sequence, Barbaud's music provides gentle accompaniment to the soloist's song in the form of sustained, descending notes on woodwind and strings, though it is barely audible given the competition of sounds between the music, lyrics and voice-over, a melding of sounds that perhaps mirrors the film's overarching theme of the merging of various binaries, such as modernity and tradition.

Although not particularly significant in terms of music, Sequence 6 refers once again to this theme of binaries and includes one of Marker's characteristically self-reflective moments, in which the narrator pokes fun at the documentary process in his commentary, which is heard over footage of a building site:

> And now here's the shot I've been waiting for, the shot you've all been waiting for; the shot no worthwhile film about a country in the process of transformation could possibly leave out – the contrast between the old and the new. On my right, the heavy-duty truck, forty tonnes. On my left, the 'telegoï' (horse-and-cart), two hundred-and-forty pounds. The past and the future, tradition in progress [...] Take a good look, because I won't show them to you again.

Sequences 7 and 8 move from machinery and construction to the Taiga and are both on the subject of reindeer. A melody marked *dolce cantible*, played on cor anglais and bassoon, accompanies the lyrics of the soloist, who praises the reindeer. Once the singing ends, another Markerian moment follows as the narrator declares that, if he had the money, he would 'shoot a spot commercial in their honour'. Within seconds, an animated advert for reindeer interrupts the film, humourously showing the omniscient control of the narrator and the filmmaker over everything we see and hear, a control that emphasises the inherently 'constructed' nature of the documentary genre.

Pushing this idea to its limits are the following scenes, in which Marker shows the same sequence of footage four times, each time with different commentary and different music, in order to highlight the relationship between music, commentary and image.[20] The first time we see the sequence of footage in question, it is accompanied by the narrator's reflections on the city of Yakutsk after hearing an Yves Montand tribute played through speakers throughout the city centre:

> As I listened to this tribute to Yves Montand, I looked around me. Undeniable energy, enthusiasm and the will to work. A faith that the future will be as bright as the past was dark. Huge gaps and a firm determination to fill them. While recording these images of the Yakutsk capital as objectively as possible, I frankly wondered whom they would satisfy. Because of course you can't describe the Soviet Union as anything but the worker's paradise, or, as hell on earth.

During this commentary, we see footage of the city of Yakutsk under construction: a red bus full of workers drives over an as yet unpaved street and passes a car driven by some administrative personnel, while nearby a crew of labourers are levelling the street-bed by dragging a heavy timber over the earth. This initial commentary is accompanied by solo, virtuosic-style piano music, its fast rhythm underlining the idea of 'energy' and 'enthusiasm' conveyed by the narrator's reflections. It is with the narrator's realisation of the tentative issue of 'objectivity' inherent in his recording of the capital that a sort of 'commutation test' on these very same images is initiated.

Having acknowledged his wish to 'test' the impartiality of the footage, the narrator accompanies the second viewing with varied commentary, as an example of one possible take on the images. On this occasion, the music accompanying the footage is dominated by brass instruments played in high registers, producing joyful, victorious-sounding music, which perfectly matches the upbeat text of the commentary. Overtly commendatory of the Soviet ideology, this version's 'progressive' commentary highlights the modernity of the city, pointing out the presence of automobiles and the work being carried out as part of the Socialist revolution. This is undoubtedly the voice of communism and so Barbaud's music is in keeping with the ideas of victory and pomp associated with its propaganda.

The third repetition of the same footage is accompanied by strongly oppositional commentary and dramatically sombre piano music, both of which clearly reinforce its negative interpretation of the Soviet regime. Lugubrious and mournful, the melody begins with piano chords in the bass, followed by extremely low notes from the brass, their doleful tones accentuating the anti-communist reading of these images. Finally, the fourth and last repetition of the footage gives us a possible 'objective' reading of the images, heard with no musical accompaniment, only diegetic street sounds. Marker leaves us in no doubt, however, about the question of whether this final version is the only 'objective' version of the footage by immediately nuancing the final showing with the following commentary:

> But objectivity isn't the answer either. It may not distort Siberian realities, but it does isolate them long enough to be appraised and consequently distorts them all the same. What counts is the drive and the variety. A walk through the streets of Yakutsk isn't going to make you understand Siberia.

In the end, Marker highlights the relativity of objectivity and the inevitable influence that all images have on the spectator's interpretation of the film. However, by removing the music, which could move us to feel drawn into the text rather than reflective about it, Marker seems to say that the 'purely informative' version of the footage is the most neutral. By introducing the concept of 'point of view', Marker thereby plays with the ways in which sound (commentary and music) can exert power over our perception of the images. In his review of the film in *France-Observateur*, André Bazin praised this aspect of the film in particular, calling it 'horizontal editing', whereby the images move laterally with what is heard.[21] This movement from the ear to the eye challenges the primacy of word over image prevalent in documentary films, making us realise the weight of sound in relation to our perception of the image.

Throughout *Lettre de Sibérie*, Marker forcefully announces his concern to de-mythologise 'objective' documentary filmmaking, using ironic juxtapositions between the soundtrack, image and narration to offer self-reflexive commentary on the film's own modes of construction.[22] The film clearly demonstrates the effects that sounds can have on image: the changing tessitura of the narrator's voice, as he passes from one tone to another, the intonations and ruptures of tone, as well as the game between music, commentary and image, all provoke us to question what we hear and what we see. We, as audio-spectators, are made to understand that this is not a 'classic documentary' with a unique, omniscient, serious voice. Rather, irony rules, not only in Marker's commentary, but also in Barbaud's musical score. As with *Dimanche à Pékin*, Barbaud once again employs conventional film music techniques, such as Mickey-Mousing, in the animal sequences. Yet, to a much greater extent than the latter film, Barbaud's music here makes fun of itself, wilfully unveiling its manipulative powers, particularly in the self-reflexive segment of repeated scenes. Music is thus more than ever part and parcel of Marker's sardonic critique of communism.

The Essay Films of the Sixties

For his essay films of the sixties, Marker intensified his politicised cinematic discourse, collaborating with an eclectic mix of contemporary composers and musicians, thus bringing a more contemporary musical dimension to his soundtracks. He nevertheless continued his commitment to accentuating the boundaries between music, the voice and sound effects, thus emphasising the singularity of each sonic element in the overall filmic construct. For the Kafkaesque film *Description d'un combat* (1960) about Israel, for instance, he collaborated with composer/sculptor Marcel Van Thienen, known in musical circles as Lalan. In the late fifties, Lalan set up his own studio for electroacoustic music. It is unsurprising, then, that his research into this genre feeds into the music he composed for Marker's film. A sombre meditation on the need to remember the past, *Description* evokes the Israeli state's struggle to remain true to the principles behind its foundation (only 12 years old at the time of filming) and its attempts to fashion a way of representing the quotidian life of Israel.[23] These themes of trial and error and constant struggle are aptly reflected in the experimental sonority of Lalan's modernist score, whose dissonant harmonics and sparse *musique concrète* provide a fitting soundscape for this reflective essay film.

Equally important are the diegetic sounds of the Israeli environment, exemplified by the cacophonous music of Jerusalem's marketplace, where traditional Israeli songs, chants and shouts combine and subsequently morph into a long passage of *musique concrète*. Later, the silence of prayer is juxtaposed with the sonic bedlam of crowds at an annual memorial procession, in which many participants are seen playing traditional woodwind and percussion instruments and singing in Hebrew. The latter cacophony is then mixed with Lalan's dissonant bass piano chords, their atonality giving the celebratory images an uncomfortable sense of foreboding.[24] Eventually, Lalan's music drowns out the crowd noises altogether and we are left once more with sparse a-rhythmical drumbeats punctuating the images. The contrast of Lalan's serious music with these apparently celebratory images suggests the need for the Israeli state to contextualise its short history of independence in light of its tumultuous past and tentative future, amidst constant warring with neighbouring Arab states. At the close of the film, Lalan's unresolved and unresolvable music underpins Marker's images and commentary by emphasising the ongoing, unresolved nature of this displaced people's fight.

In his subsequent documentary *Cuba sí!* (1961), Marker musicalises a vibrantly partisan celebration of the recent Cuban revolution with authentic Cuban music, interspersed with snippets from popular revolutionary songs and, later, electronic music.[25] The powerful rhythms of the soundtrack drive this overtly political documentary, which explores the background to the Cuban revolution of 1959, looking particularly at the Bay of Pigs invasion.[26] Moreover, as Alter suggests, the film also signals a revolution in Marker's filmic practice as he uses – for the first time – a camera that records synchronised sound.[27] The film thus showcases Marker's awareness of the potentiality of making the soundtrack an integral element of a film's construction at the point of recording the image. For example, by means of a lively, energetic style of editing, the film's montage of images parallel the rhythms of the Cuban music on the soundtrack, as well as the fractured patterns of Castro's interminably long speech featured in the second half of the film.[28] It is by means of sound mixing that Marker uses snippets of aggressive electronic music to disturb Castro's elocution, thus sonically portraying the many attacks aimed at Castroist discourse during this period, particularly from the mainstream press. In a 1961 interview, Marker disclosed that, of his films to date, *Cuba sí!* was the closest to his heart, describing it as an attempt to communicate the 'rhythm' of a decisive revolution in contemporary history.[29] As Cooper notes, the published commentary to the film strengthens the musical references, since it labels each section with a different Italian tempo description, from *Largo* to *Allegro*, with Castro's interviews labelled *Arias*, to mark the various and frequent changes of their pace.[30] Defending *Cuba sí!* against censorship, filmmakers Agnès Varda and Jacques Demy singled out the film's rhythm in their argument, declaring that Marker had 'filmed the Conga Brava' and 'made a film on a living revolution'.[31] Marker's combination of electroacoustic and electronic music with the national musics of Israel and Cuba, respectively, thus emphasises his wish to engage with experimental, contemporary music whilst also stressing the authenticity of these emerging nations in their respective struggles for independence.

From his playful travelogue essays to his more serious, politically-driven documentaries, Marker continually used the soundtrack as a powerful tool to critique, parody, comment upon and enrich the documentary film genre. His unrelenting commitment to provoking us, the audio-spectators, to question both what we see *and* what we hear resulted in an undeniable reinvention of the essay film; an achievement for which Marker will fondly be remembered as one of the most distinctive documentary filmmakers of the twentieth century.

Notes

1 Timothy Corrigan, *The Essay Film: From Montaigne, After Marker* (Oxford: Oxford University Press, 2011), 2.
2 Nora M. Alter, 'Composing in Fragments: Music in the Essay Films of Resnais and Godard', in *SubStance #128*, 41:2 (2012), 25.
3 Sarah Cooper, *Chris Marker* (Manchester: Manchester University Press, 2008), 2.
4 Catherine Lupton, *Chris Marker: Memories of the Future* (London: Reaktion Books, 2005), 13.
5 William F. van Wert, 'Chris Marker: The SLON Films', in *Film Quarterly*, 32:3 (Spring 1979), 38.
6 Ibid., 39.
7 Bazin's quote appears on the jacket of Chris Marker's *Commentaires I* (Paris: Editions du Seuil, 1961).
8 Jeffrey Ruoff, 'Conventions of Sound in Documentary', in *Sound Theory, Sound Practice*, ed. Rick Altman (London: Routledge, 1992), 218.
9 Jack C. Ellis and Betsy A. McLane, *A New History of Documentary Film* (New York: Continuum, 2005), 217.
10 Tammy Stone, '(Non)Fiction and the Viewer: Re-interpreting the Documentary', in *Journal of Moving Image Studies* (Autumn 2003), at http://www.avila.edu/journal/fall03/StonePaper.htm (accessed April 10, 2010).
11 Ellis and McLane, *A New History of Documentary Film*, 216.
12 Ibid., 217.
13 Ruoff, 'Conventions of Sound', 217.
14 Ibid., 218.
15 Ibid., 221.
16 Cooper, *Chris Marker*, 18.
17 '*Lettre de Sibérie*: Filmnotes at PFA', in *Chris Marker: Notes from the Era of Imperfect Memory*, at http://www.chrismarker.org/2008/04/lettre-de-siberie-filmnotes-pfa/ (accessed May 15, 2010).
18 John Grierson, the man who coined the term documentary and came to be considered the father of British and Canadian documentary film, was a proponent of this tradition.
19 Altman, *Sound Theory, Sound Practice*, 202.
20 Unfortunately, the music for this sequence of the film and for some of the sequences which follow are not in the score held at Barbaud's archives in Paris.
21 André Bazin, 'Review of *Lettre de Sibérie*', *France-Observateur*' (October 30, 1958); reproduced in Bazin, *Le cinéma français de la libération à la nouvelle vague* (Paris: Cahiers du cinéma, 1983), 257.
22 Jonathan Kear, 'The Clothing of Clio: Chris Marker's Poetics and the Politics of Representing History', in *Film Studies*, 6 (Summer 2005), 50.
23 Ibid., 51.
24 For more on the use of atonal and dissonant harmonies to denote foreboding, see *Music in the Horror Film: Listening to Fear*, ed. Neil Lerner (New York: Routledge, 2010).
25 Lupton, *Memories of the Future*, 73.
26 Cooper, *Chris Marker*, 32.
27 Alter, *Chris Marker* (Champaign: University of Illinois Press, 2006), 68.
28 Kear, 'The Clothing of Clio', 51.
29 Marker, quoted in Cooper, *Chris Marker*, 33.
30 Ibid.
31 Agnès Varda and Jacques Demy, quoted in Cooper, *Chris Marker*, 33.

Chapter 6

Water Music
Scoring the Silent World

Mervyn Cooke

> There is, one knows not what sweet mystery about this sea, whose gently awful stirrings seem to speak of some hidden soul beneath; ... here, millions of mixed shades and shadows, drowned dreams, somnambulisms, reveries; all that we call lives and souls, lie dreaming, dreaming, still; tossing like slumberers in their beds ...
>
> Herman Melville, Moby-Dick.[1]

> He began, in a tone of great Taste and Feeling, to talk of the Sea and the Sea shore – and ran with Energy through all the usual Phrases employed in praise of their Sublimity, and descriptive of the undescribable Emotions they excite in the Mind of Sensibility. – The terrific Grandeur of the Ocean in a Storm, its glassy surface in a calm, ... and the deep fathoms of its Abysses, its quick vicissitudes, its direful Deceptions, ... All were eagerly and fluently touched; – rather commonplace perhaps ...
>
> Jane Austen, Sanditon.[2]

Rarely have composers, artists, filmmakers or writers regarded the oceans as commonplace and Austen's deliciously bathetic use of the term in the passage above (penned in 1817) was a curt dismissal of the clichés routinely trotted out by those who subscribed to the extravagant romanticism of Byron and his followers when confronted with the sea. In the visual arts, painters by the mid-seventeenth century had already been depicting vessels tossed on stormy waters in a way that 'substantiated popular conceptions of the sea as an untrammelled force of nature', a preoccupation that culminated in Turner's highly expressive conception of seascapes.[3] Like Byron, Turner was furthering the concept of the 'sublime', an attempt to come to terms with nature's sometimes inhospitable grandeur that in a maritime context dates back to a statement published by Joseph Addison in 1712, in which he writes of his 'pleasing astonishment' and 'agreeable horrour' when contemplating an expanse of water; the notion of the sublime was later formulated by Edmund Burke.[4] The crucial factor here is the oxymoronic conjunction of pleasure and terror: as John Mack puts it, the romantic sublime was 'a kind of fretful pleasure which was held to be both uplifting and inspiring'.[5]

The preoccupation meshed well with the majestic but often turbulent and inhospitable expanses of the oceans, which when calm could also encourage contrastingly relaxed emotions rooted in notions of tranquillity and beauty, and between these two extremes inhabit the 'gently awful' region described by Melville.

In literature, the sea proved itself to be almost uniquely universal as a symbol or metaphor. Auden compared it to the (waterless) desert, since both lack a sense of community and 'historical change for better or for worse' and, as a result, promote alienation and solitude.[6] In the eighteenth century, literature (including lyrics for hymns) so habitually treated the oceans in symbolic and metaphorical terms that they ceased to be recognisable as a real domain.[7] Metaphorical treatments of the seas, from the Renaissance to the present day, have proved fruitful not only to writers with personal experience of ocean travel (Conrad, Melville) but also to at least one who richly explored the ocean's potential as a symbol for the human condition without, in all probability, having ever set foot on a sea-going vessel (Shakespeare). The central idea that 'the writer who goes to sea [or considers it from a distance] finds himself confronting a disturbed reflection of his own age, personality, and preoccupations' is neatly suggested by the title of Conrad's collection of autobiographical essays, The Mirror of the Sea (1906).[8] At the same time, however, the deep ocean can be a metaphor for the utterly impenetrable. For example, Jean-Pierre Melville's debut feature Le Silence de la mer (1948), based on Vercors' story about the French Resistance, has a wonderfully evocative title; but neither sea in particular, nor water in general, play the remotest part in the film. They are never seen, or even alluded to, and the title instead refers to the prolonged silence of non-cooperation on the part of the mute leading characters and to the sea as a metaphor for 'the submerged life of hidden and conflicted feelings, desires and thoughts'.[9]

For composers, evocative treatments of the sea in literature have long been a potent source of inspiration and fine concert works written on maritime topics are far too numerous and well known to list here. One, however, deserves singling out for the major impact its style exerted on film composers during, and since, the so-called Golden Age of Hollywood feature films. While the stylistic norm in nondiegetic orchestral film scores in the 1930s and 1940s was heavily dependent on the idiom of Richard Strauss – and appropriately so, since his symphonic poems had perfectly fused detailed programmatic suggestion with autonomous structures (an ideal to which much conventional film music aspired) – more vivid colouring was occasionally provided by hints of Russian exoticism and French impressionism. Debussy's symphonic poem La Mer (1905) became much imitated in scores to films with ocean-going scenes and even more so in the theatrical documentaries with which the present chapter will primarily be concerned. In particular, Debussy's novel approach to orchestral textures, specifically the layering of ostinati based on different rhythmic patterns (an idea intensified by his seminal encounter with the Javanese gamelan), seemed perfectly attuned to the need to portray musically the swelling motion of the ocean waters. Furthermore, the same basic approach could be readily adapted to different motions and patterns of both water and light: gentle lapping, sunlight sparkling on the surface, swells and surges, huge waves breaking and so on.

The Movies Go to Sea

Since music for mainstream ocean-set documentaries has always been heavily indebted to the compositional formulae of narrative feature films, it may be helpful briefly to examine a few representative examples of musical treatments of seascapes in fictional movies before examining the documentaries themselves.

The Straussian opulence of Erich Wolfgang Korngold's score to the Errol Flynn vehicle *The Sea Hawk* (1940) is primarily concerned with capturing the antics of the swashbuckling hero. Apart from one exterior shot of a ship at sea (27'), in which orchestral flourishes memorably double the rise and fall of simultaneous harp glissandi, the latter device is so ubiquitous – indeed, it was a mannerism for which orchestrator Hugo Friedhofer was criticised at the time – that for the most part it fails to carry its traditional (Debussyan) watery connotations, even occurring during interior scenes. Nevertheless, the harp glissando and harp timbres in general were to remain stock illustrative devices when film composers were required to deal with the sea. The apogee of this tendency was Bernard Herrmann's music for *Beneath the 12-Mile Reef* (1953), a film whose principal strength is the combination of vivid aquatic CinemaScope photography (sometime presented in a quasi-documentary manner, as at the opening) and an evocative score that includes nine harps. Multiple harp glissandi enhance various watery scenes, clashing discordantly to create the wave effects in the main title sequence and recurring as a diver is first menaced by sharks and then taken up to the surface, assumed dead (46'–47'), creating a lush accompaniment to a couple's romantic underwater swim (69') and producing a deranged sonic wash as a diver is attacked by a giant octopus (93'). But the harps are also used less conventionally, with Herrmann exploiting the instrument's normally neglected bass strings to create deep, throbbing ostinato patterns that evoke the movement of large sea creatures or the heaviness of a deep-sea dive (87'). When divers explore underwater vegetation towards the end of the film, the harps provide, as Christopher Palmer describes it, 'a shadowy, murmurous continuum against which drums, low winds, electric bass and organ pedals heave and writhe as if to resist the enormous pressure of the water'.[10]

Apart from the use of harps, Herrmann's score deploys other familiar musical gestures associated with the sea and later frequently used by documentary composers: isomorphic rhetoric (e.g. music rising when someone climbs aboard a boat and descending for diving into the water), waltz rhythms for underwater swimming and Debussyan layered-ostinato textures supporting slow, sustained melodic tones. This last manner of composing is particularly useful, since rhythmicised ostinati can suggest inexorable movement even within a very slow harmonic rhythm, and the conjunction with a slower melody captures the swell of the ocean or stiffness of the wind while retaining a sense of expansive grandeur.

Ostinato-based textures can also quickly shift to suggest tension and anxiety (85') as well as natural phenomena or serenity.

Few later maritime film scores came even close to the level of resourcefulness demonstrated by Herrmann. John Barry's dreary response to Peter Benchley's story *The Deep* (1977), a wooden attempt to cash in on the huge success of Steven Spielberg's film of the same author's book, *Jaws* (1975), did not have the benefit of John Williams's famously energising music: Barry's contribution to the follow-up is ponderous enough to make even the action sequences seem inactive. Since then, some sea films have elicited emptily clichéd musical responses from their composers, while others have not stood the passage of time well, including Eric Serra's dated electronic score for Luc Besson's diving yarn *The Big Blue* (1988) which, like *Beneath the 12-Mile Reef*, includes underwater sequences shot as if for a documentary. Besson had originally intended to use a symphonic score and in preparation Serra spent three years absorbing music by composers such as Debussy and Ravel; but Serra (on his own admission) could not read the scores adequately enough to analyse them effectively, so the idea was abandoned in favour of 'something more corresponding to our culture'.[11] Serra's score contains effective touches: the combination of heartbeats, sonar bleeps and electric-bass riffs, for example (27'), along with a parody of Kubrick's use of *The Blue Danube* waltz in *2001: A Space Odyssey* (95'), which suggests an equation between the underwater world and deep space. Both these ideas are also to be found prominently in the scores examined below.

The Silent World of Jacques Cousteau

Writings about the sea changed significantly when the development of oceanography in the second half of the nineteenth century produced a new literary genre that was 'half science, half adventure'.[12] This label also serves as an excellent description of the work of the famous French maritime explorer, Jacques-Yves Cousteau, author of the popular English-language memoir *The Silent World* (1953) and director of three of the best known of all ocean-set theatrical documentaries: *Le Monde du silence* (1956), *Le Monde sans soleil* (1964) and *Voyage au bout du monde* (1976). Of these, the first two won Academy Awards for Best Documentary Feature; the first also won the Palme D'Or at the Cannes Film Festival.

Cousteau's co-director for *Le Monde du silence* was Louis Malle, soon to be a director in his own right, but still only 20 years old and fresh out of college at the start of what proved to be a three-year apprenticeship with the explorer on his famous ship *Calypso*. Malle learnt to dive and how to operate a waterproof camera, and in addition functioned as editor and sound recordist on the project. He recalled:

> I was in a state of wonderment about what we were filming. We had to invent the rules ... The camera by definition – because we were underwater – had a mobility and fluidity; we could do incredibly complicated equivalents

of what, on land, would be a combination of crane movements plus enormous tracking shots – and we would do it just like breathing because it was part of the movement of the diver.[13]

Then heavily under the influence of the austere style of director Robert Bresson, Malle found himself disapproving of Cousteau's commercial instincts, which tended towards hybrid 'docu-drama' and 'conventional spectacle' rather than objective reportage; he felt both Cousteau and his financial backers (National Geographic) were preoccupied with finding the 'human touch' and cited gratuitously 'cute' moments such as a dog barking at a lobster on deck and the toning down of the (nonetheless controversial) attack on marauding sharks by angry sailors.[14] Malle objected to Cousteau's choice of music, too:

> I remember having a discussion about music with Cousteau during editing. And I said, "What you're trying to do, this is not documentary, this is show business. It is not what it should be, it is becoming like Walt Disney." Walt Disney was making those "True-Life Adventure" documentaries in those years, very closely edited to music, trying to please the crowds.[15]

Disney's 'True-Life Adventures' had been launched in 1948 with *Seal Island*, scored by Oliver Wallace (better known for his music for *Dumbo*, *Cinderella*, *Alice in Wonderland*, *Peter Pan* and *Lady and the Tramp*). In this film, the female seals of the Aleutian Islands – referred to in the voiced-over narration as 'ladies' – swim en masse to the island to the accompaniment of a lumbering waltz-time variation of 'Here comes the bride', an old-fashioned method of thematic allusion harking back to the days of silent film.

Cousteau's evocative title is, of course, misleading: the underwater world is far from being silent, although in an earlier age it was traditionally regarded as such.[16] Sound waves travel four times faster under water than in the air and confuse the human ear to the point that divers 'perceive underwater sound as omniphonic: coming from all directions at once (and because of sound's seemingly instantaneous arrival, often as emanating from within one's own body)'.[17] Furthermore, sounds under water are full of high frequencies which are rarely reflected in sonic soundscapes purporting to be the sounds of the ocean deep.[18] Composers confronted with the challenge of writing music to accompany underwater images often attempt to create unfamiliar sounds that may plausibly have originated in water, however inauthentic these may be, in addition to dramatising the pictures in more conventional ways. These two considerations inevitably merge when the aim is to suggest a mysterious or forbidding atmosphere, and here a parallel between the underwater world and outer space is frequently evoked – especially where strange, unfamiliar and sometimes terrifying life forms emerge from the depths. Furthermore, real underwater sounds – principally divers' amplified breathing and sonar bleeps – can be integrated into the musical fabric to blur the distinction between the diegetic world and the musical commentary. All these underwater devices, which are sometimes threatening or claustrophobic in effect, can be made to contrast sharply with more conventionally expressive and extrovert music designed to capture the expansiveness of the (far noisier) ocean surface of energising winds and crashing waves above.

The score for Le Monde du silence was written by Yves Baudrier who, along-side such figures as Messiaen and Jolivet, belonged to a generation of composers dubbed 'La Jeune France'.[19] The latter's manifesto declared their common musical aims to be 'youthful, free, as far removed from revolutionary formulas as from academic formulas'.[20] Baudrier was also the author of the book Les Signes du visible et d'audible, of which the first part was Le Monde sonore, published in 1964 by the Institut des Hautes Etudes Cinématographiques, where Malle had been a student. Baudrier had a passion for nature, which he said 'is not an escape, but a way of measuring more freely the limits of what it is to be a human being'.[21] Reviewing a 1936 performance of Baudrier's Raz de Sein (1936), André Coeuroy declared it to be 'a seascape which does not seek to be picturesque but aims to express a Breton tragedy, and perhaps a tragedy pure and simple'.[22]

Certainly a sense of drama pervades Baudrier's score for Le Monde du silence, in marked contrast to Cousteau's laconic voiced-over narration and the occasional snatch of (seemingly rehearsed) dialogue. The main-title sequence elicits eerie artificial harmonics from the violins and a groping theme in the lower strings: the predominant underwater mood is one of foreboding, rather than the excitement of exploration, and the music immediately becomes more amiable when we see the divers on their ship in bright sunshine. This abrupt musical shift from below to above the surface is soon repeated at a similar edit (8'). Chamber-music textures are often preferred to full orchestrations, in keeping with Baudrier's admiration for the earlier film music of his compatriot Maurice Jaubert, and the unsettling soundscapes call at times upon the electronic timbre of the ondes Martenot which – like its cousin, the theremin – is well suited to promoting a sense of the alien, supernatural or irrational.[23] Dissonance levels can be high, as in the cue when a diver is threatened by nitrogen narcosis (10') and in the combination of the ghostly ondes and impressionistic harp glissandi when a shipwreck is encountered (38'), both cues using subdued dynamic levels to make their points. Sometimes the music is arresting in its unusual characterisations: porpoises are greeted in their antics with a brass fanfare and percussion writing, by turns stirringly militaristic and starkly eccentric, before stopping dead at the scene's conclusion (13'). Muted strings as night falls are a familiar romanticising gesture, but here the music darkens mysteriously as the divers descend to the depths of an unknown 'world of rapture' where the coral assumes 'nightmare shapes' (19'); as in the main titles, artificial harmonics float eerily above low-tessitura groping. 'Rapture of the depths' was a phrase used by Cousteau to describe the state of delirium caused by nitrogen narcosis, which can induce hallucinations and lead divers unwittingly into highly dangerous situations.[24]

The music's emotional responses can be ambivalent: the controversial use of dynamite to kill a large sample of fish for census purposes sets out with a huge orchestral explosion, followed by an affecting lament for the dead specimens, but quickly lapses into easy-listening mode as the scientists conduct their examination of the grisly fallout (22'). Other cues are unashamedly comedic: circus-style music akin to Shostakovich in his most flippant mood captures the fluttering of sea-anemone tentacles, for instance, this style presumably having been suggested by the appearance of a clown fish (21'). Emotionally neutral scoring is supplied when factual information is imparted by the narrator, notably when the content is uncomfortable (e.g. statistics about divers killed or maimed) and in the notorious scene where a baby whale is bloodily injured by the ship's propeller, harpooned and then shot in a mercy killing (50'–52'); here the chromatically-descending octatonic chords for the death throes hail straight from the sound-world of *film noir*. Music is generally not supplied when the camera enters the ship's interior and the film deals with day-to-day life on board, but the divers are a crucial part of the narrative and in Cousteau's films, as he asserts in his narration, 'no [scientific] instrument can replace a man'. At times the shots of the heroic divers are more prolonged than those of their surroundings, as in the lengthy sequence in which two men ride underwater electric scooters and 'fly in space' (25').

As in numerous music tracks to other wildlife films, waltzes accompany the ballet-like movements of sea creatures. Thirty sharks dance a grim waltz (described in the narration as an 'underwater dance of death') after they have descended on the unfortunate whale's corpse (55'), the clouds of diluted gore scored with recapitulations of the moody octatonic chords before the sailors avenge the dead mammal by killing the sharks. This is one of the scenes which Malle felt to be unsatisfactory, but it cannot be denied that Baudrier's dynamic scoring of the entire brutal sequence is compellingly tense without being unduly manipulative emotionally. A sophisticated dance sequence for exotic species of fish, in which the jovial music is foregrounded as the narration falls silent, also includes a waltz (71'). When the divers befriend an ugly grouper fish, the narrator jokingly asks as the beast swims inside a circle of the men: 'Ulysses, may I have the next waltz?' (76'). The cue here is a fittingly eccentric combination of the ondes with a banal dance idiom. In his memoirs, Cousteau described attempts by his colleague and co-author Frédéric Dumas to persuade octopuses to behave in the luridly threatening way described by Victor Hugo, who fantasised that they ate humans; in reality they were rather shy and Dumas became 'a sort of dancing instructor' who coaxed an octopus into gyrating with him by 'taking his pupil by the feet' and leading it 'through some balletic improvisations'.[25]

On the release of *Le Monde du silence*, Eric Rohmer and André Bazin said it had opened up 'new vistas of experience' and Malle was more specific: 'It felt very close to what the first astronauts must have felt'.[26] The parallels between deep-sea exploration and outer space became far more explicit in *Le Monde sans soleil* (1964), not least because the saucer-like submarine used by the explorers looks uncannily like a spaceship as it plumbs the murky depths with its spotlights. Clad in futuristic all-silver wetsuits, the film's scuba divers would not look out of place in outer space (figure 6.1) and Cousteau makes the astronaut parallel explicit at the end of the film, when he describes their explorations as 'only the first steps into our new space'. Both Cousteau's narration and the opening credits appropriately dub the divers 'oceanauts' and, as in the previous film, the content is at times more about their experiences than presenting objective reportage of their watery environment. His apparent nods towards the genre of science-fiction (with obvious shades of Jules Verne) led the critic of the *New York Times* to question the veracity of some of the film's scenes, even alleging that certain of the least plausible – those involving the activities of the divers in their underwater living complex – had been fabricated in a studio as a kind of 'hoax' (a suggestion vigorously denied by Cousteau). At the same time, however, the film was warmly praised for its 'pictorial poetry ... and an excellent musical score'.[27]

Figure 6.1 Space walk or deep-sea dive? One of Cousteau's silver-suited 'oceanauts' outside their underwater village in *Le Monde sans soleil* (Jacques-Yves Cousteau, 1964).

The music was composed by Serge Baudo, who had conducted Baudrier's score for *Le Monde du silence*. Baudo's style is more modernist and greatly indebted in places to the propulsive ostinato techniques of Bartók, even where this seems at odds with the serenity of the visual images (for example, as the diving saucer glides through the water at the opening); the effect at these moments is in much the same vein as an exciting action score by Jerry Goldsmith. This opening cue is later reworked to accompany shots of fish trying to break into plastic bags holding live specimens of other fish, in order to eat them (29'). Ideas similar in concept to those in the earlier film include the avoidance of nondiegetic music for the interior shots of the (well-lit) submarine and the use of circus-like music (56') to depict various humorous scenes. Waltzes are heard as we see strange nocturnal fish (40') and creatures likened to 'gazelles on a sea-bed desert' (81').

When Baudo's music is atonal, or nearly so, the viewer/listener is presented with the same paradox engendered by many contemporaneous *nouvelle vague* films with modernist music tracks: is the dissonant idiom intended to scare or create tension, or (as Alain Resnais believed) simply to place the audience in a responsive state that encourages deeper contemplation? The edit where the camera's point of view suddenly shifts from the interior of the under-water village into the ominous darkness outside (12') is a prime example of this ambiguity, and the modernist cue here is abruptly followed by a confus-ing appearance of Bach's Third Brandenburg Concerto (presented, 1721) as we see the entire complex (13'), the diving equivalent of a space station. We then suddenly realise that the Bach is being played by a tape machine inside. Avant-garde fragmentary textures in an athematic, dissonant idiom, often fea-turing glassy sonorities, are akin to formulaic cues for the genres of horror and thriller (e.g. 16', 25', 41' and 49'), but cues of this type are generally brief and do not promote a sustained sense of threat; in fact, at times they are evidently tongue-in-cheek, as when spiky pointillism portrays a crab colony (82'). There is a prominent shift in musical mood as warmer, more lyrical string writing emerges for footage of coral (26') and lush vegetation in an underwater valley is furnished with close-position trombone harmonies in a popular tonal style, complete with pizzicato bass and superimposed harp ostinati (45'), this material also duly passing to the strings. The pizzicato bass moves fully into jazz territory soon afterwards, joined by harmon-muted trumpet and lightly-brushed drums.[28] The jazz material accompanies shots of divers amongst the weeds (50') for no apparent reason – though jazz in French cinema had, since the late 1950s, been a common enough resource for new-wave directors and was famously used by Malle in *L'Ascenseur pour l'échafaud* (1958).[29] Later jazz cues in Cousteau's film involve a muted trombone (61', 84') and always have the pizzicato bass as an idiomatic sonic marker; they are highly chromatic and often dissonant, so do not jar alongside Baudo's orchestral style.

A notable feature of the soundtrack is the attempt to suggest sonar-like noises musically. These instrumental sound effects are sometimes achieved by using punctuating notes for solo wind instruments doubled with xylophone (5', 76') and also by vibraphone, piano and timpani pulses in a nocturnal scene (33'), rapid monotone pulses and rotating ostinati for the harvesting of micro-organisms (35') and in conjunction with footage of the diving saucer (68'). In the mov-ies, this idea dates back to *The Cruel Sea* (Charles Frend, 1953, with a score by Alan Rawsthorne), a tale of a Royal Navy corvette hunting U-boats, in which the beeping of sonar (ASDIC) becomes a sonic character in its own right, frequently replacing the traditional function of nondiegetic music to create tension; intent listening for sonar echoes then quickly became a cliché of depictions of Cold War submarine actions. During the climactic deep-sea descent in Cousteau's film, tension is at first created through a prolonged absence of music that allows the mechanical whirrings of the diving saucer to come to the fore (74'), though the end of the 'vertical desert' is marked by the appearance of a scarlet fish that reintroduces dissonant modernism from Baudo's ensemble. The divers' noisy breathing – also a cliché of movies involving underwater action – in this film often sounds like a rasping percussion instrument and its prominence is plausible in the light of Cousteau's comment in his memoir that the sea 'is a silent jungle, in which the diver's sounds are keenly heard – the soft roar of exhalations, the lisp of incoming air ...'[30]

Baudo's last collaboration with Cousteau was far less creative. The captain's third theatrical film, *Voyage au bout du monde* (1976), was an account of his Antarctic expedition of 1975–76, again featuring the diving saucer but now embracing a more expansive world view by including aerial footage shot from a helicopter and hot-air balloon. A score had been commissioned from François De Roubaix, a diving enthusiast who had supplied music for the French television series *La Mer est grande* (1973), but Cousteau disliked the contemporary sound of De Roubaix's electronics and rejected his score after a preliminary private screening.[31] In its stead, the music track was compiled from various gobbets drawn from numerous orchestral and chamber works by Ravel, specially recorded by the London Symphony Orchestra under Baudo's direction. These are deployed as generally rather brief cues, and a sense of bittiness in the music track is scarcely remedied by the loose stylistic coherence provided by Ravel's idiom. For example, snippets of no fewer than four different scores accompany a sequence in which chinstrap penguins swim like porpoises, then act out their courtship ritual before swimming again underwater (18'–26'). Even when pre-existing music is involved, certain conjunctions of timbre, form and image remain stereotyped: the harp (*Introduction and Allegro*, 1905) occasionally features prominently (91') and the swimming penguins are given a waltz (*Valses nobles et sentimentales*, 1911). Unlike the first two films, however, there is a notable absence of eeriness or the threat of the unknown: this is a well-lit and pure, white world in which the vegetation underneath an ice floe is described as 'delicate and warm [!]' and red algae greet the divers with 'a waving, inviting welcome'. Ravel's music is always beautiful and never ominous, but occasionally suggests an awe-inspiring grandeur when the camera lingers on huge ice cliffs (Concerto for the Left Hand, 1929–30) or breathtaking aerial panoramas (*Daphnis et Chloé*, 1909–12). No dramatising music is provided for the storms that twice threaten *Calypso*, however, the second damaging the ship's propulsion system and endangering the lives of all on board, or for the diving saucer's epic descent to 1000 feet. While at once prolonging French cinema's love affair with classical music and celebrating the rich national heritage of musical impressionism, the film's score could nevertheless with some justification be described as 'the limit of musical vandalism'.[32]

Deep Blue

The general trajectory of Baudrier's score in *Le Monde du silence* marks a progression from the mysterious opening to the nail-biting climax of the bloody encounter with the whales and sharks, followed by a sense of relaxation as the music presents a series of more varied dance-like cues accompanying an assortment of vividly coloured specimens of marine life. Baudo's score for *Le Monde sans soleil* is made up from brief individual cues: this is music of the moment, in accordance with a modernist aesthetic of fragmentation familiar enough in the concert hall, rather than a score with a clear long-term structural trajectory. Neither of these two scores attempts to emulate a traditional symphonic approach by which thematic developments and long-term structural considerations bind the music together in a way that would assure it success as an autonomous listening experience. A contrastingly coherent musical experience is, however, provided by George Fenton in his orchestral score for *Deep Blue* (Alastair Fothergill and Andy Byatt, 2003), a feature-length theatrical spin-off from the BBC TV natural-history series *The Blue Planet* (2001). Such is the cohesive power of many of Fenton's wildlife scores that he has been much in demand to conduct his music in live screenings, without narration (apart from short oral introductions to the set-piece segments) and with front-rank orchestras such as the Berlin Philharmonic and Philharmonia. These touring performances, with the visual images projected on large high-definition screens, are in effect a living continuation of the venerable tradition of silent-film exhibition. In addition, the DVD release of *Deep Blue* included an isolated track for music and sound effects, allowing the voiced-over narration to be removed altogether if desired.

For *The Blue Planet*, Fenton had departed from the electronic soundscapes that had characterized many previous BBC wildlife series – a representative example is Elizabeth Parker's score to 'The Open Ocean', episode 11 from *The Living Planet* (1984), which embodies familiar thriller or sci-fi type scoring for the mysteries of the deep, as well as integrating sonar-like beeps with the synthesised music. Instead, he took something of a gamble in spending his music budget on a full-orchestral and choral score conceived along traditional symphonic lines. Certainly, its often memorably melodic nature, deft musical characterisations of sea creatures (some verging on the anthropomorphic) and ability to suggest elemental force, grandeur and majesty all accounted for a good deal of the score's appeal.[33] But the structural sophistication that binds these set-pieces together in their reworking for *Deep Blue* is notable: the music's cohesion in the cinema version derives ultimately from the resourceful reworking of a handful of basic motifs and a reluctance to recapitulate the main theme (the expansive signature tune from the television series) except at structurally significant moments.

Familiar tropes include several dance-like cues associated with animal movements: dolphins (1'30"), fish, with French-style parallel harmonies (21'), seahorses (33'), rays (37'), penguins (41'), as a continuity link between shots of a ray, the open sea and various creatures swimming underwater (56') and for bizarre, luminescent organisms (69'). Humourous touches include a funky Latin-style cue for crabs (17'), rounded off with a cheeky tag ending for a straggler; moments such as these provide effective contrast and lighten the mood after some of the more harrowing footage. The harp occasionally provides a watery timbre; used sparingly as a solo instrument, it is often present in the bubbling ostinati of the orchestral textures. A nightmarish mood pervades a nocturnal sequence featuring coral cannibalism and frightening predators on the prowl; here we have horror rhetoric, with electronics and sustained semitones in the violins (23'–29'), culminating in a Rózsa-like thriller flurry for a shark attack. Jellyfish elicit fantastic quasi-sci-fi music with wordless voices (34'). When a futuristic-looking submersible descends into 'perpetual night', the music is glassy and glittering in a fantasy vein reminiscent of Herrmann, the narrator making the Cousteau-like comment that 'more men have been into space than have visited the deepest reaches of this alien world' (64'). Eerie electronics return as the craft encounters luminescent creatures like alien monsters (67'). Fenton makes full use of the versatile texture of expansive melody presented over rhythmicised ostinati within a slow harmonic rhythm, for example to accompany shots of tempestuous waves (29'30"). These Debussyan layered patterns are first presented at an early stage in the film when the narration describes the ocean's 'endless cycle of birth, death, renewal' (10').

In a number of set-pieces, the music plays continuously for some considerable time as it adapts its moods and thematic developments to ongoing action on screen. For example, dolphins power through the surface waters to a scherzo in a hard-driving compound metre (7'), with the Lydian-tinged brightness of (non-threatening) Hollywood action cues, but the music darkens as the camera goes underwater and sharks attack a shoal of fish (8') before turning more majestic as killer whales appear; it lightens again for diving birds, with a solo trumpet riding above Debussyan ostinati. In a later scene (50'–55'), compelling continuity is achieved where the killer whales re-emerge with all the menace of marauding U-boats in a war movie; sombre brass intone a minor-key chant as militaristic drums beat deep tattoos with a sense of impending doom. The killers are targetting a grey whale calf, the heavily edited footage compressing what was in reality a six-hour chase into just five minutes of breathtaking action. Fenton constantly reworks a four-note motif in various forms throughout this sequence, sometimes foregrounding it melodically (figure 6.2 in plain minims) and at other times submerging it into his layered ostinato textures (figure 6.3 in successive rhythmic diminutions); the motif is related to the first part of the main theme (cf. figure 6.5 below).[34] A stinger as the calf's blood rises to the surface is followed by a gentle elegy for the doomed creature, also based on the four-note motif but now with poignant changes of harmony (figure 6.4) as its body sinks to the sea bed and the viewer is left contemplating the stillness of the open ocean.

As noted above, the deployment of the main theme from the television series is sparing and always telling. Expansive in nature, the first part of the theme (figure 6.5) is generally associated with the elemental power of the waves and tends to accompany majestic footage on or above the surface; it is first

Figure 6.2

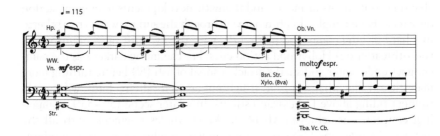

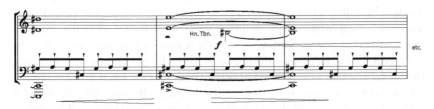

Figure 6.3

stated during the opening shots of dolphins leaping through the waves (2'). The second, climactic segment (figure 6.6) coincides with stupefying footage of a massive breaking wave (3'), the image (figure 6.7) inevitably conjuring up the famous coloured print by Hokusai ('Under the Wave, Off Kanagawa' ['The Great Wave'], c. 1830–1832), which Debussy had printed on the front cover of the first edition of the orchestral score of *La Mer*.[35] After this unforgettable conjunction of music and

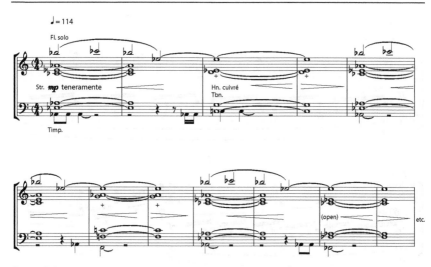

Figure 6.4

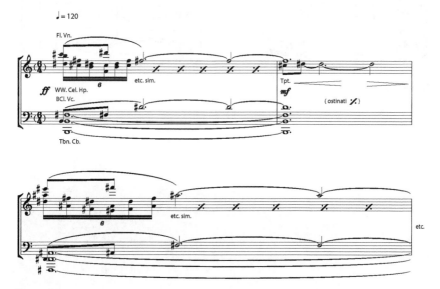

Figure 6.5

image, however, the two components of the theme only reappear as subtle suggestions of their falling intervallic patterns: examples occur at footage of tranquil vegetation (31'), when a sequence with penguins climaxes in their leaping out of the water (41') and in darker tonal garb for the grey whales (49') who are soon to be pursued by their killer cousins. At the climax of the whale attack, the

Figure 6.6

Figure 6.7 The great wave in *Deep Blue* (Alastair Fothergill and Andy Byatt, 2003).

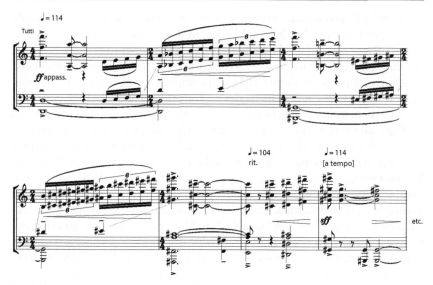

Figure 6.8

orchestra prepares us for what sounds as if it will be a minor-key recapitulation of the theme (figure 6.8), but this is cut off abruptly before the melody can take flight (53'). Having been hinted at throughout the film in this way, it seems inevitable that the theme must at some point make a fully-fledged reappearance and its eventual recapitulation at the conclusion is carefully prepared. A sense of epic expansiveness is first established in conjunction with deep-sea shots of the Mariana Trench (sombre and slow, in minor mode, as seemingly befits the darkness of the extreme deep and merging with the sonar bleep of the submersible); then the wordless choir joins in for the movements of elegant underwater life forms and the voices remain for the subsequent aerial shots of dolphins presented, significantly, with no sound effects so the music is foregrounded (77'); the scoring becomes higher in texture, lyrical but still slow and awe-struck, and gradually harmonic suggestions of the climactic part of the theme are introduced; the full orchestra, in the stately 6/4 quasi-waltz metre that always characterises this material, re-establishes the first part of the main theme (78'), based on a three-note motif (figure 6.5), which is recapitulated as seabirds and predatory fish congregate on the surface to feed on a shoal (79'); and finally the second part of the theme (equivalent to figure 6.6) bursts forth inexorably and triumphantly, twice, before subsiding into a gentle, slow chorale as we are left with an aerial shot of the stillness of the surface, in which serenely floats a blue whale.[36]

Since at least the 1960s, it has been abundantly clear that musical scores by no means need to aspire to the level of autonomous structural cogency achieved by Fenton in order to work well with the films for which they are specifically conceived. Both Baudrier and Baudo, in their music for Cousteau, demonstrate different approaches: the former creates a general arch-like trajectory suiting the three principal subdivisions of the film, while Baudo savours the moment and constantly adapts his modernist style to the implied terrors of the ocean depths. More recently, seaborne documentaries for both cinema and television have continued to demonstrate considerable variety in their scoring practices, even when dealing with ostensibly similar subject matter. Consider, for example, two projects concerned with fishing boats. Arguably no such documentary has proved quite so nightmarish or viscerally disturbing as *Leviathan* (Lucien Castaing-Taylor and Véréna Paravel, 2012), examined elsewhere in the present volume, which contains no music and inhabits that disconcerting realm between hyper-realism and avant-garde experimentation. On the other hand, the Discovery Channel's popular docu-soap *Deadliest Catch* (launched in 2005 and in its ninth season at the time of writing) subscribed to the predictable reality-TV formula of a pounding, excitement-generating synthesised rock track to enliven endlessly repetitive footage of crab cages being emptied unceremoniously onto a trawler deck.

The theatrical documentary *Planet Ocean* (Yann Arthus-Bertrand and Michael Pitiot, 2012), with music by Armand Amar receiving its own isolated title card at the very start of the film, continued to engage with the time-honoured maritime tropes of waltzing creatures and sci-fi electronics (algae are described as being like 'distant galaxies'), thriller-like pounding percussion (a sailfish attack on a shoal), expansive scoring for majestic aerial photography and the occasional dash of emotionally-neutral minimalism. The film's lacklustre narration by Josh Duhamel continued the tradition established by Cousteau's own remarkably laconic voice-overs and continued by Michael Gambon in *Deep Blue*, of providing basic and emotionally neutral factual information and allowing the films' resourceful composers to tease out as much emotional and atmospheric suggestiveness as seems appropriate in the endlessly fascinating 'silent' world of the deep sea.

Notes

1 Herman Melville, *Moby-Dick*, chapter 111, in *Redburn, White-Jacket, Moby-Dick*, ed. G. Thomas Tanselle (Library of America; Cambridge University Press, 1983), 1308.

2 Jane Austen, *Northanger Abbey, Lady Susan, The Watsons, Sanditon*, ed. James Kinsley and John Davie with an introduction and notes by Claudia L. Johnson (Oxford: Oxford University Press, 2003), chapter VII, 321.

3 John Mack, *The Sea: A Cultural History* (London: Reaktion Books, 2011), 32.

4 Addison's letter to *The Spectator*, written in response to an article on 'the pleasures of the imagination', is reprinted in *The Oxford Book of the Sea*, ed. Jonathan Raban (Oxford and New York: Oxford University Press, 1992), 80–83. Burke's treatise was published under the title *A Philosophical Enquiry into the Origin of our Ideas of the Sublime and Beautiful* (London: R. and J. Dodsley, 1757).

5 Mack, *The Sea*, 95.

6 W. H. Auden, *The Enchafèd Flood, or The Romantic Iconography of the Sea* (London: Faber and Faber, 1951), 25–6.

7 Mack, *The Sea*, 17.
8 Raban, *The Oxford Book of the Sea*, 3.
9 Vercors [Jean Marcel Bruller], *Le Silence de la mer* (Paris: Minuit, 1946), 48, quoted in Ginette Vincendeau, 'Le Silence de la mer', liner notes to Blu-ray/DVD release of Melville's film (Eureka EKA 70066), 11.
10 Christopher Palmer, *The Composer in Hollywood* (London and New York: Marion Boyars, 1990), 271.
11 Eric Serra, quoted in Gergely Hubai, *Torn Music. Rejected Film Scores: A Selected History* (Beverly Hills, CA: Silman-James Press, 2012), 227. Made in English and dubbed into French as *Le Grand Bleu*, the film was significantly revised for US distribution and in the process Serra's music was jettisoned in favour of a new, more melody-based score by Hollywood composer Bill Conti that nevertheless remained rooted in 80s electronic timbres.
12 Raban, *The Oxford Book of the Sea*, 29.
13 Malle quoted in *Malle on Malle*, ed. Philip French (London: Faber and Faber, 1993), 8.
14 Ibid., 17.
15 Ibid., 8.
16 Cousteau justified the title of his book *The Silent World*, even though 'aware that wide publicity has recently been given to the noises of the sea' by declaring that underwater sound recordings by scientists' hydrophones had been 'grossly amplified': Cousteau with Frédéric Dumas, *The Silent World: A Story of Undersea Discovery and Adventure, By the First Men to Swim at Record Depths with the Freedom of Fish* (London: Hamish Hamilton, 1953), 199. For more on the sea as 'a cacophony of sound', see Michel Redolfi's comments in Daniel Charles, 'Singing Waves: Notes on Michel Redolfi's Underwater Music', in *Contemporary Music Review*, 8:1 (1993), 63.
17 Stefan Helmreich, 'Underwater Music: Tuning Composition to the Sounds of Science', in *The Oxford Handbook of Sound Studies*, ed. Trevor Pinch and Karin Bijsterveld (New York: Oxford University Press, 2012), 157.
18 Ibid., 169 n. 7.
19 Rollo H. Myers, 'Some Reflections on French Music Today', in *Musical Times*, 88 (1947), 18. The group had been set up, on Baudrier's own initiative, in 1936: see Martine Cadieu and André Jolivet, 'A Conversation with André Jolivet', in *Tempo* new series, 59 (1961), 3. For more on Baudrier's career, see Alain Lacombe and François Porcile, *Les Musiques du cinéma français* (Paris: Bordas, 1995), 85–6.
20 Nigel Simeone, 'La Spirale and La Jeune France: Group Identities', in *Musical Times*, 143 (2002), 15.
21 Ibid., 16.
22 Ibid., 16–17.
23 An American film-music critic once commented that it was impossible to discern whether Baudrier's tendency to use economical instrumentation in his film scores was driven by aesthetic or financial considerations: see Lawrence Morton, 'Film Music of the Quarter', in *Hollywood Quarterly*, 5:3 (1951), 283.
24 For Cousteau's experiments to investigate this phenomenon in the 1940s, during the course of which one diver lost his life, see *The Silent World*, 126–31.
25 Ibid., 164–5.
26 French, *Malle on Malle*, 6.
27 Bosley Crowther, '*World Without Sun* (1964): Movie of Undersea Study at Cinema II', in *New York Times* (23 December 1964), at http://www.nytimes.com/movie/review?_r=2&res=9B04E7D91E3BE13ABC4B51DFB467838F679EDE& (accessed 19 December 2013).
28 The main titles credit an unspecified 'musical theme' to (guitarist) Henri Crolla and (composer) André Hodeir, which is presumably part of the jazz material. For Hodeir's collaborations with Cousteau, see *The André Hodeir Jazz Reader*, ed. André Hodeir and Jean-Louis Pautrot (Ann Arbor: University of Michigan Press, 2006), 5.

29 Malle's score was specially created by Miles Davis: see Mervyn Cooke, *A History of Film Music* (Cambridge: Cambridge University Press, 2008), 222.
30 Cousteau with Dumas, *The Silent World*, 199.
31 De Roubaix died in a diving accident before Cousteau's film was released. Music from the rejected score appeared posthumously on the CD *Le Monde électronique de François De Roubaix* (Universal Music Jazz France 981 808-9, 2004) and the double (vinyl) album *L'Antarctique & autres séances électroniques Rue de Courcelles* (WéMè 018) in 2009. Stéphane Lerouge's liner notes to the former release recount the circumstances of the music's rejection.
32 Lacombe and Porcile, *Les Musiques du cinéma français*, 293.
33 Fenton's (albeit sparing) anthropomorphising tendencies were criticised by one reader of *Radio Times*, who wrote to the magazine after watching episode 5 of the BBC series *The Trials of Life* (1990) to complain that the epic Hollywood-style march accompanying the bizarre sight of a huge single-file column of lobsters fleeing from turbulent waters along the sea bed trivialised the animals' heroic struggle against nature. At the time of writing, this sequence is a popular video clip on a number of websites.
34 I am greatly indebted to George Fenton for sharing the full score of *Deep Blue* with me and to his assistant Samuel Pegg for providing much helpful advice and material relating to the film's music track. All music examples in this chapter have been arranged for short score by the author and are © Shogun Music Ltd, 2003.
35 For a detailed discussion of the links between Debussy's orchestral impressionism and artists whose seascapes he admired – including Turner, Hokusai and the impressionists – see Edward Lockspeiser, *Debussy: His Life and Mind* (Cambridge: Cambridge University Press, 1978 [1965]), vol. 2, 15–32.
36 This is not the end of the musical journey, however, since Fenton then provides a substantial end-credit cue (82'–87'), a characteristic gesture of musical thanks to his orchestra – in this case, the Berlin Philharmonic – for following him through the vagaries of ocean life.

Chapter 7

Music and the Aesthetics of the Recorded World

Time, Event and Meaning in Feature Documentary

John Corner

Some 12 years ago, I wrote a short article about the use of music in documentary film and television, which considered both the positive and negative consequences of various types of application.[1] In this chapter, I want to revisit some of the issues raised there in the light of what has been happening to documentary since, as well as in respect of my own further thinking about documentary form. I shall start with some general observations and then try to develop my ideas further by looking at a number of quite recent, and very different, examples of music at work within the documentary frame. Most of my examples involve, among other things, a consideration of music's role in shaping the manner and mood in which key events are anticipated by exposition and narrative, given audiovisual portrayal within a temporal frame and positioned for retrospective assessment.

One factor to emerge from any consideration of soundtracks in documentary practice is that the more self-consciously 'artefactual' a documentary production considers itself to be (including the possibility of it being offered for viewing as, primarily, a piece of 'art'), then the fewer inhibitions are likely to surround the use of music.[2] Conversely, the more that a production privileges other aims, including journalistic integrity or the veracities of direct observational recording, the likelier it is that music will become a more sensitive issue. The risks of 'imposition', of an imposed 'externality' which is seen either as somehow contaminating the documentary record or as introducing an emotionally manipulative dimension to it, or both, are likely to be weighed in the balance. Music is an important element of *aestheticisation*, as my above comments suggest, and therefore the core issue of music's relation to documentary involves ideas about the relationship between aesthetics and knowledge. Although it is certainly possible to argue for the ways in which aesthetic design supports rather than impedes the generation of knowledge (and not simply by the crude ploy of 'sugaring the pill'), the close relationship between aesthetics and pleasure and between aesthetics and appreciation of *form* rather than of *content* sometimes sets up tensions within documentary perspectives. It does so, even though as my earlier essay pointed out, the pioneers of documentary actually saw documentary as a way of advancing filmic aesthetics and used music extensively and imaginatively in the promotion of this goal.[3] Clearly, the specific forms of knowledge, and the forms of *knowing*, at work in a given production are important factors to keep in mind when analysing how music works within its audiovisual design. This is not at all to say that matters of knowledge are absent from the rich range of fictional cinema and television – modern societies 'know' a lot from various forms of fiction – but to note that the forms and operations of knowledge in documentary are of a distinctive and prominent kind and that they are central to its *generic imperative*.

In the period since I wrote the article, the expansion and diversification of documentary forms have been extensive, including in the area of online practice. 'Documentariness' of different kinds, the use of sound and image to 'document' aspects of reality, has become a dominant feature of the audiovisual landscape and it might be said that there is more 'documentariness' now occurring in productions which do not define themselves as 'documentary' than there is in productions which do. This would include a whole range of entertainment, travel, special interest and promotional forms and it would extend, of course, to web activities. The impossibility of clearly defining documentary is an issue recognised right from the term's beginnings in the 1920s, but any sense of specific generic space and generic guidelines has become further complicated within the new terms of audiovisual culture (and audiovisual economy).[4] One effect of the increased 'messiness' of the territory is, I believe, an expansion of musical opportunity. This expansion is part of the attempt to provide new answers to the question 'what works?' in an intensified and segmented cultural marketplace where the requirement to capture and maintain attention is at a premium. The growth and success of feature work designed initially for cinema distribution has been one, much discussed, part of recent documentary history. Here, the increased desirability of sensory and affective impact, of a viewer experience that approximates at points to that of watching feature fiction, is clearly an important factor, as my examples below will illustrate.

Musical Relations and the Documentary Frame: Story, Exposition, Observation

As other chapters in this volume variously demonstrate and discuss, the ways in which music is employed in documentary relate to the often very different structures and sequences out of which documentaries are made. We can, with some approximation, divide these into three categories as indicated above, each of which suggests a rather different range of musical possibility, even if there are considerable overlaps and allowing for the fact that many documentary productions move between very different types of approach across their full length. My first two examples below work primarily around the imperatives of narrative, of storytelling and of exposition, the presentation of evidence, description and proposition. I shall later look at one or two instances of sequences led by observation of interaction. However, both my initial examples contain extensive use of interview testimony. There is a sense in which in-shot interviews work in part as 'observation' for the viewer, even if their organisation prevents that sense of overlooking and eavesdropping on an 'unaware' world which is so powerful a feature of watching much observational work and which often lends itself quite directly to kinds of musical 'addition'.[5]

As part of the analysis of musical relations, I am interested too, like writers on film music generally, in the levels at which documentary music operates in respect of viewer consciousness.[6] How far does it call attention to itself as a part of the communicative design, even perhaps involving recognition (a known song, an identified composer, a specific set of prior associations)? How far, by contrast, does it work to provide a layer of unconsciously registered ground tones, a set of cues for interpretative navigation and for mood? In analysing most instances of its use, we can be confident that, without it, given scenes would be different in their perception by audiences and, in addition, that substitution with different music would be likely to produce changed interpretations (variables which have been tested out by researchers).[7]

Analysis of music in documentary faces the challenge of making itself comprehensible to readers who may not have extensive musical knowledge and who might not have ready access to the material under discussion. I start here by looking at two quite recent Oscar-winning documentaries widely available on DVD – James Marsh's *Man on Wire* (2008) and Charles Ferguson's *Inside Job* (2010). I shall give more attention to the first of these, since the range and function of music within it deserve greater analytic attention. The films have usefully contrasting approaches to documentary design and a discussion of them leads productively to questions I can then pursue by taking brief examples from other material, also available easily on DVD.

Man on Wire (James Marsh, Wall to Wall, 2008)

Man on Wire (MOW) is a useful documentary to consider in the context of musical applications since music perhaps plays a more sustained and significant role in the overall meanings projected by the film than is usually the case. MOW tells the story of the 1974 wire walk between the twin towers of the World Trade Centre in New York, a feat accomplished by Philip Petit, a French acrobat and high-wire specialist (figure 7.1). This act (which finally involved several crossings between the towers) required extensive planning and preparation. All of this was achieved by subterfuge and stealth, since access to the towers was by permit only and the crossing itself constituted a criminal act (the attractively minimalist title of the film is taken from the incident and charge sheet of the New York Police Department after Petit's arrest).

Marsh's film involves no commentary and no moments of 'observational' footage and it is essentially a combination of interviews, mute dramatisation and archive materials (including newsreel material and self-documentation from Petit's previous adventures and his preparations for the New York project). We are thus primarily in the realm of 'story', an unfolding narrative, strongly biographical

Figure 7.1 Man on Wire (James Marsh, 2008).

and autobiographical, focused on the culminating event of the wire-crossings. The viewer will continually be gaining knowledge but this will come largely from the descriptions offered by the interviews and the actions portrayed in the dramatised and archive footage. The music is assembled from several sources but preexisting work by Michael Nyman, some of it previously used in the soundtrack to cinema fictions, is prominent and of major significance throughout.[8]

The film has a distinctive 'economy of time' working across its different parts, a framework within which historical time is connected to durational time, the time allocated to particular sequences. The archive material and the interviews present the viewer with different periods of 'time past', a past which includes not only the earlier exploits of Petit, but also the building of the WTC. The dramatisation of events inserted at points into the flow of the film presents a dramatically immediate 'time present', the reconstruction of the final preparations, entry into the towers and the rigging of the wire recounted as time-past in the interviews but enacted as ongoing action on screen, in this respect following the temporal profile of feature fiction. The walk itself takes up seven minutes of screen time and is constructed from around 30 still shots taken of the event itself from different angles and 'worked' upon with zooms and reverses, reframing the image and repositioning the act itself within the space of the sky, the buildings and the ground. The images are intercut with interview comments from those involved. I call the temporal character of this section of the film 'climactic' time, a 'magical' time out of time in which the act which we have seen being prepared for against a range of obstacles is finally performed. There is a transcending tranquillity about this sequence, a quality grounded in its use of stills. This clearly provides the film with its strongest moments and serves to generate those 'inspirational' feelings to which many viewers and critics testified. Insofar as the film can be said to project a philosophy, however indirectly, it is in the portrayal of the walk itself, together with the comments made about it, that this is primarily achieved.

Music has a great deal to do in an overall documentary design of this kind. It has to work both in affective organisation, cueing and modifying the kinds of emotional engagement active within the viewing experience, and in signalling the shifts and the connections across the different 'chapters' of the story.

It would be unproductive to try to describe the musical contribution on a scene-by-scene basis. Among other challenges, this would require a formidably extensive description of visuals and of speech. However, in trying to account for the musical profile of *Man on Wire*, for the way in which watching the film is a musical, perhaps quasi-operatic, experience, it is worth looking at a number of different moments of musical usage under four subheadings.

a) Generic Expectations
The opening sequence of the film, running for several minutes before the title frame appears, is a rapid succession of images of preparation. Crates are being packed and nailed shut, items of kit are being checked, diagrams and planning sheets are lying around. Then, watches are glanced at, van doors are shown opening and closing; there are shots of a city from the inside of a moving vehicle and a man is shown holding a camera close to his body, apparently photographing the interior of a building as he walks through its lobby. Snatches of interview speech refer to schedules and anxieties, the context not yet clear. Over this, an orchestral score ('Leaving Home' by Josh Relph) gives a brooding bass presence, with strong percussion, across which strings set up a sense of tension. The whole combines to provide an entry into the world of something close to an action movie – some 'crime' (perhaps a 'heist') portrayed in the fragmented terms of its urgent last stages of preparation, with the intriguing promise of a forthcoming 'big event' which will provide retrospective coherence. The music does not simply play a support role here: it *drives* this sense of generic shadowing, almost of generic parody, beginning a line of narrative development, which, intermittently, is carried through almost to the end.

b) The Towers
Images of the towers within different kinds of footage occur throughout the film, but the first images, taken from archive footage of the building under construction, establish their presence strongly. This is after Petit's former girlfriend has described his early obsession with the structure. Nyman's *Fish Beach* (originally written for Peter Greenaway's 1988 'experimental' film, *Drowning by Numbers*), with its stately but mournful two-note development on trombone, is the music used for a sequence of colour-faded archive images, beginning with a shot of what in 2001 became 'ground zero' at the point when it was the busy site for establishing structural foundations.[9] These shots of building work – cranes

swinging girders into position and various perspectives on the dizzying heights involved – has no speech accompaniment, and therefore the music is more fully active in the production of meaning than in those cases where it is placed over speech or over images carrying a strong narrative line. As at other points in the film, the later tragic history of the Twin Towers contributes to the overall tonality, always staying in the background against depiction of the astonishing feat of 1974, but placing what we see against a known future and giving certain moments an added poignancy. It is through the music's rather 'grand' repetitive elegy that this subtle and sad component is embedded effectively in the viewer's consciousness.[10]

c) The Sydney Precedent

Petit had accomplished several major wire-walking feats before his attempt in New York and the film has extensive footage of one of the most spectacular of these – a crossing between the Northern Pylons of Sydney Harbour Bridge. Partly because the subsequent portrayal of the Twin Towers crossing can only use still footage (no film record was made), it is important for MOW to give the viewer time to consider Petit's skills *in action* on a real and dangerous project, rather than in the kinds of low-level practising and rehearsals which feature in other archive sequences. This again, like b. above, involves looking without commentary and, for some time, without interview voice-over. The music chosen here is Peter Green's 1968 hit *Albatross*, as recorded by Fleetwood Mac. Perhaps the choice of this relaxed, soothingly rhythmic tune, with its two chord repetitions and its wave sounds, risks a level of cliché, but its established cultural position as a tune signifying freedom, weightlessness and natural space (all those pop concert crowds swaying with their arms extended!) connects perfectly with what is seen. For some viewers, it will work through recognition and prior cultural association while for others it might operate solely through its immediate sonic appropriateness to the actions viewed and their connotations.

d) Practising

Sequences inserted at different points in the film show the refinement of Petit's skill, often in a rural or expansive garden setting. These are essentially moments of 'playfulness' and pleasure, they constitute a kind of temporary time out from the main flow of the narrative although they deepen the viewer's sense of Petit's ability and dedication. There is a comic jauntiness about some of these scenes and Nyman's busy 'Baroque' mode works well with them, its bouncy rhythms both driving the narrative flow while at the same time having enough of parody about them to place what we see within a softly ironic frame. In one sequence, however, Marsh wants to signal something more about the tranquillity of mind, not just the driving ambition, of Petit and to connect this with the Arcadian settings, in such contrast with the New York scenes. Again, perhaps risking cliché, he uses the soaring, fluttering strings of Vaughan Williams' *The Lark Ascending* (1914, rev. 1920) over monochrome footage of a bare-chested Petit practising with his friends on a low-wire rig set somewhere amidst trees and meadows. Once more, restraint in the use of interview speech gives the overt spirituality of the music considerable space, making the viewing experience one of marked musical pleasure. The score moves to become an almost equal partner with the visualisation. As well as being about setting and action, about a musical connection with *externality*, this sequence also works, like several others, to connect with *interiority*, with the special and mysterious quality of Petit's own consciousness of himself and of the world.

e) The Walk

I have noted how the time of the walk itself, after frantic last-minute preparations beset with risks of discovery and of technical failure, is a kind of 'magical' time, the film's 'special time' to which all we have seen and heard has led up and to which everything we take away from the film will relate. Across the sequence of stills of Petit on the wire, Erik Satie's *Gymnopédie No. 1* (1888) is used. Its *'lent* and *douloureux'* movement (two major seventh chords and a repeated nine note piano figure) reinforces the sense of poise and of calm, precise development that the images generate. The see-saw movement and repetitive balance of the music provides a quite direct formal complement to what we see as a series of moments of 'stopped time'. The music is at once static (the repeated chord oscillation) and forward looking (a slowly developing melody). This sequence is a time for awe and wonderment at the true magnitude of the accomplishment, feelings reflected in the comments of those involved as well as by the shots of awestruck spectators on the ground gazing upwards. Although Satie's piece has been used elsewhere in film soundtracks, its employment in this core scene with its distinctive durational values makes it, alongside Nyman's *Fish Beach*, the defining music of the film (it was used as the soundtrack for the menu on the DVD release).

At many points in MOW, music forms what we might call its 'conventional' function in supporting narrative development and reinforcing changes in intensity of action and of mood. Here, the range of Nyman compositions is central. These compositions work alongside other thematically 'appropriate' applications. For example, there is Grieg's *In the Hall of the Mountain King* (1875) used over the semi-comedy of a policeman being involved in a 'hide and seek' relationship with team members as they wait for dawn on the day of the attempt (a sequence which *becomes* comic through the music). There is the bright, snappy disco pulsing of *A Fifth of Beethoven* by Walter Murphy and the Big Apple Band (1976), placed across the first surveillance of the building after the team's arrival in New York. In these instances, music has an important structural role to play in both separating and connecting the various strands and time frames out of which the film is built. However, in the selected sequences described above, the music does not merely contribute to the filmic experience but regulates and controls it through the salience it is given. This helps the film's meanings to move beyond the documentation of a specific, daring act towards a much broader, if indirect, statement about terms of living and the relationship between 'special' and 'normal' experience.

Inside Job (Charles Ferguson, Sony Picture Classics, Representational Pictures, 2010)

By contrast with Man on Wire, Inside Job is essentially an expositional film, grounded in a commentary (spoken by the actor Matt Damon). It involves both a detailed chronology of events surrounding the financial crisis of 2008 and an exposition of the complex character of the financial products at the centre of this crisis together with the strategies and accounting practices that contributed to 'meltdown'. Within its structure, a wide range of interviews appear, some of them including tense as well as revealing exchanges, alongside various type of archive footage of events, including official inquiries.

The score (mixed by Andy Richards) works discreetly underneath many of the scenes, providing a tonal supplement to the commentary and interview speech and underpinning the sense of unfolding significance across various interior and exterior spaces. Unlike most sequences of Man on Wire, this does not provide a conscious musical experience for the viewer, to be registered alongside other components (I note the exceptions to this below). It performs instead the function of giving continuity across scenes involving different speakers, generating in the process a ground tone suggestive of the magnitude of the issue undergoing expository development (in sharp contrast to the narrative pace of MOW). In the opening shots of the beautiful Icelandic landscape, for example, as the film starts to describe the scale of the banking crisis in Iceland and its causes, the music ('Iceland' by Alex Heffes, with slow tempo, sustained strings in the lower register and 'ambient' keyboard) performs the conventional task of supporting the visual experience. It gives viewers a strong aural frame in which they are positioned with 'time to look' at the quietly intense drama of outstanding natural beauty, but without this frame significantly modifying, or commenting upon, what is otherwise seen and heard.

At a number of points in the film, however, this approach is exchanged, if only briefly, for a very different application. This involves the use of rock songs, the volume and energy of which cut through the audiovisual mix to become dominant (sometimes aggressively so) and which have lyrics reflecting directly on the settings and situations under analysis. The use of these songs occurs in a mode which we can call 'punctuation and comment', operating in transitional sequences as points of implicit evaluative consolidation before further development. The first of these occurs in the shift from the six-minute pre-title sequence about Iceland to the titles sequence itself. This sequence runs Peter Gabriel's hit Big Time (1986) over a four-minute section of aerial shots of New York (comprising angled shots of panoramas and skylines and shots directly downwards on to the urban grid of roofs and streets) together with interview fragments from material to come later. The sequence ends in a rapid montage around 'wealth', including images of boats and of private planes at an airport. As I have suggested, it is not just the energy of the music combining with the force of the images that pulls the viewing experience into a more intensive mode of engagement; it is also the lyrics. Gabriel's song is about money and the city, including highly relevant lines such as:

'I'm on my way and I'm making it'

'I've had enough, I'm getting out to the city, the big big city'

and remarking:

'I'll be a big noise, with all the big boys'

'how my life is one big adventure'

This rowdy performance combined with such strong visuals interrupts the flow of sober analysis with which the film begins and officially 'opens' the film at an exciting level to which it will occasionally return but which its very subject matter prevents it from sustaining. This 'rock video' moment gives it, albeit temporarily, another dimension of appeal beyond that of its evidence and analysis.[11]

At a later point, Bachman-Turner Overdrive's *Takin' Care of Business* (1973) erupts across the developing account of institutional malpractice and Ballard's *New York Groove* ('I'm back, back in the New York groove', recorded by Hello, 1975), is run across montage shots which include those of expensive houses, the beaches of The Hamptons and yachts in a marina.

The film's final credits roll through to the quiet, slow, reflective irony of MGMT's *Congratulations* (2010), e.g.:

'But I've got someone to make reports

That tells me how my money's spent'.

If the visual portrayal in these aesthetically marked scenes is about the urban topography of financial power (with Manhattan located at the centre of the global economy) and about the trappings of extreme wealth (cars, yachts, private jets, beach house retreats), the lyrics provide an ironic view of the sensibility of those who endorse the dominant values. The view of the architecture and externalities of the new order is thereby complemented by a critically caricatured voicing of perspectives from 'within'. The slangy frankness of the lyrics together with the energies of the music work as a critique/rejection of the greed and deception we are hearing about, one issuing from 'popular space' rather than the specialised spaces both of the activities under documentary investigation and the investigation itself. As well as adding an engaging vitality, the music enters 'the argument' of the documentary in a way that contrasts interestingly with MOW's very different project of capturing a particular physical feat and the values that surround it.

Spaces and Sounds

To explore a little further some of the different applications of music to documentary discourse and to different kinds of 'documentary space', I want to look now at two quite recent examples in which the function of music is absolutely essential to whatever else is heard or is seen. The important role that can be played by music in constructing the meaning of a sequence has been illustrated in my examples above, but here the removal of music would not simply result in depleted meanings but in sequences that 'would not work', producing a severe breakdown in the communicative flow.

I take my first example from the remarkable Israeli film, *Waltz with Bashir* (Ari Folman, Bridgit Folman Film Gang/Sony Classic Pictures, 2008). This highly praised production is a landmark in 'animated documentary', consisting for most of its length of artwork images rather than those 'captured' on film. Over these animated scenes, voices in conversation and commentary construct a story about an attempt by an Israeli army veteran to come to terms, many years later, with an experience had while serving in West Beirut during the 1982 Lebanon war. During this time, he was involved in a major act of atrocity, when Israeli soldiers held a perimeter around the Palestinian Refugee Camp of Sabra and Shatila and illuminated it by flares while the Lebanese Christian Phalange militia carried out a massacre. The film is about his attempt to assess the degree of his guilt in these events, as he tries to form a clearer sense of the precise nature of his involvement by working with what are often incomplete and contradictory memories of the incident.

Initially, his own memory of what happened is a blank, but after talking to a friend who was also there and who suffers from regular nightmares, he has a dream in which some aspects of the surrounding realities of the event appear, transformed into an hallucinatory flow. This sequence, about eight minutes into the film and just over a minute long, shows naked soldiers bathing in the sea at night from a Beirut beach, tall apartment blocks lining the palm-fringed promenade. The viewpoint is from the sea, behind the bathing soldiers (who are floating face upwards) and looking towards the beach and the promenade. The images are a mix of blacks and yellows. They show shadows playing over the rippling water, while the bathing bodies, in their stillness and posture, almost resemble corpses. Flares appear in the sky, falling slowly down. The soldiers stand up and walk out from the sea with only their dog tags on, gathering their weapons (figure 7.2). We see their emergence from a side view, moving in apparent slow motion and then, as they are silhouetted, putting on their clothing. From a viewpoint on the promenade, we watch them slowly walking up the steps from the beach and we are in front of them as they walk through the war-damaged streets, adjusting their kit. At an alleyway junction, a crowd of distressed, weeping women floods past them. We see this initially from behind the head of one of the soldiers and then the viewpoint moves round to show his front and to close in on his face and his eyes.

This sequence (repeated in part later) becomes such an engaging and disturbing one, used in the trailer for the film, through its music. Max Richter's score here, an exercise in electronic minimalism (*The Haunted Ocean*), develops a steady, deep and repetitive progression, cumulatively setting up slow tensions. It strengthens the sense of a dream world but its cadences also point

Figure 7.2 Waltz with Bashir (Ari Folman, 2008).

towards the imminence of something bad. Richter himself noted how a 'sort of unresolved, weightless, lost melancholia' was his aim.[12] The combination of slow, animated movement and music provides a choreographic dimension which distances it even further from conventional documentary reality than the fact of animation would achieve on its own, moving it close to dance in its precision of aligned movement; its weird aesthetic grace. As in some of my earlier examples, the score provides an auditory frame, which is also an affective frame, in which to look intensely at the screen for a period during which nothing is said and when actions unfold only gradually and without immediate meaning. Within this context, music and image give a viewing experience that partly parallels the experience of the dreamer in its intensity and its power to intrigue and disturb. Without the music, the scene would be likely to fail because the images alone would not generate an adequate density of aesthetic and cognitive connection. They would not 'mean' fully enough to sustain the required level of viewing engagement. If a commentary voice were placed across them instead, they would be pushed towards an 'illustrative' realism (even if that of representing a dream recounted by the voice) which would radically diminish their symbolic centrality.

I can describe my next example with greater brevity. It is from *La Vie Moderne* (Raymond Depardon, Soda Pictures, 2009). This documentary works within a broad and varied 'tradition' of documentaries that explore rural life through a mixture of interview and close observation. The contrast with the life of the city and with dominant ideas of 'the modern' often gives an implicitly contrastive edge to such film-making, provoking reflection on the values of 'our' ways of living as against 'theirs'. Here, Depardon returns to a little hamlet in the Cevennes that he visited a few years before for an earlier film.

The film opens with a long take of his approach to the village over the rolling hills and passes of the last few miles of road. It is clear but cloudy. There is an expansive view of further hills stretching to a distant horizon. The shot is as if from the front of a car but no part of the car appears in it since its presence would set up a rather different set of viewing relations. The shot lasts for almost a minute and a half and effectively finishes when the car stops almost at the bottom of a hill to allow sheep on to the road from the hillside. The shepherd at work with the flock knows him and he will be one of his interviewees in the film. They exchange greetings. At the end of the film, before images of those who have participated in it appear briefly together with their names, there is effectively a reversal of this shot, as he leaves the village and we see the same landscape as if from the back of the vehicle. It is a sunny evening. This time the on-screen journey runs for longer, almost three minutes, taking us back down the road past the point where we started in the opening sequence.

Both at the start and at the finish, only wind and road noise are heard. However, almost half-way into the opening sequence, the sad, slow cello melody from Fauré's *Élégie op. 24* (1880) is introduced and this continues for 30 seconds before we return to wind and road noise and finally to some brief comments by Depardon ('first come the roads, and at the end of the roads are the farms'). We learn that it is 9.30 pm on a July evening. In the final sequence, it is over one and a half minutes before the music begins. During this time, there are brief comments over the road noise. We are told that it is 6 pm in the autumn and that 'tonight I am filming in a light that is like no other'. A few further remarks are made before the music begins and this then runs for another minute of road journey before being used across the two closing minutes that show for the last time the people whose accounts of life we have heard.

There is nothing particularly original about the use of an 'entry and exit' shot of this kind, even when the exit so directly reverses the entry, although the duration of the sequence in both cases is unconventional and arresting. Significantly, in the opening, the music is used sparingly; we are 'required' to gaze at the peace and beauty of the landscape both close and distant and to experience the movement of entry into the village in a way that positions us vicariously as visitors too. The initial paucity of sound immediately places us in a direct, 'observationalist' relationship with what we can see. The arrival of the music intensifies what is now an established pictorial experience, aestheticising it further but only for a short while before we return to wind and road noise only, although perhaps with the music still lingering in our heads. In the 'exit' sequence, an even longer period without music occurs at the start of the road travel footage, much of it without any speech. When the music begins, it works to 'colour' the affective experience of leaving, an experience which now 'gathers up' all that we have seen in the body of the film, gaining further significance by its 'repetition with a difference' of the arrival scene. Finally, it is used as a connective, articulating the *collectivity* constituted by the various participants who appear briefly before us once more.

It is the restraint of the application here that I think is of particular interest. It produces a situation in which the music is essential to our thinking and feeling in these two defining parts of the film without its constitutive role becoming too heavily marked.

The Specificity of Documentary

Documentaries, even when fully dramatised, do not usually invite us to *immerse* ourselves in the worlds they portray in the same way that feature fiction typically does. Although their discourse may be richly imaginative, the dynamics of *understanding* something in relation to specific *realities* finally take priority, whatever the complexities and ambiguities involved and whatever the affective as well as cognitive depth of our engagement. We watch documentaries from a position in the same world as the events, circumstances and people depicted in them, although it may seem at points to be an alien world. Our interpretative coordinates generally reflect this framing of the actual rather than the imagined, connecting us 'back' and grounding our viewing position even in those moments where we are closest to the forms of our involvement in fiction. Music performs some of the referential and formal tasks that it does in fictional narratives but its play upon and beneath the record of the real, as an agency both of expansion and of focus, gives its use in documentary accounts a distinctive role. At certain points, as noted in my remarks on *Inside Job*, this role can involve entering the expositional design with a contrastive, ironic or comic force.[13] In most cases, whether its use is pronounced or restrained, intended to be noticed or to work upon perception unregistered, music in documentary requires a rather different kind of critical appreciation from that accorded to its use in feature fiction. I hope my examples above have contributed, alongside other chapters in this book, to the exploration of at least some of the possible terms of this difference, a difference that takes us to the heart of the tensions, and the continuing attractions, of what is now a highly diverse, international documentary culture.

Notes

1 John Corner, 'Sounds Real: Music and Documentary', in *Popular Music*, 21:3 (2002), 357–366.

2 Aesthetically ambitious documentary and video art are now sometimes hard if not impossible to distinguish. The extent to which aesthetic density is given priority over referentiality is one criterion, although in practice it may be a hard one to apply.

3 Clearly, such a goal became subject to modification or competition when the 'journalistic' potential of documentary form, and then later the 'observational' possibilities allowed by new camera and sound technology, established themselves, bringing with them a degree of aesthetic austerity.

4 Recent essays on this and related issues can be found in *The Documentary Film Book*, ed. Brian Winston (Basingstoke: Palgrave Macmillan, 2013).

5 Such addition can enhance the watching of observed silent action and interaction, but used over spoken exchange, however quietly, it may have the effect of displacing the 'eavesdropped' speech into something close to dramatic dialogue, thereby weakening the reality effect.

6 Among the many commentaries on this question, that of Claudia Gorbman in *Unheard Melodies: Narrative Film Music* (London: British Film Institute, 1987), has received frequent citation, including in Scott Lipscomb and David Tolchinsky's useful survey, 'The Role of Music Communication in Cinema', in *Musical Communication*, ed. Dorothy Miehl, Raymond MacDonald and David Hargreaves (Oxford: Oxford University Press, 2005), 383–404.

7 Here, a case-study by Iben Have deserves mention, 'Attitudes Towards Documentary Soundtrack – Between Emotional Immersion and Critical Reflection', in *Mediekultur*, 48 (2009), 48–60.

8 Interestingly, an earlier film on Petit, Sandi Sissel's 30-minute observational documentary *High Wire* (1984), used music from Philip Glass's 'Glassworks' (1982).

9 Like other pieces for *Drowning by Numbers*, *Fish Beach* was derived from passages in the slow movement of Mozart's *Sinfonia Concertante* in E-Flat Major (1779) and its quirky solemnity soon won it widespread recognition.

10 The very austerity and inward intensity of minimalist work – static temporality, lack of clear tonal progression and difference through repetition – perhaps make it particularly useful for certain kinds of documentary sequence, such as those in *Man on Wire*, where intensive and sustained looking at ongoing and otherwise largely silent action is encouraged.

11 Ferguson himself referred to it in these terms: see Adam Lashinksy, 'Inside Job Director on Geithner, Goldman and Criminal Bankers', in *CNN Money* (March 15, 2011), at http://finance.fortune.cnn.com/2011/03/15/inside-job-director-on-geithner-goldman-and-criminal-bankers/ (accessed December 2013).

12 Anonymous interviewer, 'Composer Max Richter Talks the "Haunted" Music of *Waltz With Bashir*' (20th February 2009), at http://theplaylist.blogspot.co.uk/2009/02/composer-max-richter-talks-haunted.html (accessed December 2013).

13 The works of Michael Moore show comic subversion through music as a hallmark styling, but the usage is widespread in the history of documentary and could benefit from more attention. See, for instance, Sarah Keith, 'Half of it is Just the Fun of Finding the Right Music: Music and the Films of Adam Curtis', in *Studies in Documentary Film*, 7:2 (2013), 161–178.

I am grateful to Holly Rogers for her help in developing some of the points in my discussion.

Chapter 8

Irish Sea Power
A New Version of *Man of Aran* (2009/1934)

K.J. Donnelly

In recent years, cinema has seen the phenomenon of musicians providing live music for silent films, converting them into singular and often special events. Indeed, silent cinema is more prominent now than it has been since the 1920s. Festivals and archival showings abound and silent films are now part of education, entertainment and art.[1] Where there are silent films, there are almost always musical accompaniments. However, there is a smaller fragment of this where early sound films have their soundtracks masked and are treated in effect as silent films to be accompanied by live and often new music. A fine example of this is British Sea Power's new score for Robert Flaherty's celebrated documentary *Man of Aran* (1934). This English rock group has provided distinctive new music for this landmark film, which resembles their own musical output rather than traditional film music. They have since provided a score for Penny Woolcock's *From the Sea to the Land Beyond* (2012) and a new score (a replacement) for the Romanian film *Out of the Present* (originally released in 1999 and directed by Andrei Ujica), both of which are also documentary films.[2] Initially, British Sea Power's *Man of Aran* was a live performance at the film's screening at the British Film Institute in April 2009, followed by the CD and DVD release in May. So, how far is this new *Man of Aran* more a musical event than a film? It seems crucial that the DVD comes free with the CD.[3] Music changes the psychological and emotional landscape of films. Therefore, I would argue that different music yields a different film, and that the new version of *Man of Aran* illustrates this well.

Man of Aran was directed by American documentary film maker Robert Flaherty (1884–1951), who had previously made *Nanook of the North* (1922) in the Arctic, arguably the ur-documentary feature film. Amongst other films, he also directed *Moana* (1926) in Samoa, worked with F. W. Murnau on *Tabu* (1931) in Tahiti, worked with the Kordas on *Elephant Boy* (1937) in India and directed *Louisiana Story* (1948). Flaherty's work inspired the making of ethnographic films and helped found the field of 'visual anthropology' as pursued by Gregory Bateson and Margaret Mead in the 1930s and Jean Rouch in the 1960s. *Man of Aran* was acclaimed and indeed remains a canonical film, but it has also carried with it much controversy.[4] It is now considered 'docufiction' in that Flaherty directed locals to act in a certain way, including sharkfishing using a technique that had not been employed on the islands for decades. Set on the stark and waveswept Aran Islands off Ireland's west coast, *Man of Aran* shows hardy islanders growing food in extremely poor conditions aided by seaweed and pulverised rock, catching fish from a cliff and a crab from the rocks and the lengthy process of killing a massive basking shark with harpoons from a very small boat. Due to the degree of fabrication, the film is now often framed by debates about 'authenticity' rather than an appreciation of the poetic imagery and exciting filming and perhaps quite unfairly the anthropological value of its depictions is often ignored.[5]

Music in documentary films can often be seen as manipulative, with its 'Hollywood' patterns and sounds and its clear emotional brief. It is often considered an element that can obscure the veracity of the location images and sounds. Mervyn Cooke notes, 'From the earliest newsreel years, sceptical observers questioned the legitimacy of borrowing manipulative narrative techniques from the fiction film … This concern proved even more troubling when emotively suggestive music was also present …'.[6] Flaherty's film was scored by John Greenwood, a seasoned composer of music for dramatic films. However, Greenwood's score, as noted in a title card at the start of the film, was '… based on the original Irish songs of the Aran Islands …'. In this way, the film's original music appears to add a degree of authenticity to the film, and indeed asserts as much.

'Silencing Film': Historicism and Reframing

The current, almost frenzied interest in history manifests a cultural trend in the face of rapid change and the destruction of senses of nationality and destiny. We are at a point where much of the recent past is on the verge of being beyond direct memory—which is perhaps why current culture is so pathologically mining images of the past to reformulate it as contemporary entertainment. The remarkable explosion of live music for silent films since the 1990s is a part of this craze for historicism, which involves rediscovering old (sometimes nearly lost) culture, and might be approached as an aggressive colonisation of the past as part of a process of cultural renewal. While this marks a different form of 'historicism', one that perhaps historians might not recognise, or might even repudiate, it is part of a particularly vehement interest in past culture, evident also in museums and dramatic depictions of the past.

The radical reframing of a film through the addition of new music appears geared explicitly towards a new context of consumption for the film. It is no accident that the increase in live music for films has developed hand in hand with the increase in film festivals that will sanction such showings. This removes old films from the archive and repositions them as 'viable' films for contemporary audiences. Some of these novel versions wield a rhetoric of cultural renewal or 'updating' in their aspiration to make the silent film a valued object to a wider contemporary audience. Thomas Elsaesser bravely defended the disparaged Giorgio Moroder version of *Metropolis* (1926), an early example of this process released in the early 1980s with a soundtrack of electronic dance music and songs. He suggested that Moroder's modern music allowed the audience to appreciate Fritz Lang's film as again being imbued with a sharp feeling of modernity, which it would have had upon its initial release in the late 1920s.[7] Modern music might allow a point of entry for audiences unfamiliar with the conventions of older cinema, functioning as a *frame* for the film by updating the experience to render a difficult and antiquated work fit for more contemporary tastes.

Returning to *Man of Aran's* soundtrack, we should remember that the film was not silent but has had its original diegetic sound recording and musical score masked to allow its replacement by British Sea Power's music. This means that the new version violates the original intentions of the filmmakers. However, it does not necessarily mean that the film is made into something of which they, and Flaherty specifically, would not have approved. However, it does detract from the historical value and the integrity of the film as a historical object. Remembering that Greenwood's score is ostensibly based on original Irish songs of the Aran Islands, the issue here is not only that of replacing an original intention, but also of replacing an integral component of the film that had an anthropological connection with the culture depicted on screen. The process of 'masking' immediately removes respect for original intention. Music as an addition is able to remove or add to the original intentions of the film significantly. There are some notable historical cases where recorded soundtracks are masked and original intentions of film makers dismissed. For instance, avant-garde composer Mauricio Kagel wrote a new score for *Un Chien Andalou* (1929) to replace Luis Buñuel and Salvador Dalí's stipulation to use discs of Wagner's *Liebestod* from *Tristan und Isolde* (1859) and an Argentinean tango.[8] However, what might be considered more significant is that as a part of the process of making *Man of Aran* ready for new music, its original diegetic sound has been erased. One of the dominant aspects of the original soundtrack is the recording of the sea and wind. The British Sea Power soundtrack includes a fair amount of sea sound, although this has a dislocated quality due to its lack of direct synchronisation with the images. This is similar to the extensive and dislocated sea sounds in Flaherty's original. However, these generic sea sounds tend to function as 'filler' material between the main bodies of the British Sea Power pieces of music, or as quiet parts within those pieces. While on one level, these generic sounds constitute a part of conventionalised representation, the sounds also contribute to a misrecognition of what is seen and what is heard, which ultimately problematises the relationship between the film and the 'real world'.[9] Another question arises: are these diegetic sea sounds or are they an integral part of British Sea Power's music? While conventionally they appear to be the former, aesthetically they are clearly the latter. This constitutes a seeming mix of nondiegetic music with diegetic sounds.

Many documentaries have proceeded from the position that the music should not detract from, nor in any way challenge, the primacy of the representations on screen. As a consequence, many filmmakers have eschewed the use of dramatic incidental music as an accompaniment to images and diegetic sound. These elements alone appear to transmit reality very directly while nondiegetic music, particularly in its Hollywood-style score variety, appears the epitome of emotional manipulation and aestheticising 'addition' to a documentary record. However, this is a relatively modern conceptualisation.[10] British documentaries of the 1930s, such as those made by John Grierson and Humphrey Jennings, tended to use a fair amount of incidental music. A pair of fine examples of this convention are Coal Face (1935) and Night Mail (1939, directed by Basil Wright and Harry Watt who had worked on Man of Aran), both with orchestral scores by Benjamin Britten. Flaherty's film is part of this early documentary tradition, indeed it was produced as a British documentary by Michael Balcon at Gainsborough Studios. As a consequence, it was not considered anomalous to have copious amounts of nondiegetic music.[11] Of course, there is nothing intrinsic to documentary that negates the use of musical scores and in recent years most television documentaries include incidental music of one sort or another, while even news items on television might find themselves awarded some subtle musical accompaniment. In the case of British Sea Power's score for Man of Aran though, the music is prominent almost to the point of dominating the film. This arguably follows a tradition outside mainstream cinema, where occasionally silent films have been accompanied by live music as a more art-based event than regular cinema projection. Gillian B. Anderson suggests that in these situations the music might be conceived as an equal partner with the silent film, but in some cases it manifests more than a partnership, designating the film as secondary.[12]

It is a critical issue that the British Sea Power version removes diegetic sound, an elimination that perhaps most crucially erases the characters' voices. The original version of Man of Aran has plenty of talking from the characters on screen, in both English and Irish (Irish Gaelic as some would have it). It should be noted that much of it is phatic language with little semantic content (for example, when a bundle is hoisted up a cliff: 'Get it up, there!'). Indeed, apart from a few points where minimal narrative information is furnished, the dialogue, rather than bearing great semantic content, has more of an aesthetic function. The voices are an essential component of the film's sense of authenticity and its depiction of the culture of the Aran Islands. Yet it is clear that the sound is almost wholly post-synchronised, making for a 'plesiochronous' accompaniment to the images and consisting of sea and to a lesser extent wind noises, along with the Islanders' voices and a few other sound effects.[13] Clearly, the recording of location sound for each shot was too difficult and the lack of direct synchronisation, even of the spoken word and moving mouths at many points, lends the film a sense of dislocation and the feeling of being based upon the principles of silent cinema. As such, British Sea Power's new music is not as disruptive as it might have been.

What is striking when comparing the two different versions of *Man of Aran* is just how different an experience they deliver. Greenwood's original orchestral music, although making much of its authenticity in terms of using Irish song melodies, in fact sounds in many ways like a fairly conventional orchestral score for a mainstream film of the period, although it differs in that the amount of music in the film is far larger than was conventional for a British-produced dramatic film of the period.[14] This is no doubt due to *Man of Aran* containing less dialogue sequences and more scenes of 'silent' action, which call out for some sonic accompaniment. Indeed, this is why British Sea Power's new music works successfully.

Greenwood's score, while including some identifiable Irish song melodies and a couple of dance-based sections, provides some direct support and anchoring to the film's meanings. The opening film titles have some grand and bold music, which suggests something of the nobility of the people of the islands (the 'Man of Aran' of the film's title). During the first sequence in the house, which illustrates the animals living alongside the people, Greenwood supplies jaunty, comic music. In contract, in British Sea Power's version, the music is far more tentative and improvisational, with a number of instruments making short interjections and the music failing to move into an easily understood piece. Rather than Greenwood's rather ponderous humour, which might almost be construed as laughing at the primitive living conditions of the islanders, British Sea Power's music is darker, perhaps suggesting something of the austere living situation which dictates such a mode of housing. In fact, this is one of the crucial differences between the two soundtracks: Greenwood's score is far 'lighter', embracing humour on a number of occasions as well as sounding upbeat and jokey, even during the epic shark fishing sequence. As we shall see, British Sea Power's music is less 'obvious', with humour far less to the fore and indeed the overall character of the music being often unerringly serious.

Sea Power

British Sea Power, as indicated by the group's unusual name, is a distinctive and highly adventurous British indie rock band. Based in Brighton, the group released their first record in 2001, followed by their debut album in 2003. Signed to Rough Trade records, an archetypal independent record label, they seem to embody an idea of current 'indie' music. At the time of *Man of Aran*, the group consisted of six musicians: Scott 'Yan' Wilkinson (vocals, guitar and keyboards), Neil Hamilton Wilkinson (bass, keyboards and vocals), Martin Noble (guitar and keyboards), Matt Wood (drums), Abi Fry (viola) and Phil Sumner (keyboards, cornet and guitar). Arguably, this was a remarkable and surprising point in the group's career to embark upon producing music for a film. The previous year, the third album *Do You Like Rock Music?* had become its most successful, reaching no.10 in the UK charts and no.5 in the US (Billboard Heatseekers Albums chart). One might have expected British Sea Power to have concentrated their efforts on retaining such top-selling status by focusing on a highly-polished follow-up recording. Instead, they chose to provide music for a film made 75 years earlier. Yet this was not so surprising if the group's concert activities were taken into account. The band has constantly confounded expectations about where rock concerts ought to be performed, preferring individual concert 'events' in a variety of outlandish locations to conventional concert tours.[15]

In addition to this, British Sea Power is perhaps best known for producing distinctive and original songs that in many cases contain anthemic choruses and build towards a climactic and repetitive statement of these. The group's sound is electric guitar-led and arguably inspired by garage band-type music.[16] There is a desire to sound organic and to avoid elaborate studio effects. Songs are strongly melody-led and insistently memorable, accompanied often by quite basic and disciplined arrangements and little in the way of musical pyrotechnics. This electric guitar-led sound was augmented by the addition of viola player Abi Fry in 2008. British Sea Power tends to extended melodies, and indeed evinces a strong interest in melody, which sometimes are more like traditional folk-style song lines rather than the often simplistic and fragmented ones upon which many contemporary pop songs are based. In dynamic terms, the group's songs are often based on the principle of building up intensity, with much use of repetition and modular elements. Rhythms are certainly insistent but not inspired by dance music and bear more closely a resemblance to the 'motorik' 4/4 beat beloved of 1970s 'Krautrock' rather than the snappy traditional backbeat which lifts and emphasises the second and fourth beats. In a period when popular music is often heavily treated to give a regularity to sounds and performances, British Sea Power revels in a more organic sound based on textural dynamics and live-sounding group performances rather than studio produced standardisation. A sense of musical cohesion across the film is supplied by the ensemble's limited range of timbres and a restricted but effective palette of musical strategies. This includes the dynamic contour of building up the pieces in terms of intensity, the use of regular continuous quaver 4/4 rhythms for energy and the use of short and repetitive solo guitar arpeggios as ostinato bases. In addition, the music that opens the film is founded upon a repeated ostinato played on single notes on the piano, which has a similar structure and character to the guitar arpeggios. The group has translated the essence of their musical oeuvre into an effective accompaniment for film with their score for Man of Aran. The sensitive but insistent qualities of their music seem well suited to Flaherty's singular dramatised documentary.

Film and Music: Pulling Apart?

In the 1940s, composer Aaron Copland posited five functions for incidental music. These are: '... creating atmosphere, highlighting the psychological states of characters; providing neutral background filler, building a sense of continuity; sustaining tension and then rounding it off with a sense of closure'.[17] George Burt points to incidental music's many material functions, such as regularly exerting an enormous influence on the pacing of events and 'emphasising the dramatic line'.[18] British Sea Power's music for *Man of Aran* successfully completes all these functions even though it is not based on the more precise traditions of musical scores for films. Consequently, there is more of a sense of music as at times a semi-autonomous parallel to the images, with the concomitant effect of rendering the film as perhaps a less manipulative medium in terms of concentrated and specific effect on the audience.

The 2009 version of the film has a tendency towards 'segmentation'. This is less an effect of the structuring of Flaherty's film itself and perhaps more to do with the approach taken by British Sea Power. The 76-minute film is accompanied by distinct musical pieces, often with sea sounds between them. The CD divisions and titles reinforce this, as do the DVD divisions which are based largely on the musical pieces. Almost all of the group's musical pieces are extended and repetitive, based on gradual unfolding and often building up in intensity. They are thus long pieces and tend to cover substantial sections of the film, where certain activities are depicted. So, rather than matching the momentary dynamics of events on screen, the music provides a blanket, unifying and furnishing a general ambience to the (often dramatic) events recorded by the film. Indeed, the score consists of a number of 'grooves', which in some cases prove highly uplifting in their dynamic build up. Interestingly, the DVD cover publicity for *From the Land to the Sea Beyond* calls the film itself 'uplifting'. I was not convinced that the film deserved this description. However, British Sea Power's music certainly has that quality, and in abundance at certain points in Woolcock's film. The same goes for the earlier *Man of Aran*, with the music lifting the sense of pace and excitement, particularly in comparison with some of the same sequences scored by Greenwood.

British Sea Power's music for the film tends to work on repetition and cumulative effect, rather than variation or alternation of material. A few pieces in the film had originally been conceived as songs and the film includes a song in the score which appears as an isolated instance. Certain characteristic *timbres* and mixtures tend to dominate the music. There is a good amount of guitar notes played with e-bow, a magnetic device that vibrates the strings, giving a quality similar to bowing them. This is often added to the string instruments (viola and some cello). Another notable strategy is the use of regular quaver (eighth note) pulses, led by guitars strumming chords but often supported by viola. This encapsulates one of the characteristic sounds of British Sea Power and at times here it becomes their default sound, which they wield highly effectively. Indeed, there is a preponderance of regular quaver pulses in each piece that build up gradually, with the focusing of the rhythm and the full involvement of the drums bringing the music to higher levels of intensity. Rather than simply leaving this up to the drums, or the guitars, which should have been a fairly conventional approach, British Sea Power often uses the viola as a rhythm instrument too, in an extremely unconventional move. The often subtle and atmospheric music partners the film effectively, although there are almost no clear synch points or moments where the music changes its dynamics precisely to match screen activity.

The film opens with title cards that slightly precede the inauguration of the haunting opening piece of music. With the main title card, a piano arpeggio starts slightly tentatively, locking into a high-register eight-note ostinato which runs throughout the whole piece and lasts for over three and a half minutes. It sounds echoed, perhaps with some electronic reverb but mostly though being played with the sustain pedal depressed and recorded in a room with reflective surfaces.[19] The piano motif simply repeats *ad infinitum* without development, although at certain points it is apparent that it is manually produced as its speed and fingerfall varies. Over the top of this, e-bowed electric guitar and strings in unison make extremely slow sustained rising pitches on an A major scale (from C sharp to G sharp and then downwards).[20] This makes for a slow melody, indeed so slow that it hardly registers as one at all, as it has more of an effect of simply rising pitch and enhancing the feel of it being organic music. This piece has no real dynamic connections with the images of *Man of Aran*, accompanying first the opening title cards of the film (including, of course, the one that credits John Greenwood's music based on Aran Island songs). After this, the images depict Michael, the boy of the central family, catching a crab from a rock pool. During this activity, the rising melody disappears, leaving only the piano arpeggio, which then returns and the piece concludes with sea sounds. These sounds have a stylised quality to them; indeed they sound remarkably like some of the sea sounds on Flaherty's original soundtrack and similarly have a slightly dislocated quality to them. A different version of this piece appears towards the conclusion of the film, accompanying images of a school of basking sharks in the sea, boats going out to them and the woman at the boiling cauldron.[21]

The four-minute sequence illustrating the laborious process of growing food begins with sea sounds accompanying dramatic images of the raging sea, leading into a song. The singing starts over one of the film's iconic images, of the woman with a gigantic cargo of seaweed strapped to her back in a basket (figure 8.1). The song has an interesting genealogy. 'Come Wander with Me' is a preexisting cult song, written by film and television composer Jeff Alexander with words by screenwriter Anthony Wilson, which had appeared in an eponymous episode of the television series *The Twilight Zone* (season five, first broadcast in 1964).[22] British Sea Power only uses the chorus of the song, a folk-inspired melody which simply repeats, with lyrics referring to someone who 'came from the sea' sung by a male voice doubled by a female voice. The instrumental backing is subtle and understated, with guitar arpeggios marking the chord changes, some viola scrapes and drum kit played quietly with brushes. The song does not sound out of place in that it has a folk quality that perhaps distantly owes something to Irish folk music, while its plaintive tone and potentially ambiguous invitation to 'come wander with me' provides a serious and slightly morose cast to the events on screen.[23] This is underlined by the home chord of A minor having its fifth augmented (from E to F) in alternating chords at the conclusion of each verse. After the sung verse, the melody again is stated by cornet and morose wordless vocals before

Figure 8.1 Woman with basket in *Man of Aran* (Robert Flaherty, 1934).

concluding with sea noises. The use of a song like this is not a traditional form of accompaniment and appears to suggest the primacy of British Sea Power's music over the film.

The whole shark fishing sequence lasts over 20 minutes and is the centrepiece of the film. As a film sequence, it not only concentrates on the men in the boat confronting the shark, but also includes sections dealing with the woman and boy on land. It embraces three different piece of music by British Sea Power, which aim at atmospheric effect rather than musical cohesion. After extensive shots of the boy climbing down the cliff and looking downwards, the appearance in shot of what the boy is beholding inspires momentary silence in the soundtrack. The startling close-up shots of the gigantic basking shark are then accompanied by isolated single-note metallic-sounding electric guitar wails, using electronic distortion and reverb. This sounds reminiscent of whale singing. It appears not only representative of the 'otherworldliness' of this monstrous but passive shark, but also of the agony of the fish being brutalised and killed. It is also representative of the process of close quarters combat with it, where the Aran men have their boat tied to the basking shark in a bid to weaken and kill it. The guitar wails becomes more frantic with the screen activity, now doubled by a heavy drum beat alongside synthesiser and guitar outbursts. The drums enter at the point where the men have managed to tether the shark to the boat. Taking some time to build into a riff, the chaotic montage is accompanied by a heavy 4/4 tom-tom beat. As the battle becomes more frenzied, an exciting tremolo picked guitar lead enters, racking up the intensity further. While the strings make a regular quaver pulse on the same notes, the guitar playing includes Jimi Hendrix-style wails. At the point where the shark is dramatically harpooned, the music has reached a cacophonous crescendo. This is in effect a lengthy montage sequence with a wealth of dramatic shots edited together.[24] Despite the fact that the music is not aimed at making strong points of synchronisation with screen activity, the shark is harpooned on an emphasised first beat of a bar, redoubling the effect.

A screen title card informs the audience that it took two days to 'win the shark's oil for their lamps'. Immediately, another, different repeated solo guitar arpeggio with a little electronic reverb giving it some space and atmosphere begins as the foundation of the succeeding piece of music ('Coneely of the West'). This guitar figure is related only distantly to the earlier one ('Boy Vertiginous'). In effect, it gives the impression of three falling notes with the final note each time sustaining for a bar to leave space for breath in the continuing concentration of shark fishing on screen. This time-consuming operation is emphasised by the intercutting of shots of the woman and boy now in the house waiting anxiously. The music is far calmer than before and lends an air of resignation to the proceedings, suggesting that the battle is won but patience is still required.

To accompany two other boats going out to help bring in the defeated shark, the music begins a new piece ('The North Sound'), with yet another unaccompanied guitar arpeggio (again with descending chromatic high notes, same lower string notes), which forms the foundation for the piece and builds in energy, despite the images suggesting that the main work is completed. Despite some outlandish echoed sounds, this is perhaps the most conventional rock piece, as it exploits energy to express something of the excitement of the community about the killing, with a chain of people pulling the fish carcass ashore with a rope while the woman protagonist boils a cauldron. Deep ominous booming notes signal that this is not quite the victory it appears, indicating the possibility of the music's comment framing a new interpretation of the 1934 images.

Man of Aran concludes with some startling and stylised images. Flaherty clearly wished to leave a strong and emotional impression of the family and has some iconic but mannered static images of the boy in close-up looking to the side and a long shot of the family along with harpoon in dramatic silhouette. The music during this sequence begins in a similar manner to some earlier pieces with a motif based on three guitar arpeggios, which later develop into strong rhythmic movement based around chord changes and with prominent cornet.[25] Flaherty's shots of the sea are absolutely astounding and their intermittent regularity gives the film its central visual character. Another version of this piece of music had already appeared on the British Sea Power album *Do You Like Rock Music?* (2008) as 'The Great Skua'.[26] The music closely resembles a song, built around a guitar arpeggio based on three chords (G-D6-CM7). It has a cornet melody and a section that alternates two chords (C-F) and then, as it builds to a dramatic and uplifting climax, the chords change to a progression of

C - D Minor - F for the conclusion. Yet it was not a song originally but an instrumental piece. If the original recording was intended to convey something of the soaring seabird, then it also appears perfectly to fit Flaherty's highly evocative and pyrotechnic closing stages of the film, showcasing a montage of towering waves breaking on dramatic barren cliffs and shots of the heroic central family. The climactic conclusion of the song coincides with dramatic static close-up shots of the man and the boy, interspersed with images of the waves and then one of the family unit in silhouette (figure 8.2). This proves a far more dramatic finale for the film than in the original 1934 release and the increase in drama comes not only from the music's effective partnering with Flaherty's poetic and life-affirming imagery, but also from the dynamic materiality of the music itself.

Figure 8.2 **The family in silhouette:** *Man of Aran.*

Conclusion

Man of Aran is a startling film, with poetic images in abundance as well as dramatic and exciting sequences. Such films are able to bear the weight of substantial musical addition, and this is proven by British Sea Power's new version of the film. The new music has a number of effects on Flaherty's film. One is that the music *emphasises* the veracity and age of the images, through a process of 'framing'. This is clearer than in the original score. Freed from music that underlines the 'reality' of the images (Greenwood's music based on Irish melodies), the new soundtrack is able to express an inner emotion and empathy for the islanders not available earlier. Furthermore, it is able to do so by using a more contemporary musical language. While this might well make the film more accessible for a contemporary audience, the new music's 'framing' of the images also, I would suggest, makes them seem more 'past'.

In the process of 'renewing' Man of Aran, British Sea Power's music adds a sense of doubtful 'historical status' to its existing doubtful 'authenticity'. Yet these additions might not be important. The film certainly 'documents' the reality of the location if nothing else, and as such it is a valuable documentary record of past events, no matter how 'authentic' they might or might not be. New music, while detracting from the past-ness of the event depicted, aestheti-cises the film, in a way matching Flaherty's dramatically aesthetic approach to Man of Aran. The film embodies the notions of 'manipulation', reconstruction and inauthenticity with respect to documentary film. Does British Sea Power's music reproduce Flaherty's folk culture romanticism, embellish it, or even com-ment on it? There certainly is a distinct romanticism in British Sea Power's desire for an 'organic' rock sound, not to mention their eccentric choice of loca-tions for concerts. Their music for the film certainly does not 'speak down' to it, or comment in any knowing or negative manner. There was already a quality in British Sea Power's songs that has enabled their music to make an effective transition to the scoring of moving images.[27] This is primarily down to mood and energy and while proving the band's versatility, it also confirms the versatil-ity of certain films for musical retrofitting.

This process of masking an original soundtrack and re-scoring the film illus-trates a profound difference in the conception of film: on the one hand, seeing them as historical documents, works of art essentially imbued with the period of their production and on the other, seeing them as living objects that have new life breathed into them by the new moment of the film's experience with novel music. The former approach represents the important current notion of the cultural museum, while the latter represents the vertiginous possibility of reappropriation, which can produce startling novelty but in some cases involves the crude coopting of existing culture into something of questionable value. Yet the British Sea Power version of Man of Aran is a highly effective film, removing the dialogue that lacks direct synchronisation with the images and Greenwood's jaunty, 'telegraphing', wall-to-wall orchestral score in favour of a darker musi-cal framing of the film. British Sea Power certainly took the film seriously, as their music gives a more solemn cast to the images throughout, as well as the extremity of events depicted being subject to the band's keen sense of musical dynamics, which build up to startling musical climaxes that not only comple-ment Flaherty's dramatic images, but also create a much wider sense of mood and excitement for the film. British Sea Power's Man of Aran is in effect a new film rather than simply an amended version, although the prominence of the music perhaps helps remove the film from its documentary context and move it instead towards the status of musical event.

Notes

1 Rick Altman, *Silent Film Sound* (New York: Columbia University Press, 2004), 4.

2 Although also a documentary with music by British Sea Power, *From the Land to the Sea Beyond* appears a wholly different prospect. The band was brought onto this documentary project through the producers being fans of the group's music and wanting a live performance by the group at the Sheffield Documentary Festival. This was conceived much more as a collaboration between the group and director Penny Woolcock and British Sea Power used a number of existing songs that had appeared on earlier records, which they rearranged as well as incorporating new material: 'Making *The Sea and the Land Beyond*' documentary extra on the *From the Sea to the Land Beyond* DVD (BFI, 2012).

3 The DVD includes a number of different soundtrack options to accompany the image track. These include 'Studio', 'Studio 5.1', 'Live', 'Live 5.1' and 'Bonus Soundtrack' (which is almost wholly ambient and electronic and assembled by the group's principal singer Yan).

4 Upon its initial release, Roderick Flynn and Patrick Brereton attest that, 'When the film was first seen by the political elite [in Ireland], it was said that Eamon de Valera – the leader of the *Fianna Fáil* political party who above all others helped define a post-Civil War identity that continued well into the 1950s – wept at its heroic portrayal of Irish people. The film reflected a preoccupation with the West as defining a pure strand of Irish identity and was marketed internationally as a realist document of life in that period.' Flynn and Brereton, *Historical Dictionary of Irish Cinema* (Lanham, MD: Scarecrow, 2007), 259. Ruth Barton sums up its current status: '*Man of Aran* now occupies a troubled position within Irish cultural life, representing for many the falsification of Ireland by the many cultural invaders who plundered it for its transformative powers, and of local Irish willingness to collude in this process. Since its release, it has become a marker of both artistic excellence and compromise.' Barton, *Irish National Cinema* (London: Routledge, 2004), 48.

5 The film is now seen as a 'fictional documentary', using reconstruction of practices that had ceased years earlier and depicting a central nuclear family who were not actually related to one another. See George Stoney's documentary *How the Myth Was Made* (1979) and Mac Dara O'Curraidhin's *A Boatload of Wild Irishmen* (2011).

6 Mervyn Cooke, *A History of Film Music* (Cambridge: Cambridge University Press, 2008), 267.

7 Thomas Elsaesser, *Metropolis* (London: BFI, 2000), 58–59.

8 This was composed and recorded despite the tradition that the film should be accompanied by discs suggested by the directors.

9 Indeed, current television convention means that documentaries using silent film footage almost always accompany them with some sort of spurious diegetic sound.

10 Brian Winston, 'Documentary: How the Myth Was Made', in *Wide Angle*, 21:2 (March 1999), 71.

11 John Greenwood (1889–1976) scored almost 50 films, including *Elephant Boy* (1937), *The Drum* (1938), *Pimpernel Smith* (1941), *San Demetrio, London* (1943), *Hungry Hill* (1947), *Eureka Stockade* (1949), *Quartet* (1949), *The Last Days of Dolwyn* (1949) and *The Gentle Gunman* (1952). John Huntley points out that Greenwood was a symphonist and conductor and wrote a vast number of film scores: *British Film Music* (London: Skelton Robinson, 1947), 206–207.

12 Gillian B. Anderson, *Music for Silent Films 1894–1929: A Guide* (Washington, D.C.: Library of Congress, 1988), xv.

13 The voices sound as if they were recorded in a different, more enclosed space as well as synchronising precisely only occasionally. For more discussion of such plesiochrony and its use in documentaries, see K. J. Donnelly, *Occult Aesthetics: Synchronization in the Sound Film* (New York: Oxford University Press, 2014), 181–183.

14 I already noted that *Man of Aran* was what must have been one of the first symphonic scores, certainly for a British film. Indeed, it is more 'wall-to-wall' than was standard for British films throughout the later 1930s: Donnelly, *British Film Music and Film Musicals* (Basingstoke: Palgrave, 2007), 18.

15 For example, Carnglaze Caves in Cornwall, Grasmere village hall, the Scillonian Club on the Scilly Isles, the Czech Embassy in London, the Monaco Hotel on Canvey Island (which was broadcast on BBC2's *The Culture Show*), appeared on *Later With Jools Holland* (BBC, Feb 2008) alongside Cumbrian wrestlers and the London Bulgarian Choir, Berwick village hall, Jodrell Bank Observatory, the CERN physics lab in Geneva, the Centenary Gala for Poet Laureate Sir John Betjeman in 2006 (Prince Charles was guest of honour, Nick Cave and Dame Edna Everage also appeared), the Great Wall of China, the Chelsea Flower Show, the Natural History Museum in London and on an island in the Arctic.

16 Perhaps at times reminiscent of the Velvet Underground, or more recently Stereolab, in that the guitars usually provide continuous rhythm and will move through a handful of chords rather than articulating repetitive riffs as a foundation for the music.

17 Aaron Copland, 'Tip to the Moviegoers: Take Off Those Ear-Muffs', in *The New York Times* (6 November 1949), section six, 28.

18 George Burt, *The Art of Film Music* (Boston: Northeastern University Press, 1994), 4, 79.

19 The piano arpeggio is reminiscent of Harold Budd's echoed piano on his collaborations with Brian Eno on *The Plateau of Mirror* (1980) and *The Pearl* (1984).

20 This may be understood bitonally as a rising Phrygian scale on C sharp to its fifth and back.

21 The opening track is called 'Man of Aran' on the CD and the reprise is called 'Woman of Aran'.

22 In the episode, it is sung by actress Bonnie Beecher and has a supernatural function, able to enchant a singer in search of a song to record. The verses of the song are added to throughout the episode, inexplicably fitting recent events and foretelling future ones.

23 British Sea Power only uses some of the song words from the original: 'He came from the sunset, he came from the sea. He came from my sorrow and can love only me. Come wander with me love, come wander with me. Away from this sad world, come wander with me'.

24 These include long shots and close ups of the boat, the shark thrashing in the water, the woman and boy watching from the shore and the boat being taken on a 'Nantucket sleighride' (being pulled along by the speared shark).

25 The track is titled 'No Man is an Archipelago' and runs for 4'49".

26 And indeed, two other pieces had already appeared in different versions as 'North Hanging Rock' and 'True Adventures' on the band's album *Open Season* (2005).

27 Indeed, this quality is evident in an effective fan video for 'North Hanging Rock', which accompanies the song with a short German silent film from the early years of the Twentieth Century ('Lights and Shades on Bostock's Circus Farm'). The film depicts a farm of 'pensioner' animals, including an elephant that dies and is moved with great effort and its body burned: at http://www.youtube.com/watch?v=7sRaN209ARs, (accessed 10 January, 2014).

Chapter 9

Excavating Authenticity
Surveying the Indie-Rock Doc

Jamie Sexton

As the second decade of the twenty-first century unfolds, the visualisation of music continues to increase. The emergence of YouTube in particular has been crucial in advancing this process, containing as it does a huge collection of official and fan-produced music videos, music performance clips and a range of other audiovisual materials. One particular symptom of music's escalating visualisation is the rise of the music documentary, which has enjoyed a boom since the 2000s. As Simon Reynolds has remarked, a huge number of music documentary films were released in the 2000s as compared to the 1990s, when production was rather sparse.[1] Made-for-television music documentaries have also increased, stimulated by the exponential growth of television channels enabled by cable, satellite and digital technologies. Reynolds cites the expansion of cable and digital channels as one factor behind the music documentary boom, alongside the fact that they can be made with small crews and are relatively cheap to produce. This latter factor has also contributed to a more general documentary boom in recent times. According to Thomas Austin and Wilma de Jong, documentary films released theatrically in the US grew significantly during the new millennium, 'from an average of 15 in the late 1990s to around 40 in 2003 and 50 in 2004'.[2] Despite this heightened presence at the cinema, they note that most documentaries remain 'very much a niche taste' and are more commonly viewed on television, DVD/Blu-Ray, or as digital streams/downloads.[3] Music documentaries are also generally niche in their appeal, but many do have the benefit of catering to an already existing fan base, which, although varying in size and devotion, invariably constitutes the prime audience for such material.

While Reynolds discusses the 'rock documentary' in general, this chapter will examine music documentaries that focus on American indie/alternative musicians. The 'indie-rock doc' has also flourished in line with the broader documentary boom, with a number of notable films being released over the past decade.[4] Examples include *Pavement: Slow Century* (Lance Bangs, 2002), *Dig!* (Ondi Timoner, 2004), *The Devil and Daniel Johnston* (Jeff Feuerzeig, 2005), *The Flaming Lips: The Fearless Freaks* (Bradley Beesley, 2005), *We Jam Econo: The Story of the Minutemen* (Tim Irwin, 2005), *Loudquietloud: A Film About the Pixies* (Matthew Cantor and Steven Galkin, 2006), *All Tomorrow's Parties*

(Jonathan Caouette, 2009), *Hit So Hard: The Life And Near Death Story Of Patty Schemel* (P. David Ebersole, 2012), *I'm Now: The Story of Mudhoney* (Adam Pease and Ryan Short, 2012), *Shut Up and Play the Hits* (Will Lovelace and Dylan Southern, 2012) and *The Punk Singer: A Film About Kathleen Hanna* (Sini Anderson, 2013). Before examining some major formal and thematic aspects of these documentaries, though, I will first outline how I am using the term 'indie'.

Mapping Indie

'Indie', of course, is an abbreviation of 'independent', but the two terms are not quite synonymous when used as cultural markers. In the sphere of music, 'independent' generally refers to production and distribution processes, most commonly indicating music distributed outside of the major commercial networks. 'Indie' can be used in this manner, but is more frequently employed in a generic sense: frequently, it denotes a broad spectrum of guitar-based music primarily influenced by 1960s garage and psychedelic rock and 1970s punk, with a tendency towards lo-fi production values.[5] Such a brief generic classification is necessarily very broad and does not capture the specificities of different types of music which have been classified as indie. A universally valid definition is impossible due to the ways in which the meanings of indie can change historically and geographically, and because there is a push and pull between commercial and audience uses of the term. Additionally, indie often connotes more than just sonic referents and also encompasses a set of values. According to Wendy Fonarow, 'indie is the spirit of *independence*, of being free from control, dependence, or interference. Self-reliance, not depending on the authority of others, has been the guiding value of indie music, as has the autonomy of the artist'.[6] This DIY ethic also feeds into a widespread anti-mainstream sensibility amongst indie communities, even though musicians recording for major labels can be considered indie if they are seen to embody autonomy within such a structure and/or if their sounds conform to prevailing generic parameters of musical expression.[7]

While the sonic parameters of 'indie' are broad, they are much less so than 'independent', which is not limited to any musical style (i.e. any kind of music released on an independent label can be considered independent). The development of indie as a generic marker reflected the dominant sounds permeating the independent record charts, particularly within Britain, which undoubtedly influenced its use within the U.S. Indie was used within Britain in the 1980s more than in the U.S., where terms such as 'alternative rock' or 'college rock' were more commonly employed, but has become more widespread within the U.S. since the early 1990s and the breakout success of Nirvana and grunge, due to the perceived mainstreaming of the 'alternative rock' scene.[8]

In this chapter, I am going to use the terms 'indie' and 'independent' synonymously, and rather loosely, to refer to artists who are generally received as independent from, or 'alternative' to, the musical mainstream. While some of the artists featured within these documentaries have had or do have contracts with major studios, the majority do not. Importantly, a number of these documentaries articulate, to differing degrees, an anti-corporate discourse, positioning big record companies as enemies of artistic integrity, and therefore reflect many of the values that Fonarow has identified as crucial within indie music cultures.

Retromania and the Archive

Reynolds connects the surge in music documentary production to an increasing retro culture which also encompasses 'band reformations and reunion tours, expanded reissues of classic albums and out-take-crammed box sets, remakes and sequels, histories and biographies, retro-oriented magazines finding endless new angles on the same old history and, not least, new bands recycling old styles'.[9] Retro culture has been analysed more exhaustively in Reynolds' book *Retromania*, in which he bemoans the increasingly backwards-looking nature of popular music culture: a culture that once epitomised ephemerality and 'nowness' has become swamped and stunted by excessive historical baggage.[10] While the reasons for this shift remain complex and multi-causal, a particularly important influence that Reynolds scrutinises is the ever-expanding archive of materials that accrue on the web and which can be accessed with little effort.

The archive, unsurprisingly, also plays a key role in a number of more recent indie-rock docs, though the types of archive material included and the ways in which such material is employed can vary. Archival recordings can be audiovisual, though they may be audio- or visual-only; they can be 'professional' or 'amateur', 'official' or 'unofficial'; and if such recordings have sometimes been used in previous films, at other times, their use in a documentary will be their first public airing. Recent indie-rock documentaries testify to the range of archival material through inclusion of all of these forms of footage. Yet what about the ways in which such footage is utilised? According to Stella Bruzzi, documentaries tend to employ archive material in two main ways: for largely illustrative purposes; or in a more critical fashion. In the illustrative mode, footage functions 'as part of a historical juxtaposition to complement other elements such as interviews and voice-over'; in the critical mode archive material is used in a more questioning manner and frequently employed 'dialectically or against the grain'.[11] While the bulk of indie-music documentaries adhere to the former mode, the actual range of archive material drawn on in fact complicates Bruzzi's general categories because they rely on a rather limited notion of the archive. Bruzzi's discussions are largely centred on archive material stemming from official collections; even though some of her discussion focuses on archival film originating within an amateur context, such material was quickly incorporated into more official archives because of its importance (the key piece of footage here being the Zapruder film of Kennedy's assassination).[12]

Official archives are, however, being increasingly complemented by a huge wealth of 'unofficial' archival material, which has grown in terms of output (affordable digital technologies enabling more people to create their own audiovisual recordings) and in terms of access (the internet hosting a massive amount of amateur documents). Jaimie Baron has elaborated on this development:

> Online databases and private collections, in particular, threaten to unseat official archives as the primary purveyors of evidentiary audiovisual documents. Indeed, while amateur photography, film, and video have always existed in an uneasy relationship with official archives, the increased availability of still and video cameras, analog and then digital, has led to a proliferation of indexical documents outside of official archives.[13]

As such, Baron argues that previous distinctions between 'archive' and 'found' footage begin to blur and that 'foundness' should be regarded as a 'constituent element of all archive documents, whether they were "found" in an archive or "found" in the street'.[14] This is pertinent to a number of music documentaries as they don't only rely on recordings stemming from official archives. Increasingly they are incorporating sounds and images that have been sourced in other ways, including personal collections (as in Daniel Johnston's extensive personal stash of recordings in *The Devil and Daniel Johnston*; or director Bradley Beesley's own personal collection of films he had made about the Flaming Lips) and amateur documents recorded by fans of particular musical artists. Fan footage is now used in many music documentaries and will sometimes comprise the entire film (as in *All Tomorrow's Parties* as well as the Beastie Boys concert film *Awesome: I Fucking Shot That!* [Adam Yauch, 2006] and the Nine Inch Nails concert documentary *After All is Said and Done* [A Tiny Little Dot, 2013]).[15]

All Tomorrow's Parties is a particularly interesting example of a music documentary which utilises the increasing presence of 'unofficial' archive material and fan footage. 'All Tomorrow's Parties' (or ATP) is a British 'alternative' music festival which first took place in 1999. It is notable for its unusual locations – seaside holiday camps – and for being curated by musical artists.[16] The documentary itself is a collage constructed from diverse footage, the majority of which was shot by fans and which was either sent in by attendees following requests by ATP organisers, or found through trawling YouTube.[17] Other footage was sourced from musicians, while newly-shot footage was also created by Luke Morris of Warp Films and Jonathan Caouette, the director of acclaimed documentary *Tarnation* (2003), who was commissioned to work on the film and is officially credited as its director.[18] Over a two year period, Warp received over 600 hours of footage; the final film was edited down to 82 minutes and features material provided by over 200 contributors.[19]

For a film comprising such a diverse array of footage of varying quality – shot with a range of devices including DV, Super-8 and mobile phones – and culled from numerous sources, there is a surprising degree of seamlessness to the film. Though the collage aesthetic is emphasised particularly through the unconventional refusal to linger on any musical performance at length, and while shifts in both sound and image quality are evident at different moments, sound plays a crucial role in stabilising the fragmented kaleidoscope of edited images by bridging cuts. It is important that sound and music in the film are largely mixed together into a seamless flow through techniques such as fade ins/outs to avoid abrupt transitions. At times, the film employs more than one audio layer, but even when it does so there is care to avoid an over-busy soundtrack: if two different tracks are used, then one will be foregrounded and another one will underpin it.

A good example of sound providing continuity across a rather hectic series of images occurs near the beginning of the film: following some vintage movie footage of British holiday camps, the rhythmic opening of Battles' 'Atlas' is heard on the soundtrack, gradually replacing the diegetic sounds of holiday goers. There then commences a rhythmic montage of multiple-screen action (with up to four separate images occupying the screen); footage of Battles on stage is juxtaposed with the vintage holiday clips and these are edited so that movement within the separate images and the appearance of images onscreen loosely synchs with the pronounced beats of the music, with a repeated loop of a girl throwing a ball towards the camera meshing with a synthetic audio swish (figures 9.1 and 9.2). These opening scenes also demonstrate how sound here motivates the organisation of moving image fragments. Furthermore, they announce one of the major themes and underpinning structures of the film, the 'old' versus the 'new': old archive footage is juxtaposed with newer archive footage; old traditions of British leisure are overlaid by newer traditions; and there is a sense of 'old' citizens being replaced by 'young' citizens, in that the majority of people in the vintage shots are elderly, whilst most of the attendees of ATP are much younger.[20]

Like *All Tomorrow's Parties*, *The Devil and Daniel Johnston* utilises the archive extensively, though is more conventionally structured and draws on

Figure 9.1 Multiscreen action in *All Tomorrow's Parties* (Jonathan Caouette, 2009).

Figure 9.2 Footage of a girl throwing a ball towards the camera is edited in a repeated, rhythmic loop in *All Tomorrow's Parties*.

the personal archive of Johnston himself. Whereas *ATP* adopts a (largely) non-linear collage format, *The Devil and Daniel Johnston* is more chronologically focused around the life of a single artist; and whereas *ATP* incorporates a dizzying array of fan footage, reflecting its emphasis on community and participation, *TDaDJ* relies most heavily on Johnston's personalised archive and newly-shot interview footage, reflecting its exploration of a single subject. While *TDaDJ* does include a number of other archival clips (including a fragment from Richard Linklater's early short 16mm *Woodshock*, 1985), the recordings Johnston made himself occupy a central position within the film as a whole. Johnston was a person who, from an early age, produced an enormous amount of creative work – including his music recordings, his drawings, Super-8 films and sound recordings of everyday life – and much of this provides access to his subjectivity and personal life.

In *ATP* there is an emphasis on the people who go to these events and a sense that they constitute an alternative community; contrastingly, *TDaDJ* is much more artist-focused. There are a few points in the film where the broader culture within which Johnston largely operated is glimpsed: Linklater's footage of the 1985 Woodshock festival; Johnston's relationship with Kathy McCarty and association with her band Glass Eye; and his trip to New York when he is accompanied by Sonic Youth. There is, however, no emphasis upon the importance of alternative music scenes within the film's discursive structure. It belongs more to a biographical/historical mode of the indie music documentary, in which a narrative is based around the dramas, tensions and development of a musical artist or band, but which only very briefly refers to broader contexts (*Pavement: Slow Century* and *The Fearless Freaks* are also examples of this kind of indie bio-doc).

The chronological, biographical approach is most common amongst the indie-rock documentaries I have surveyed, but as opposed to films which play down a band's links to any particular scenes (or community), many such films combine a biographical focus with an emphasis on context, often linking subjects to other independent artists or labels (e.g. *I'm Now: The Story of Mudhoney, We Jam Econo*), to gender politics (*The Punk Singer* and, to a lesser extent, *Hit so Hard: The Life and Near Death Story of Patty Schemel*) and sometimes locality (for example, *I'm Now* looks at the importance of Seattle within the early 1990s grunge explosion). Notably, all of these films make extensive use of diverse kinds of archive footage and combine these with newly-shot interview material.

Narration

One feature common amongst most recent indie-rock documentaries is the absence of voice-over narration. Of the films I have looked at, only *Dig!* is propelled by voice-over narration. Generally, though, there is a reluctance to adopt this often-maligned technique within indie-rock docs. Though narration exists in a number of films, it is often constructed through brief expository scenes and the structural arrangement of interview material. A good example of this can be found in *The Punk Singer*. The film begins with a grainy archive clip of Kathleen Hanna performing poetry (with synchronous sound) in a small venue in Olympia and is followed by another archival clip of Hanna staring into a camera combined with the artist stating how she got involved in music following a talk with Kathy Acker (the sound now non-synchronous, taken from a newly produced interview). This gives way to the opening of the Bikini Kill song 'Rebel Girl' (1993), accompanied by credits, stills of Hanna in performance and, most prominently, different archival images of her singing the song (some of which is loosely synched with the sound). As the archival images of Hanna in performance continue, the song is faded into the background of the mix as different interview snippets summing up her attitude and importance are foregrounded. This continues with the performance footage now interspersed with newly-shot footage of some interviewees (matching the speech on the soundtrack); after a couple of interviewees express curiosity as to why she quit music, we hear – for the only time in the film – the interviewee ask a question (asking if they know why she quit) accompanied by a title (because of low quality sound). After Kaia Wilson and Joan Jett answer in the negative, there is a cut (in both sound and image) to Hanna filmed bathing by a swimming pool, accompanied by a radio. The soundtrack now contains an introduction of a radio interview she did, with a presenter introducing her (this acts like a more conventional voice-over narration, even though it is not strictly so) and this is followed by Hanna recounting her own childhood over family photographs.

The Punk Singer is typical of the more biographical strains of the indie-rock documentary in its construction and avoidance of voice-over narration. It follows a largely linear trajectory through the life of Hanna, through emphasising her importance within a broader context of the Riot Grrrl movement and feminist politics and in this sense is quite conventional in formal terms. In order to avoid voice-over narration and yet still communicate basic aspects of who Hanna is for the less initiated viewer, it employs an introductory sequence – as outlined above – which communicates such information as well as introducing a key feature of the documentary: the revelation as to why Hanna stopped making music in the mid-2000s. Similar types of introductory sequences of varying lengths can be found in *The Devil and Daniel Johnston*, *Hit so Hard: The Life and Near Death Story of Patty Schemel*, *I'm Now: The Story of Mudhoney* and *The Flaming Lips: The Fearless Freaks* (although there are a couple of moments in this film when director Beesley does provide voice-over narration, albeit very briefly). In all these films, such openings act as a framing device and are followed by a broadly chronological, sometimes thematically clustered, structure based around interviews. There is also frequent recourse to the use of titles in these films, sometimes to introduce section headings, sometimes to impart basic narrative information and sometimes to clarify dialogue.

There is, then, an evident resistance to voice-over narration within biographically-oriented documentaries. This is so within other modes of indie music documentary as well: for example, *Loudquietloud* is a different kind of film in its incorporation of concert film and direct cinema techniques, and as such would be expected to avoid voice-over narration; and yet it is still notable that even when it needs to convey expository information, it resorts to using the intertitle as opposed to the voice-over. *All Tomorrow's Parties* is also a very different kind of documentary, a kind of kaleidoscopic compilation, but which nevertheless does contain narrative elements such as an outline of how the festival came about and the ideals that underpin it. These are again communicated via interview material rather than voice-over narration.

On a practical level, the avoidance of voice-over narration could be linked to the substantial amount of music on the soundtrack. As musical content in these films is an important part of their appeal, voice-over narration may have been minimised in order to lessen the disruption of musical flow. While there may be some truth to this line of thinking, it does not account for how the voice still takes prominent place within the majority of these films. Voice and music dominate the soundtracks of these documentaries to different degrees, but it is the voice that assumes priority (with the exception of *All Tomorrow's Parties*). As such, when interviewed voices are placed on the soundtrack, then music – if it has been playing – will either be phased out or lowered in volume so that it switches from a central to a supportive soundtrack element. This technique follows a long line of conventions in filmmaking more generally in its privileging of the human voice. As Michel Chion has argued, 'the presence of the human voice instantly sets up a hierarchy of perception' as humans have learned to prioritise the voice over competing sounds (he calls this *vococentrism*).[21] He further argues that classical cinema followed this privileging of the voice through techniques such as reducing other noises as far as possible to maintain vocal intelligibility.[22] In this sense, many of these documentaries are quite conventional in terms of how they treat the voice of the interviewee as paramount.

Music itself can function in different ways in indie-rock documentaries, but there exist loose diegetic and nondiegetic conventions. Diegetically, when a live performance with synchronised sound is shown, then music tends to combine with the image and function as archival testimony: not only a record of the artist(s) in performance which may be interesting enough in itself for a fan, but often as a means of narrative illustration, providing evidence to support what is being spoken about. To cite a brief example, in *The Flaming Lips: The Fearless Freaks*, the director provides a rare segment of voice-over narration when he mentions how a representative from Warner Bros. turned up for one of their 'fiery freakout' gigs in Oklahoma, 1990, after which they were signed to the major label; this is accompanied by low-resolution footage of the very gig. There follow interview segments in which participants (such as Donahue, then a member of the band) recount experiences of the gig. Here the performance, replete with tinny sound, acts to flesh out the spoken words, providing the viewer with a sense of what the performance was like in a way that words alone cannot; but the live archival clip is also fleshed out by the speech, which contextualises and narrates the performance, indicating its importance within the band's career. Nondiegetically, music often functions emotionally and prevalent use of underscoring adds emotional weight to particular moments in many of these films: in *Hit So Hard*, for example, Patty Schemel's tearful discussion of being replaced by a session drummer for the *Celebrity Skin* (1998) album is accompanied by a sparse piano line as if underlining the emotional and dramatic importance of the incident; similar music is employed in *The Devil and Daniel Johnston* to accompany Johnston's tearful father when he recounts how his son interfered with his piloting of a plane and forced him to crash land. At other times, nondiegetic music often functions to provide a kind of dynamic momentum to the vocal track by filling its gaps and silences.

Another possible factor influencing the avoidance of voice-over narration may be the legacy of direct cinema and its connections with the rock music documentary. Rob Strachan and Marion Leonard have noted such links, claiming that not only did rock music emerge as a distinct musical form around the same period as direct cinema came into existence, but that they were both attached to discourses of authenticity and seriousness.[23] As many direct cinema films also documented rock musicians, this mode significantly influenced the conventions of the rockumentary.[24] Certainly within many forms of independent music culture, the concept of authenticity (as well as seriousness) is crucial, though authenticity itself is a very malleable concept that can signify different properties according to the contexts within which it is mobilised. For example, progressive rock in the 1970s was often tied to discourses of authenticity, but it was so in a very different manner than, say, ideas of authenticity circulating in punk music culture (which is often seen as a reaction to progressive rock). While independent music is a very broad concept and is an outgrowth of hybrid traditions, and thus difficult to pin down exactly, it shares more commonalities with punk than it does with progressive rock: Kaya Oakes and Amy Spencer both argue that independent culture grew out of punk and was attached to the central tenet of *do it yourself* (DIY), involving a commitment to lo-fi cultural production (music as well as zines and other art) which moved far away from the large-scale bombast of progressive rock.[25]

Direct cinema should be considered an important influence on a number of independent music documentaries (some more than others), though the plethora of interview material, frequent use of archive material and plentiful use of non-synchronised sound in many of these also highlights differences from that tradition. The influence of direct cinema is most evident in the qualities of authenticity, immediacy and roughness. Authenticity is evident in many films through a commitment to documenting 'genuine' artists, sometimes contrasting them to less authentic, commercialised cultural actors and artefacts and in particular a recurrent anti-corporate discourse. Immediacy and roughness – the outcome of direct cinema's use of lightweight, mobile technologies and the prioritising of capturing events as they happen over the production of audiovisual material of optimal technical quality – is also apparent in many indie-rock documentaries, though in slightly different ways. Commitment to cheaper technologies is usually here a necessary byproduct of financial limitations, though there is also a more general privileging of lo-fi aesthetics within segments of indie cultures. The sense of immediacy imparted in many of these films, though, stems less from the footage shot by the filmmakers themselves as it does from the archive material used, as a good deal of performance material featured is amateur footage, while newly-shot material is dominated by interviews.[26] Even the indie-rock documentaries that I would associate most closely with direct cinema – *Loudquietloud* and *All Tommorrow's Parties* – nevertheless differ from some common traits associated with the form. The former film, for example, while following the band around on a tour and featuring mostly newly-shot footage, does feature interview material and also a newly-composed soundtrack (by Daniel Lanois). *ATP* diverges further: though it features a lot of footage marked by 'immediacy', this is crafted into a dense, non-linear collage style.

Another factor to consider in the general avoidance of voice-over narration is a longstanding hostility towards this technique by critics, practitioners and theorists. Bruzzi notes – though herself counters such attitudes – how the voice-over has gained a reputation as the 'unnecessary evil of documentary', often perceived as both unimaginative and didactic.[27] As independent music and film cultures are often committed to discourses of creativity, the circumvention of voice-over narration may indeed be a result of its general status as a documentary cliché. Such a self-conscious avoidance of clichéd conventions is particularly evident in *I'm Now* when Mark Arm starts discussing his heroin problems; as he begins to discuss these, he mentions how he hates the way drug problems are often presented in music documentaries: 'The music kinda gets all kinda sappy and things slow down', he states, briefly accompanied by ironic sounds (a plaintive piano segment) and images (slowed down and mixed concert images).

Countering the glorification of such stages in life as pivotal and important, he notes how he is embarrassed by this period of his life and admits that he himself became a cliché. Similar to how many indie music documentaries are primarily narrated out of the interviewed voices of the subjects, this distancing from overused conventions also arises out of interview material and is not presented as a stylistic gesture forced onto the material by the filmmakers.

While many of these documentaries (again, with the possible exception of *ATP*) are far from being innovative on an aesthetic level overall, it would appear that the voice-over is perceived by the respective filmmakers as particularly suspicious. As such, the few times when narration is included in these films, there is still care to eschew 'voice of God' narration, the most conventional mode. As mentioned, many indie music documentaries feature audio that functions as narration, but these are either selected extracts from interviews with subjects or samples from archival material. The more objective 'voice' standing outside of the documentary space is not in evidence. In *Dig!* – the only film I have surveyed which does feature more sustained voice-over commentary – narration is provided by one of the subjects of the film itself (Dandy Warhol's frontman Courtney Taylor-Taylor), though not its main protagonist and, interestingly, someone who is often denigrated by the primary subject of the film, Anton Newcombe of The Brian Jonestown Massacre.

Conclusion: The Subjective and the Formal

The general sidestepping of voice-over narration in a number of indie-rock documentaries can be linked, at least implicitly, to a denial of objectivity. While not explicitly articulated, such a position can be supported by the more general distrust of the voice-over and its status as a technique denoting objective distance. It is important that the majority of narration in these films is formed by the extraction and placement of interview material without the interference of interviewer questioning.[28] Narration in most cases, then, emanates from the *subjects* of the film and is not an interpretation pasted onto the film from above. Of course, the interview material is generated from questions guided by the filmmaker and does not merely stem from the subjects; the filmmaker must select what material to include and exclude, decide where to place things within the film and whether to emphasise certain moments (for example, by accompanying interview passages with prominent nondiegetic music). The aesthetic results give an impression of the importance of the subject and play down the presence of the filmmaker. Directors themselves rarely appear in these films, a strategy that again emphasises the importance of the subjects involved in the events being depicted and how they are crucially involved in the film's overall narrative. While the makers of these films originate the project and shape the material in certain ways, their role is one very much steered by the available material (both archive and newly-produced interviews). In this way, their role is like that of a DJ, in the sense of creatively piecing together fragments into a coherent unity.

The emphasis on the subjective within narration can also be linked to a broader indie ethos, in particular the sense in which participants in such cultures have often distanced themselves from mainstream culture. If voice-over narration and an objective depiction of historical events are more typical of the mainstream documentary, then the strategy of avoiding such techniques can be read as an attempt to offer more marginal histories in different ways, mainly through emphasising the lived experiences of the people involved. This can be seen as a particularly important strategy in those films that document female artists, such as *Hit So Hard* and *The Punk Singer*, as they are portraying doubly-marginal cultures (independent music cultures have still tended to be dominated by men). Not only has the 'voice of God' style of narration been linked to objectivity, it has also been linked to male authority. In refusing this technique, *Hit so Hard* and *The Punk Singer* also signal their negation of official, male histories in their exploration of more marginalised events and perspectives. This gendered perspective is especially crucial to *The Punk Singer* because of its focus on Hanna's role within the Riot Grrrl movement and how it radically opposed male dominance and misogyny within the independent music sector.[29]

As mentioned, *Dig!* does employ voice-over, but it does so in an unusual fashion, a strategy that fits in with its broader – at times rather clichéd – exploration of creativity and constraints. The film firmly privileges the view that increased commerce is equal to creative compromise, celebrating the possibilities afforded by working independently. The Dandy Warhols are represented as the more ambitious band in the documentary, willing to discipline their behaviour in order to be able to make a living out of music; while The Brian Jonestown Massacre are depicted as ill disciplined, uncompromising and unpredictable. The film focuses on Anton Newcombe as sole artistic genius of the band, a man troubled and sometimes unpleasant but whose artistic integrity is never in any doubt. While occasional critique of his uncompromising stance is voiced, this is rare; it is the Dandy Warhols' decision to sign to a major label which is revealed as most damning, revealed through lengthy sequences of them tussling with their record company. Taylor-Taylor's narration fits the previously mentioned avoidance of objectivity as he is a major protagonist within the film, but he is not *the* major protagonist. Once again, this subjective dimension to the narration can be seen as a technique that signifies a modest difference from convention, a strategy which relates to broader themes of creativity integral to the film.

Nondiegetic music, on the other hand, tends to be employed more conventionally within indie-rock documentaries. John Corner has noted how the late 1940s/early 1950s saw a shift in documentary spectatorship as it 'in effect "migrated" from the cinema to television', a shift which affected its modes.[30] Sonically, it led to a less 'declamatory' and more 'intimate' mode of narrative voice, 'with a reduced commitment to affective impact'; this led to changes in how music was used within documentaries.[31] Corner states that in certain types of documentary – particularly those that lean more towards the artistic as opposed to the more journalistic – music came to play an increasingly affective role, in terms of creating a particular tone, for example. The majority of indie-rock documentaries continue such sonic conventions, but in other ways they can be more firmly linked to contemporary modes of spectatorship. Today, documentary films are shown on cinema screens and television screens, as well as on a variety of different mobile screens; they can be viewed in many different locations, both public and private; they can exist on film prints but they are more likely to be stored in digital form, accessible via DVD, Blu-Ray, downloading or streaming. Films are now viewed upon differently-sized screens and often exist in multiple versions. For example, the fan-sourced Nine Inch Nails documentary *After All is Said and Done* was available to order on DVD and Blu-Ray, placed on YouTube in low and high resolution versions to stream and was available to freely download in four different versions from the A Little Tiny Dot website (with recommendations as to which device such versions are most suited to). The hybrid nature of many of these documentaries – mixing newly recorded and archive material, shot by amateurs and professionals and including qualitatively variable footage captured on a range of devices – is therefore suitably apt to contemporary spectatorship, where viewing is increasingly fragmented across a number of different platforms. As a majority of footage featured within indie music documentaries tends to be low fidelity, it is not only suitable for viewing on most devices but also reflects an ideological/aesthetic commitment to a lo-fi aesthetic across a number of independent music cultures. In this sense, the current climate is particularly suitable for both the production and reception of indie music documentaries and it is a mode of filmmaking that is likely to increase over the coming years.

Notes

1 Simon Reynolds, 'Tombstone Blues: The Music Documentary Boom', in *Sight and Sound*, 7: 5 (May 2007), 32.
2 Thomas Austin and Wilma de Jong, 'Introduction: Rethinking Documentary', in *Rethinking Documentary: New Perspectives, New Practices*, ed. Austin and de Jong (Maidenhead: Open University Press, 2008), 3.
3 Ibid., 4.
4 There have also been documentaries on British indie musicians and labels, including *Shadowplayers: Factory Records 1978–81* (James Nice, 2006), *Joy Division* (Grant Gee, 2007), *Upside Down: The Creation Records Story* (Danny O'Connor, 2010), *The Stone Roses: Made of Stone* (Shane Meadows, 2013), not to mention a plethora of television documentaries, which often appear on BBC4. I am largely focusing on American documentaries in this chapter due to limitations of space. The only exception to this is *All Tomorrow's Parties*: though this was a British documentary about a British-based event, I have included it here as it was principally directed by an American and features a number of American independent music acts.
5 For definitions and historical foundations of indie music, see for example: David Hesmondhalgh, 'Indie: The Institutional Politics and Aesthetics of a Popular Music Genre', in *Cultural Studies*, 13:1 (1999), 34–61; Michael Azerrad, *Our Band Could Be Your Life: Scenes from the American Indie Underground* (New York: Black Bay Books, 2001); Holly Kruse, *Site and Sound: Understanding Independent Music Scenes* (New York: Peter Lang, 2003); Amy Spencer, *DIY: The Rise of Lo-Fi Culture* (London: Marion Byers, 2005); Wendy Fonarow, *Empire of Dirt: The Aesthetics and Rituals of*

British Indie Music (Middletown: Wesleyan University Press, 2006); and Kaya Oakes, *Slanted and Enchanted: The Evolution of Indie Culture* (New York: Henry Holt and Company, 2009).

6 Fonarow, *Empire of Dirt*, 51.

7 It is also the case that some independent labels will be partly owned by majors yet still retain a degree of independence from them and therefore still be considered independent.

8 Ryan Hibbett, 'What is Indie Rock?', in *Popular Music and Society*, 28:1 (2005), 58.

9 Reynolds, 'Tombstone Blues', 32.

10 Reynolds, *Retromania: Pop Culture's Addiction to Its Own Past* (London: Faber and Faber, 2011).

11 Stella Bruzzi, *New Documentary, Second Edition* (London & New York: Routledge, 2006), 26.

12 To be fair to Bruzzi, she was writing this at a time when the flurry of interest in amateur archives – particularly generated by YouTube and the increasing prevalence and affordability of audiovisual recording technologies – had not quite kicked into gear. Nevertheless, footage existing outside of official archives has a long history, particularly accruing around various subcultures and fan communities. As Henry Jenkins has written: 'If YouTube seems to have sprung up overnight, it is because so many groups were ready for something like YouTube; they already had communities of practice that supported the production of DIY media, already evolved video genres and built social networks through which such videos could flow.' Jenkins, 'What Happened Before YouTube?', in *YouTube: Online Video and Participatory Culture*, ed. Jean Burgess and Joshua Green (London: Polity, 2009), 110.

13 Jaimie Baron, 'The Archive Effect: Archival Footage as an Experience of Reception', in *Projections*, 6:2 (2012), 102.

14 Ibid., 103.

15 I am including *Awesome: I Fucking Shot That!* as an example of music documentary more generally here, as opposed to claiming that it is an 'indie-rock' documentary.

16 The first festival was set in Pontins holiday camp in Camber Sands and was curated by Mogwai. Subsequent festivals have occurred annually at either Camber Sands or the Butlin's holiday camp in Minehead. There have been occasional festivals curated by non-musical artists: for example, Matt Groening curated the 2010 ATP, while fans who booked a chalet or purchased tickets co-curated with ATP organisers in 2007 and 2009. There have also been ATP events held outside the UK – including Australia, Iceland, Japan and the USA – and associated UK events such as 'Nightmare Before Christmas' and 'I'll be Your Mirror'.

17 A significant contributor was Paris-based filmmaker Vincent Moon, who sent footage he shot of the first ATP to Warp and was invited to shoot future ATP events. He has since gone on to direct documentaries, music videos and music performances. A Kickstarter campaign to finish work on four films of ATP events he had shot was successful in October 2011. They have now been completed and are available to watch online for free.

18 It is sometimes credited to – as it is on the cover of Warp's 2011 DVD – 'All Tomorrow's People and Jonathan Caouette', though IMDB lists Caouette as the director.

19 Barry Hogan, Liner Notes, *All Tomorrow's Parties* DVD (Warp Films, 2011).

20 This does not constitute a straightforward dismissal of the 'old' populace, though. In fact there is a respect for the old and the past here, as evidenced by performances from older performers such as Iggy Pop and Patti Smith. The archive footage of the younger Smith, in which she boldly proclaims that rock 'n' roll is 'in the hands of the kids' does, however, sum up the focus here on youth.

21 Michel Chion, *The Voice in Cinema* (New York: Columbia University Press, 1999), 5.

22 Ibid., 6.
23 Robert Strachan and Marion Leonard, 'Rockumentary. Reel to Real: Cinema Verité, Rock Authenticity and the Rock Documentary', in *Sound and Music in Film and Visual Media: An Overview*, ed. Graeme Harper, Ruth Doughty and Jochen Eisenstraut (New York and London: Continuum, 2009), 284.
24 Strachan and Leonard use the term *'cinéma vérité'* but I prefer to use 'direct cinema'. While I accept that these terms are sometimes used synonymously, I personally identify them as separate (though interlinked), with *vérité* associated more with the approaches and thinking of French filmmakers such as Jean Rouch and Pierre Perrault and direct cinema coming out of a North American tradition and associated with filmmakers such as Richard Leacock, Dan Pennebaker and the Maysles Brothers.
25 Oakes, *Slanted and Enchanted*, xviii; Spencer, *DIY*, 331.
26 *The Fearless Freaks* stands as an exception here as a substantial amount of the archive footage was actually shot by the director Bradley Beesley.
27 Bruzzi, *New Documentary*, 48.
28 There is an exception at the beginning of *The Punk Singer*, as previously mentioned. This is, however, extremely rare.
29 *Hit So Hard* also stresses the difficulty of gender and sexual orientation within the music industry but in a less explicitly political manner.
30 John Corner, 'Sounds Real: Music and Documentary', in *Popular Music*, 21:3 (2003), 361.
31 Ibid., 361. Corner outlines different conventions across a number of documentary modes.

Chapter 10

More Than Background

Ambience and Sound-Design in Contemporary Art Documentary Film

Robert Strachan and Marion Leonard

It is perhaps unsurprising that discussion of documentary films has often concentrated on the visual content, editing and directorial decision making. Yet, as this book attests, it is vital to understand the way in which sound and music structure the meaning and impact of documentary film. In this chapter, we turn particular attention to the composition and importance of film sound-scape: that is, the way in which a given 'sonic environment' is represented.[1] Traditionally, the use of environmental sound has been seen as a sonic back-ground. For Michel Chion, ambient (or territory) sound 'envelopes a scene, inhabits the space without raising the question of the location of its specific source(s) in the image'.[2] In other words, the normative use of ambient sound in film naturalises (and is thereby in service of) the image by providing a fully-rounded audiovisual sense of place. It is present but unremarkable, a kind of unnoticed perceptual anchor. Using the examples of two landscape documen-taries, this chapter argues that greater attention needs to be played to the vital role that the soundscape can have in contributing to mood, narrative and the emotional impact of a film. The analysis will concentrate on the Irish film *Silence* (2010) and, to a lesser extent, the British film *sleep furiously* (2008). The chapter argues that these films are indicative and resultant of a wider historical blurring of sonic and stylistic boundaries between art film and documentary. In order to do this, we concentrate on normally understudied elements of cin-ema's audio world: the sound of acoustic environments, of transient moments of weather and wildlife and of the space between music and dialogue. In essence, the argument works towards an approach that takes the film soundtrack as a soundscape composition of the type that emerged within the acoustic ecology movement in the 1970s. The result is a reading that takes *all* the elements of a given sonic environment as redolent with meaning and cultural significance.

In placing a concentration upon soundscape, we wish to reassess the under-stood hierarchical relationship between sound and vision, where image, dia-logue and music are prioritised over locational sound. We argue that within *Silence* and *sleep furiously*, soundscape has a crucial role to play and cannot be understood simply as a complementary bed always in service of other elements of the audiovisual composite. Moreover, we suggest that these selected films form part of an enmeshed continuum between art cinema and documentary that stretches back to the 1930s where environmental sound is often used in a strategic and overtly self-conscious fashion. In acoustic ecology terms, the soundscape of films within this tradition can take what Barry Truax calls a 'variable spatial perspective' in that they employ multiple aural perspectives from representational and linear to more abstracted and symbolic.[3] As we shall discuss, within these films, ambient sound at times works as an indicator of realism, providing an (albeit constructed) sense of actuality; at others, it is used to evoke a sense of the uncanny or to create a distancing effect for the viewer.

Further, the concentration on environmental sound within this chapter seeks to contribute to an approach which takes all elements of a film soundtrack as an orchestrated whole. In doing so we are responding to Paul Théberge's call for 'an integrated approach to the study of the soundtrack that allows us to examine the various sound elements in their distribution and relation to one another and to narration' which he has identified as 'still lacking'.[4] He has argued that, while there is now a considerable body of scholarship on music in film and a smaller number of studies on sound and dialogue:

> we do not have a framework that allows us to hear the "multiplane system" as the sound designer conceives of it, as the mix engineer realizes it, and as the audience hears it: as a delicately balanced, elaborately interwoven set of sonic elements, each of which contributes to the overall narrative but does so in a cumulative and integrated fashion.[5]

Silence, directed by the Irish documentary filmmaker Pat Collins, and *sleep furiously*, by British director Gideon Koppel, are examples of art documentary practice that explore landscape and identity. Koppel's *sleep furiously* offers a portrait of the Welsh farming community of Trefeurig, while *Silence* traces a journey across the remote and protected landscapes of Ireland. The formal elements of both films situate them within a lineage of art cinema and documentary film, yet *Silence* is also very much within an Irish cinema tradition. As Martin McLoone has commented in a discussion of Ireland on screen, 'the cinematic tradition that has had the most enduring legacy has been that of rural Ireland and its wildly romantic landscapes'.[6] Both films, in common with Collins' other works, *Oileán Thoraí* (2002) and *Tim Robinson: Connemara* (2011), use similar formal techniques and aesthetic strategies in their thematic explorations. *Silence* pushes at the boundaries of the documentary form (in that its central character is fictional), and yet its techniques and feel are consistent with the documentary approach. The films conform to a poetic mode of documentary, as outlined by Bill Nichols, in that they eschew traditional narrative structure in favour of mood and a contemplative reflection upon their respective subjects.[7] The 'tonal and rhythmic qualities' of each are extremely important and soundscape is central in their experiential purchase and evocation of place.[8] These films, as Thomas Austin writes of *sleep furiously*, are 'emphatically physical' works that ask their viewers 'to feel, or at least to imagine feeling, the somatic impact of wind, rain, sun, and different textures and sounds'.[9]

Within these films (and *Silence* in particular), sound is used as a self-conscious thematic device in an unusually heightened manner. In particular, the foregrounding of ambient sound is used as both an experiential trigger and an invocation to reflect upon issues such as memory, loss and identity. We shall argue that key strategies in sound design and post-production are employed to invite a 'reflective audioviewing' in the film's audience. Adapting Katharine Norman's concept of reflective listening from acoustic ecology, Randolph Jordan uses the term reflective audioviewing to describe the way in which a self-conscious manipulation of sound in cinema prompts the listener towards an active engagement with the represented soundscape.[10] In other words, soundscape is clearly used in order to invite reflection upon the spatial, aesthetic and thematic concerns of a given work in parity with the visual.

The two films under discussion here are particularly apt for the application of such an approach given their similar treatment of sound. *Silence* follows the journey of a fictive sound recordist (played by the writer Eoghan Mac Giolla Bhríde who also co-wrote the film), who returns from his adopted home of Berlin to his native rural Ireland in order to record the sound of landscapes devoid of human-made noise. The film follows Mac Giolla Bhríde as he travels up the west coast of Ireland from County Cork to his native Tory Island in Donegal, encountering a number of differing landscapes and individuals on his way. The film *sleep furiously* is a similarly rural document that captures the life of the small mid-Wales farming village where the director grew up. The film explores aspects of change within the community through a number of devices, including following the rounds of the local mobile library and the planned closure of the local primary school. However, much of the film seeks to echo the rhythms of rural life with tableaux of work, leisure and landscape along with fragmented but gentle portraits of individuals and groups within the community.

The core of Collins' film is ostensibly the pursuit of silence. The film follows the protagonist's attempt to get away from sound produced by humans (including voices, cars, planes and the sounds of industry). To establish his success in this endeavour, the viewer has to attentively listen out for these sonic encroachments on the 'natural' soundscape. In so doing, the listener/viewer is encouraged to understand such man-made sounds as noise. Thus a clear demarcation is made between natural sound and invasive noise. His attempts are often stymied by a sonic reminder that the sounds of nature have been overridden or are constantly interrupted. In his first attempt to record in a wooded glade by the side of Loch Hyne in County Cork, Mac Giolla Bhríde encounters the distant chugging mechanical sound of a rock breaker ('Next week it's finished and then you won't hear anything here', comments a local farmer). Several subsequent attempts to capture only natural sounds are interrupted by humans or human-made noise. As Frances Morgan comments, 'It is less a film about the absence of sound than one about how sound cannot ever really be absent'.[11] The second half of the film is more preoccupied with the themes of memory, place, leaving and loss; subtleties which emerge from the soundscape as Mac Giolla Bhríde travels north.

Silence is essentially hybrid in nature, blurring the lines between documentary and narrative fiction. Whilst the main character is credited as Mac Giolla Bhríde, the actor is primarily a writer playing a role. Many scenes within the film are based upon encounters with people they met as the filming took place: they appear on screen to be having 'real' conversations, for instance (although the extent to which they are staged is unclear). Certainly, Collins' background as a documentarian had a fundamental effect upon both the film's methodology and aesthetics, as he explains:

> The people that Eoghan meets as he travels through Ireland are mostly real characters playing themselves. People we had read about or people we had met ... It's one of the great things about making documentaries—the houses you get invited into, the people you meet out and about in odd places. These encounters give the film a documentary sensibility but it is clearly fiction in my mind.[12]

In another interview, the director stated that whilst he 'wasn't looking to create a documentary authenticity', he wanted 'it to be more like real life. I think if the entire cast were professional actors, the film would be very different. It would have a different feel'.[13] This link with documentary was also apparent in the way in which Silence was filmed. Collins comments that 'many of the scenes were filmed as if we were making a documentary. Long scenes of talking that we edited back'.[14]

This slippage between forms is perhaps a natural progression given the resolute subjectivity of the poetic documentary form. Indeed, there has been a strain in documentary cinema stretching back to the 1930s which has blurred the lines between documentary and art.[15] As Koppel himself writes in a self-reflective piece on sleep furiously:

> In considering an approach to documentary film which places an emphasis on a subjective perspective and uses a syntax which evokes an experience of the world rather than making claim to an objective description, we are inevitably walking a precipice between what might be classified "documentary" on the one side, and 'art' or the avant-garde on the other. [16]

This hybridity is reflected in the sound design of Silence and sleep furiously. The soundscapes of both are highly produced, edited and, in many instances, self-consciously stylised; sound is often used to create a distancing effect where the audience is forced to reflect upon the mediating techniques and technologies and there are moments where we are invited to identify with a character's subjectivity through a marked change in audio quality.

In *Silence*, sound design is used to establish the narrative and thematic core from the beginning. As the film opens, our attention is immediately drawn to the recorded nature of sound. Accompanying a blank screen we hear the click of a tape recorder before we simultaneously see and hear a reel-to-reel recording of Mac Giolla Bhríde's mother singing the popular song 'The Breeze and I'. The song carries over to a shot of the protagonist walking outside at dusk, with bird-call and other natural sounds clearly audible. The music fades out, giving way to the wind and bird sound as the encroaching night makes the screen almost black, thus drawing the viewer into the soundworld. The key thematic importance of the contrasts between man-made and natural sound is also established at this point. The wind, sea and bird noises cross-fade to Berlin street noise, while an image of the Irish night momentarily lingers before eventually cutting to a shot of a Berlin tram. As the tram passes, Mac Giolla Bhríde is revealed, standing with a windproof microphone suspension system under an overhead Ubahn, a cut that immediately provides a stark aural contrast. This opening sequence serves both as a thematic and stylistic synecdoche for the rest of the film, which goes on to use a series of techniques to draw the viewer's attention to sound in a highly self-conscious way. These can be broadly categorised as relating to three main elements of the film's sound design: editing, sound mixing and diegetic signposting. In order to unpack this a little more, we will examine the ways in which these three elements of sound design engender a 'reflective audioviewing' in our two films and how the utilisation of sound in *Silence* serves to develop the film's core theme of place, identity and emotional memory.

Editing and Sound Design

Both films employ a number of editing conventions that accentuate the aural through the manipulation of rhythm and pace. Most striking is the predominance of ambient sound in terms of screen time. For example, dialogue accounts for only 27 minutes of *Silence*'s 87-minute duration; the rest is taken over by soundscape and music (although it is firmly balanced towards the former). The last eight minutes are given over to environmental sound and a short sonic collage evoking memory and place in Mac Giolla Bhríde's childhood. The pace of *sleep furiously* is similarly set through several extended periods where ambient sound is the only element of the soundtrack. This weighting invites the audience to be active listeners, responsive not just to dialogue but also to the other sonic elements. The very fact that sections without dialogue or music are long (and frequent) by normative cinematic standards engenders an experience in which the environmental soundscape is inescapable. Although (mostly) naturalised, unlike in Chion's classical cinema hierarchy, it cannot be ignored.[17]

The pace of both films is also maintained by the use of two types of long shot: firstly, slow moving shots that pan over a given landscape; and secondly, static extreme long shots (many lasting over a minute). These are filmed using a fixed camera and often depict a landscape which is either seemingly actionless or where action and subjects (people or animals) drift into (and out of) shot. The film *sleep furiously* includes a number of prolonged static extreme long shots. Perhaps the most striking is a three-minute sequence in which the only audible sounds are those of a persistent rain shower with the distant bleating of sheep and the barely audible hum of traffic. Two minutes of the sequence is taken up by a single landscape shot of sheep slowly moving over a hillside in two far-away lines. The landscape shot fills the screen and the sheep are so distant as to be blurred and indistinguishable, creating an almost abstracted and painterly aesthetic to the scene. The composition and feel of the shot thereby engender a meditative and most hypnotic effect for the viewer.

A section of *Silence* filmed in Mullaghmore, County Clare, is even more striking, both in its use of these shots and in its treatment of soundscape. In the five-minute scene, a number of shots show Mac Giolla Bhríde as a diminutive figure in the landscape (figure 10.1). These sequences are intercut with sections

Figure 10.1 A static extreme long shot from *Silence* (Pat Collins, 2010) filmed in Mullaghmore, County Clare.

where the landscape fills the frame to such an extent that it becomes difficult for the viewer to ascertain a sense of scale. Throughout this scene, there is no dialogue. A light summer breeze dominates the soundscape, which is only punctuated at the start of the sequence by the distant call of a bird. Later in the scene, Mac Giolla Bhríde reads out his location coordinates and the buzzing of a bee can briefly be heard. Towards the end of the section, we see Mac Giolla Bhríde listening intently through headphones to the recordings he is making. At this point, the soundscape is being shared as if the viewer is listening to the recording process. For around two seconds we hear a snippet of what appears to be a female voice singing a traditional air, so far down in the mix as to be almost imperceptible. Within the context of an extended soundscape of wind, the effect is both ambiguous and uncanny. We are unclear whether this is a voice or a recording carried on the wind, or whether it represents a memory belonging to the protagonist. In the very last cut of the section, we return to a panning landscape shot with the sound of what appears to be wind. In the extreme distance, a white dot briefly appears, a van or lorry on a road, making the listener question the source of the sounds she is hearing; we are unsure whether it is wind or distant traffic. This five-minute section presents an audio-visual combination that demands close attention to the extreme subtleties of the soundscape. The scale of the wide shots, in combination with the relatively dynamically-flat soundtrack, draws the listener in over a period of minutes until these exceptionally subtle elements become highly significant.

Although the use of the extreme long shot has a common and established use in cinema, that is as an establishing shot to signify location and locate subsequent action, its use within Silence and sleep furiously is somewhat different. Because of their extreme length, these shots, rather than being a precursor to the real 'action', are woven into the very fabric of each film's thematic core and are at least as important as dialogue and other elements of filmic representation. In auditory terms, there is a kind of training of the ear, in which the listener is invited to concentrate very closely on ambient sound within an individual shot. This is perhaps a conscious inversion of what Chion calls vococentrism: that is, the hierarchical predominance of the human voice over other sonic components within film.[18] For Chion, language is central to the filmic soundscape, even when it may not immediately seem to be. He points to classic Hollywood cinema as being a verbocentric form, whereby dialogue is reinforced and punctuated by small incidental actions ('parallel visual play' such as drinking, smoking, driving, dressing etc.) which draw the viewer back into the dialogue.[19] The use of long landscape shots, along with the minimal narrative within the majority of Silence, creates the obverse of this technique. Here, the human voice constitutes an intrusion into the predominance of ambient sound. Dialogue thus has the feeling of temporarily punctuating an extended meditation upon the soundscape.

These sections also raise issues about the blurred boundaries between documentary and art cinema. Whilst both films utilise the methodologies and approach of documentary to a certain extent, they also have the formal and technical feel of art cinema. In one sense, we can see the use of these techniques as part of an established and sanctioned formal nuance of the international art film tradition. For example, the drawn out, static shot has, more generally, become such a marker of art house cinema as to be regarded as something of a cliché. Directors from Jean Luc Goddard and Michelangelo Antonioni, through Robert Altman to Paul Thomas Anderson and Steve McQueen have been noted for their use of the technique, for instance. But in another sense, the slow, long shot is indicative of a tradition of aesthetic composition in documentary filmmaking that stretches right back to its beginnings. One only needs to go back to a foundational film such as John Grierson's silent documentary Drifters (1929) to encounter shots that are painterly in their composition, abstracted and beautiful; in this film, seascapes flow for extended periods, the top of a fishing net and buoys provide a minimal stroke across the screen and close-ups of machinery create hypnotic moving shapes.

Such a crossover is also apparent in other elements of the editing and mix in *Silence* and *sleep furiously*. For example, both films use 'sonic jump cuts', that is, abrupt audio cutting between scenes.[20] This gives the effect of a sudden change in tone and frequency range, which is immediately perceivable by the listener. The lack of music to salve between location sounds feels intended to give the viewer a visceral jolt. The balance between audio elements of the films' sound world is also unconventional at times. In *Silence*, sections of the dialogue are placed either lower in the mix than would be the case in most films or are entirely inaudible. In the scene in which Mac Giolla Bhríde is explaining his departure to his partner, for example, the dialogue is deliberately drowned out by a passing train.

These techniques clearly play with audience expectations as they subvert the normative filmic conventions relating to soundtrack, dialogue, Foley and ambient sound. Again, such a subversion is simultaneously part of a well-established documentary aesthetic *and* a feature of concurrent art cinema. The fly-on-the-wall approach of 'defer to reality' documentary movements that emerged in the 1950s and1960s (direct cinema in the U.S., free cinema in the UK and *cinéma vérité* in France) served to set up certain stylistic parameters which have had a fundamental influence on documentary over the past half century. The core approaches of these movements were facilitated by the rise in new technologies. Hand-held cameras, portable magnetic tape recorders and directional microphones afforded a flexibility that allowed filmmakers into locations and situations that would otherwise have been impossible. They also served to cement something of a low fidelity aesthetic. As Jeffrey Ruoff notes (and as we saw in the Introduction), the relatively low fidelity of the soundtrack within documentaries which only use sounds recorded on location has become something of a stylistic marker. Unlike in Hollywood cinema, the sound edits between shots within these films is not always well balanced or smooth. Similarly, a low signal-to-noise ratio means that dialogue recorded on location has to compete with ambient background sound to an extent where the viewer has to strain to distinguish what is being said.[21]

Use of hand-held microphones and tape units to record location sound thus became something of an aesthetic and ideological engagement. Influenced both by the stylistic innovations of *vérité* and the availability of these new technologies, New Wave cinema began to eschew Hollywood's use of highly directional microphones and careful amplification of foregrounded sound in favour of a 'direct transcription of all ambient sounds' (Rick Altman) by way of a single omnidirectional microphone.[22] These sonic practices were clearly in keeping with a set of formal techniques within New Wave, which sought to echo a conceptual turn towards realism, improvisation, spontaneity and narrative ambiguity within the movement. These techniques were a deliberate inversion and deconstruction of normative Hollywood techniques. As Chion notes:

> The sonic unity achieved by classical cinema … is ordered hierarchically; ambient sounds and sound effects occupy the lower rungs, functioning not continuously but at given points, as transitions or brief events; often they are incorporated into the music, which locks them into their *proper* place in the score.[23]

Whilst this might be true of classical cinema, the history of art cinema is full of purposeful inversions of this naturalised unification. For example, the muffling or loss of an actor's voice through competing ambient sound is a technique used by Jean-Luc Godard in *Breathless* (1960), when the dialogue is drowned out by the urban noise of the city penetrating through an open window.[24] The soundscape is used to different effect in Michelangelo Antonioni's *Blow Up* (1966), where the rustling of wind in trees is used as a sonic motif. Given the canonic centrality of New Wave within European art cinema, the use of these cinematic techniques is understandable as symptomatic of a particular cinematic style and a self-consciously artistic aesthetic. Thus, through the use of these particular sound practices, alongside the approaches to audiovisual editing outlined above, landscape art documentaries simultaneously evoke and draw upon both the *vérité* tradition of documentary filmmaking and a dominant strain within European art cinema of the second half of the twentieth century.

European art cinema, through directors such as Alain Resnais, Antonioni and Pier Paulo, can also be credited with exploring alienation effects within sound-image relations.[25] Distancing effects are also a core characteristic of the two films under discussion here. Indeed, Koppel describes the way in which the production team of *sleep furiously* used very intricate microphone and postproduction techniques to create distancing effects within the soundtrack.[26] For example, the sound designer Joakim Sundström used an amalgam of edits on a radio mic overlaid with layers of Foley in order to create a juxtaposition between a static extreme long shot and the sound of a character moving through the landscape in close audition. Similarly, *Silence* creates distancing effects through the use of disembodied location sound over incongruous cuts. For instance, in a driving montage (a cliché of the road movie where normally music would feature prominently), subtle wind noise is seamlessly used over a series of cuts, rather than, as in the traditional use of ambient sound, synching audio cuts to match each visual change. Instead, a constant sonic bed sutures the entire sequence. As such, there is a suggested disharmony between sound and image and listeners are encouraged to listen aesthetically rather than experience the section as a naturalised whole. Collins consciously draws the viewer towards this inversion by soundtracking two earlier driving sequences with Rory Gallagher's 'I Fall Apart' (1971) and sections of Mahler's 9th Symphony (1908-09). By comparison, the third sequence becomes unsettling. Experienced directly in relation to these scenes, the third road sequence provokes questions in the listener's mind by relating to the source of the audio and differences in the emotional cues given by music and non-music respectively.

Silence also creates distancing effects through constant diegetic signposting; that is, highly self-conscious elements within the action of a film that draw attention to source, materiality and tone of the soundscape. Examples of diegetic signposting occur from the first section of the film, when the urban sounds of Berlin are shut out of Mac Giolla Bhríde's apartment, a silencing motif repeated in the opening and closing of a West Cork hotel room window to expose and shut out human voices. The film also utilises the abrupt turning off of playback technologies, which are the sources of diegetic music or other recorded sound in the film (indeed, most of the film's music is presented diegetically). The click of recording technologies is a motif that carries though from *Silence's* opening seconds. Voices, field recordings and music are silenced by the click of reel-to-tape machines, a portable field recorder, a car stereo and computer audio editing software. This repeated strategy has a dual effect. It draws the audience's attention to the mediated nature of sound in everyday life, but also provides a series of what Walter Murch calls 'locational silences'; that is, the 'visceral effect of a sudden transition from loudness to silence'.[27]

Diegetic signposting is also used to create an aural point of view (or APOV), where we 'hear from the character's point in space' (Edward R. Branigan); in this case, the protagonist's experience of mediating sound technology.[28] In a short scene in Connemara, Mac Giolla Bhríde is shown throwing an aquaphone (a specialist underwater microphone) into the sea from the water's edge before placing headphones on his ears. The sound of a stone being thrown into water is then clearly heard from the recording being made from the submerged aquaphone (a deep sonorous thud that lacks clarity at the top end of the frequency range). The effect simultaneously draws the listener into the protagonist's head (he is wearing headphones) and creates a distancing effect whereby the limitations and sonic colouring of the mediating technology are highlighted.

Memory and Identity

Sound-design is central in both of the films' formal realisation and aesthetic strategies. However, in *Silence*, the use of sound is fundamental to the film's overall diegesis. What starts as a quest for silence ends up as an extended meditation upon the ways in which the sonic is implicated in identity and the power of sound to evoke emotion, to signify stasis, to trigger memory and to create a sense of loss or nostalgia. More specifically, the sonic is used to explore personal memory and the individual's connections to the landscape, broader national identity and the past.

The purpose of Mac Giolla Bhríde's quest for a 'pure' soundscape, unpolluted by extraneous noise, is never quite clear. At the beginning of the film, he remarks to his partner that he is going to Ireland because it is work, making it clear that he does not intend to go back to his home 'that far north'. The people that he encounters on this journey across Ireland also question his intent, and yet his replies remain somewhat opaque: 'I'm not really collecting stories. It's more quiet than that'. His journey takes him through four of Ireland's six National Parks (Burren, Ballycroy, Connemara and Glenveagh in Donegal), before he finally travels to his family home on Tory Island. The selected locations are part of a protected national heritage and the sound recordist's journey seems also to be a pursuit of an idealised sonic trace of this landscape. His interwoven personal connection to the land adds another layer to the narrative, bringing an emotional sense of belonging and also an evolving – and it seems shifting – motivation to record the soundscape. His pursuit of an undisturbed set of sounds seems to be allied with a pursuit of the past, as if it might be possible to find a bygone dimension (still present) by realising a soundscape unencroached by the sounds of modernity.

As Nuala C. Johnson has observed, Irish tourist literature and advertising has often tempted visitors with an image of Ireland that offers uninhabited 'empty space' and also as 'occupying "empty time" – where today is like yesterday and yesterday is like tomorrow'.[29] There is a sense in which *Silence* confirms this representation with repeated landscape images of 'unspoilt' landscape. Yet, the focus here is not on inviting the visitor or viewer into the country's 'empty space'; rather, we move with Mac Giolla Bhríde across the landscape as he seeks the auditory world of this 'empty time'. The final sequence of the film shows the sound recordist return to his derelict family home on the almost deserted Tory Island. While we are reminded of his personal connection to the land, the location also speaks to an enduring national heritage. Here, Mac Giolla Bhríde converses in Gaelic with the people he encounters, a change that reinforces the separation of the island and the resultant continuity of tradition where the Irish language still survives. As Patrick J. Duffy suggests: 'Because of their relative inaccessibility, Ireland's islands (both coastal and lacustrine) are sometimes the last outposts of landscape and cultural heritage'.[30] The definitiveness of Tory Island seems to present the perfect opportunity to capture the quietness of nature. Yet Mac Giolla Bhríde is instead pictured within his family house without his recording equipment, listening to the phantom sounds of his past (figure 10.2).

Figure 10.2. Eoghan Mac Giolla Bhríde returns to his abandoned family home on Tory Island in *Silence*.

The viewer shares the sounds with him: barely audible songs, sung long ago, snatches of domestic conversation and the creaks of floorboards – everyday sounds now redolent with nostalgia. The sequence reinforces the importance of sound to memory, experience and identity by using post production techniques such as multitracking and filtering in order to construct a particular affective framework. The remembered sounds are placed low down in the mix and their higher frequencies are filtered out: they overlap, fractured, indiscernible yet present. The power of these voices lies in their disembodied nature and their lack of clarity. As Brandon LaBelle argues, the blurring of clarity in acousmatic voices has a particular psychological affect in which sound 'breaks from its source to become something greater, more powerful and suggestive … a sound that comes back to haunt, returning as transformed through its diffusion'.[31]

Conclusion

Despite the power of *Silence*'s final sound collage, it is the use of ambient sound in both the films analysed that is particularly instructive. In essence, the strategies outlined within this chapter elevate ambient sound in the hierarchy of sonic elements within the soundtrack, resulting in an aesthetic which draws upon similar elements that can be found in the ethnographic and compositional soundscape movement that emerged in the 1970s. Just as the work of the acoustic ecology movement was intended to draw in the listener and heighten aural attention and awareness, so also the films under discussion work to engender a concentrated listening in their audience. In each, the soundscape becomes a defining feature of the overall aesthetic. Rather than being a background which naturalises the audiovisual meld, or providing a bed for foregrounded sound, ambient sound here speaks with a powerful voice. The essentially meditative and discursive feel that is engendered by these landscape art documentaries is facilitated by the prominence of the soundscape.

Whilst the texts under discussion here are clearly marked out by their self-conscious and integrated use of soundscape, this does not mean that the approach to soundtrack and sound design outlined above is not relevant in examinations of other forms of audiovisual media. Indeed, close attention to *all* elements of a film's sound world is an approach that can reveal much about the experiential qualities of film. It is therefore important that we take an approach to analysis that views the soundtrack holistically. Undervaluing the importance of ambient sound serves to diminish an important facet of film's sensory engagement. It also neglects to recognise that there are established tropes within location and environmental sound which both contribute to the meaning making and experience of cinema. The underlying historical line within documentary and art film hinted at in this chapter is rife for re-evaluation through a sonically holistic approach. Such a tradition (and films such as *Silence* and *sleep furiously*) is instrumental in sensitising us to the importance of soundscape and encourages us to listen more attentively to the sounds that populate the space between dialogue and silence.

Notes

1 R. Murray Schafer, *Our Sonic Environment and Soundscape: The Tuning of the World* (Rochester: Destiny, 1977), 275.
2 Michel Chion, *Film, a Sound Art* (New York: Columbia University Press, 2009), 487.
3 Barry Truax, 'Genres and Techniques of Soundscape Composition as Developed at Simon Fraser University', in *Organised Sound*, 7:1 (2002), 8.
4 Paul Théberge, 'Almost Silent: The Interplay of Sound and Silence in Contemporary Cinema and Television', in *Lowering the Boom: Critical Studies in Film Sound*, ed. Jay Beck and Tony Grajeda (Urbana and Chicago: University of Illinois Press, 2008), 66.
5 Ibid.
6 Martin McLoone, 'Landscape and Irish Cinema', in *Cinema and Landscape: Film, Nation and Cultural Geography*, ed. Graeme Harper and Jonathan Rayner (Bristol: Intellect 2010), 140.
7 Bill Nichols, *Introduction to Documentary* (Indiana: Indiana University Press, Second Edition, 2010), 31.
8 Ibid.
9 Thomas Austin, 'Figures in a Landscape: Work and Beauty in *Sleep Furiously*', in *New Review of Film and Television Studies*, 9:3 (2011), 379.
10 Randolph Jordan, 'The Ecology of Listening While Looking in the Cinema: Reflective Audioviewing in Gus Van Sant's *Elephant*', in *Organised Sound*, 17:3 (2012), 248.
11 Frances Morgan, 'Soundings: Quiet, Please', in *Sight And Sound*, 22:11 (November, 2012), 70–71.
12 Pat Collins, 'Directors Statement', in *Silence Pressbook* (2010), at http://www. newwavefilms.co.uk/assets/872/Silence_Pressbook.pdf (accessed 1 February 2014).
13 Adam Scovell, 'Interview with Pat Collins (*Silence*, 2012)', at http:// celluloidwickerman.com/2013/08/09/interview-with-pat-collins-silence-2012/ (accessed 1 February 2014).
14 Ibid.
15 As discussed by Nichols, *Introduction to Documentary*; and Austin, 'Figures in a Landscape'.
16 Gideon Koppel, 'Documentary: The Evocation of a World', in *Journal of Media Practice*, 8:3 (2007), 309.
17 Chion, *Film, a Sound Art*, 487.
18 Chion, *The Voice in Cinema* (New York: Colombia University Press, 1999), 5–6.
19 Ibid.
20 Vlad Dima, 'The Aural Fold and the Sonic Jump Cut: Godard's (Baroque) Sound', in *Quarterly Review of Film and Video*, 29:3 (2011), 237–251.
21 Jeffrey Ruoff, 'Conventions of Sound in Documentary', in *Cinema Journal*, 32:3 (1993), 24–40.
22 Rick Altman, 'The Evolution of Sound Technology', in *Film Sound: Theory and Practice*, ed. John Belton and Elizabeth Weis (Columbia: Columbia University Press, 1985), 44–53.
23 Chion, *Film, a Sound Art*, 5 (italics ours).
24 For more on this, see Dima, 'The Aural Fold and the Sonic Jump Cut'.
25 Richard Neupert, *A History of the French New Wave Cinema* (Madison, Wisconsin: University of Wisconsin Press, 2007).
26 Koppel, 'Sound sleep furiously', in *The New Soundtrack*, 1.1 (2011), 1–11.
27 Walter Murch, 'Touch of Silence', in *Soundscape: The School of Sound Lectures*, 1998–2001, ed. Larry Sider, Diane Freeman and Jerry Sider (London: Wallflower Press, 2003), 95.

28 Edward R. Branigan, *Point of View in the Cinema: A Theory of Narration and Subjectivity in Classical Film* (Berlin: Mouton de Gruyter, 1984), 94.
29 Nuala C. Johnson, 'Framing the Past: Time, Space and the Politics of Heritage Tourism in Ireland', in *Political Geography*, 18 (1999), 191–192.
30 Patrick J. Duffy, *Exploring the History and Heritage of Irish Landscapes* (Dublin: Four Courts Press, 2007), 35.
31 Brandon LaBelle, *Acoustic Territories: Sound Culture and Everyday Life* (London: Continuum, 2010), 15.

Chapter 11

Sonic Ethnographies
Leviathan and New Materialisms in Documentary

Selmin Kara and Alanna Thain

> Another thing we know is that nature makes no blunders so untoward as to allow things, including human things, to swerve into supernaturalism. Were it to make such a blunder, we would do everything in our power to bury this knowledge. But we need not resort to such measures, being as natural as we are. No one can prove that our life in this world is a supernatural horror, nor cause us to suspect that it might be.
>
> Thomas Ligotti, The Conspiracy Against the Human Race.[1]

In his first work of nonfiction, philosophical reflections on the human condition inspired by a long tradition of nihilist and pessimist thinking, renowned horror writer Thomas Ligotti urges his readers to think of the natural order in supernatural terms. True horror, he states, is nested in the depictions of 'monstrosities of paradox' – things that are neither one thing nor another – like humanity suddenly confronting its own ambiguous status in nature. As a reference point, he takes up the writings of Julius Bahnsen, highlighting the German philosopher's rendering of existence as something strange and awful (and his comparison of the world of nature to a festival of meaningless massacre and carnage). For Ligotti, reality is, similarly, the expression of a cosmic force, the movement of which is monstrous in nature, 'resulting in a universe of indiscriminate butchery and mutual slaughter among its individuated parts'.[2] It is essentially this reality that supernatural horror mirrors. If horror speaks to the often-suppressed elements of monstrosity in human experience, it can be argued that the recent ethnographic film *Leviathan* (2012) comes closest to normalising that vision, or making us suspect that *our life in this world is a supernatural horror*, from within a documentary framework. In the old 'documents' of maritime cartography, unknown waters were labeled 'here are monsters'. But rather than waters as yet unpopulated by the markers of human mastery and control, *Leviathan*'s waters are precisely a challenge to mapping modes of thought. As such, the film's sound design also speaks to the challenge of documenting sonic ecologies that retain a monstrous edge; disquieting in their ambiguity and acoustic alterity, they chart the zones where we find ourselves at the limits of habituated knowledge, often through bodily intensity itself.

Leviathan, directed by Lucien Castaing-Taylor and Véréna Paravel (both artist-researchers at Harvard University's Sensory Ethnography Lab), received much critical attention following its release in 2012 due to its foregrounding of new audiovisual technologies and sound, reflecting a post-cinematic, new materialist aesthetics. At once a documentary, an avant-garde experiment and an ethnographic study, *Leviathan* also fits into the framework of the monster film, making references through its title and eerie oceanic footage to the eponymous mythical sea monster of the Old Testament as well as other nautical creatures of terrifying grandeur, such as Herman Melville's *Moby-Dick* (1851). The film shares its setting with Melville's novel, taking place aboard a groundfish trawler off the coast of New Bedford, the Massachusetts port that was once the whaling capital of the world (and which remains the largest fishing port in the U.S.). Featuring hauntingly visceral imagery and a carefully orchestrated mix of muffled yet evocative sounds captured by GoPro cameras (hardy, small and lightweight cameras first designed for use by extreme sports enthusiasts) as well as small stereo mics mounted on DSLRs, the film is situated within the ecology of the long catastrophe of commercial fishing. However, the political impulse of Castaing-Taylor and Paravel is neither to represent this catastrophe nor to propose a solution to the current problem of overfishing. Instead of following traditional documentaries' humanist fixation on labour and the problems arising from it, *Leviathan* aims to show the bodily work involved in this practice via its audiovisual intensity, as an embodied experience and inextricable part of humanity's being-in-the-world: a turbulent affair effectively conveyed by the documentary's unsettling images and sounds.[3] Of particular note, and part of what brings out a new materialist approach in the film, is that embodied experience does not solely signal a human body, or in fact, discrete and identifiable bodies. Instead, the film's ecological approach to audiovisuality begins from the middle; from within the various forces that make up the relations the film seeks to explore.

The combination of new technologies that highlight bodily praxis and affect, the commitment of the filmmakers to giving sound a constitutive role in exploring the assemblage of human, animal and machinic existence and the contemporary ecological sensibilities that linger in the backdrop of the film's ominous tone all point towards a shift from the historical framework of *visual* anthropology toward a new, multi-sensorial ethnographic vision in nonfiction filmmaking. Sensory ethnography, as this emergent approach has come to be known as in the field, sees the machinic, natural, animal and human actors as equally powerful agents in a sensual and material ecology.[4] As the website of Harvard's SEL (Sensory Ethnography Lab) indicates, sensory ethnographic filmmaking harnesses 'perspectives drawn from the arts, the social and natural sciences and the humanities', encouraging 'attention to the many dimensions of the world, both animate and inanimate'.[5] In this context, sound gains a renewed resonance, paving the way for a formulation of 'sound ethnography' (the title of the Harvard course taught by *Leviathan*'s sound designer Ernst Karel) as an increasingly central category in anthropological filmmaking, building on already established sound-based fields: sound studies, ethnomusicology, location recording in ethnographic cinema, sound art, sound mapping, soundscape and electroacoustic composition and experimental media. Critically, in this film, this is not a prioritisation of another sensory modality as a critique of the visual, but an ecological, though non-holistic method. In what follows, we want to draw attention to the common foregrounding of sound and acoustic modes of perception in recent sensory-ethnography films like *Leviathan*, in order to highlight sound's role in portraying ethnography as a relational field and drawing out the alternative modes of knowing emerging from recent new materialist experimentations in documentary.

Of Monsters and Men

In his 2013 study of the 'Cambridge Turn' in American documentaries, Scott MacDonald locates the works that have come out of Harvard's SEL within the observational tradition that has flourished in Boston-area documentary filmmaking and analyses the Castaing-Taylor and Paravel film as a key text. *Leviathan*'s power, he argues, lies in its relentless assault on the viewers' senses:

> While the film's title seems to be a reference to the Biblical leviathan (the film's opening quotations from the book of Job confirm the biblical reference), the leviathan in *Leviathan* is the film itself. Made to be shown on the big screen with surround sound, *Leviathan* swallows us—regurgitating us out of the theater at the end of 90 minutes, exhausted and happy to have lived through what is as close to a sensory trauma as any documentary in recent memory.[6]

This description of the film as a bestial immersion by voracious sensory stimuli is fitting, as the documentary is composed of mostly unsettling and indistinct audiovisual footage pertaining to oceanic slaughter and haul, cloaked in the overwhelming darkness of extensive nighttime sequences. Much like in Abbas Kiarostami's experimental multi-screen documentary *Five* (2003) and Aleksandr Sokurov's 1998 *Confession*, the stormy night setting stretched onto an indefinite temporality in *Leviathan* presents a perfect opportunity for the filmmakers to withdraw the field of vision (and its logocentricism) from prominence and allow other senses, like audition, to step in to complicate and foreground perception.[7] Although MacDonald does not directly address the specificity of sound or nighttime sequences in the passage above, he implies that the film gains its monstrous quality by rearranging and exhausting the senses, an aesthetic sensibility he later associates with Jackson Pollock's action painting, Stan Brakhage's gestural 16mm filming of the late 1950s and the surreal vision of Georges Franju in *The Blood of the Beasts* (1949). Trevor Johnston similarly draws attention to the abstract painting and 'ocean-going

Le sang des bêtes' connection, while making a more direct comparison between *Leviathan*'s audiovisual strategies and the aesthetics of horror film:

> What fresh hell is this, anyway? Amid enveloping, galactic darkness, pin-points of light illuminate an ocean-going slaughterhouse. There are men in hoods and gore-stained overalls, the glint and swish of blades, piscine victims flapping and gasping for air. An outlet spews blood and backwash into the sea, while a metallic cacophony of grinding winches and insistent, infernal engine noise radiates out into the night. Welcome to the New Bedford chain-net massacre.[8]

The reference to the film's predominantly dark image track and overpowering cacophonic sounds is not coincidental; visceral 'body genres' like horror heavily depend on the power of sound to emphasise the embodied nature of perception, making the SEL documentary's particular aesthetics resonate more heavily with the affective register of monster, slasher, or supernatural horror film.[9] Yet Johnston establishes a further, ontological, connection between horror and documentary, channeling Ligotti: '[in *Leviathan*] the comparisons between horror and docu-mentary aren't altogether fatuous either, since both strands of cinematic endeavor aim to access the deepest, darkest truths about man and his environment. Both are about looking at the things we may not necessarily want to confront'.[10]

What *Leviathan* urges the viewer to confront are the paradoxical aspects of bodily experience: the body as ambiguously both interior and exterior. Like-wise, the ambiguity of the body extends to its embeddedness in the abstract machine of threat and monstrosity that is the driving metaphor of the film, even as the origin of this threat remains critically unassignable to particular agents. *Leviathan* rejects the clichés of rugged individualism of the world of commer-cial fishing, which remains one of the deadliest professions, whose catastrophic precarity is often romanticised through heroic portraiture (the reality TV show *Deadliest Catch* and its portrayal of rugged, cowboy-like fishermen do precisely this) as a tactical response to the sheer impossibility of thinking the mass – both human labour and fish as a population.

Instead, its aesthetics convey a sensibility more akin to that of the nineteenth-century Japanese woodprint artists, best exemplified in Katsushika Hokusai's 'Under the Wave, Off Kanagawa' ['The Great Wave'] (c. 1830–1832), which is often cited as an inspiration for Japanese monster/kaiju films as well as, most recently, for the oceanic monster battle sequence in Guillermo del Toro's *Pacific Rim* (2013). The first print in Hokusai's 'floating world' series, *Thirty-Six Views of Mount Fuji* (the title of which suggests a multi-perspectival and documentary-style approach to everyday life around the mountain), 'The Great Wave' depicts an enormous open sea wave – appearing monstrous with its claw-like crest – raging towards three fish-ing boats off the coast. Although barely discernible and off-centre, the fishermen are still visible, clinging onto their oars and heading towards the centre of a storm. The affective import of the print is quite unique; the image evokes a monstrosity that is not necessarily supernatural or residing outside the natural/human. Rather, it points to an ambiguity of relations or a sensual assemblage between the sea, the implied storm, the boats and the fishermen, which converts the awe or terror induced into an embodied, intimate experience of reality. In *The Digital Film Event*, Trinh T. Minh-ha talks about the influence of traditional Asian arts on her ethnographic filmmaking and argues that artists that devoted themselves single-mindedly to tree, mountain, or bamboo painting reflected the desire to receive the world through the mentioned materialities, rather than to become experts on or fully know them.[11] This way of 'taking in the world' imbricated in their practice suggests the possibility of finding in the Eastern arts the precedents of a different approach to ethnographic documentation. Of course, there is an irrecuperable distance between Hokusai's dreamlike/idealised pre-industrial scene of fishing and the somewhat nightmarish contemporary ecological conditions surrounding *Leviathan*, yet an affinity persists in their liminal and experiential portrayal of the human body and its environment. Also, Hokusai and *Leviathan*'s specific takes on the monstrous are both suggestive of what documentary-style media have brought and can bring to the aesthetics of horror (and perhaps one can think of the significance of the staged shark hunt sequence in the now canonical fishing documentary, Robert Flaherty's *Man of Aran* (1934), in this context too, which is discussed by K.J. Donnelly in his chapter), shifting the focus from horror's taken-for-granted unidirectional influence on documentary films.

The highly artefactual nature of the imagery produced by GoPro cameras – attached to various crew members' clothing/gear (lower and above eye-level), 5-foot booms or a 2 × 2 that Paravel termed their high tech 'wood stick' – decentre vision, making the viewer switch back and forth between the seemingly interchangeable points-of-view of the fishermen, the ship, the ocean (conveyed through underwater shots), seagulls and the fish gasping for survival (figure 11.1). The long takes and absence of narration recall observational cinema's

Figure 11.1 A bird's-eye shot from *Leviathan* (Lucien Castaing-Taylor and Véréna Paravel, 2012).

fly-on-the-wall aesthetics, yet the viewfinder-less use of the cameras strip vision of any guiding sense of human intentionality.[12] The film's 'fly' or agents behind the camera are not only at times non-human, giving the animal metaphor in the phrase a new meaning, but also a monstrous assemblage of bodies that move but don't have a vision of their own (the body that the camera is mounted on becomes the eye), more like the body of *Leviathan* composed of many faces on the famous frontispiece of Thomas Hobbes's political treatise. Together they present fragmented, kaleidoscopic impressions (insect vision, fisheye lens look, bird's-eye view? Animal metaphors easily proliferate) of the world of fishing, which is sensual yet devoid of a unifying/sovereign narrative or affects.

In *Ugly Feelings*, dealing with the aesthetics of negative emotions in literature, film and theoretical writing, Sianne Ngai describes a detachment in contemporary art from the classical political passions theorised by Aristotle or Hobbes (who made affect, and more specifically fear, central to his formulation of modern sovereignty through a seventeenth-century reimagining of *Leviathan*).[13] She argues that the contemporary moment calls upon a new set of feelings – ambivalent and more suited in their ambient nature for new models of subjectivity – to be reflected in them. Ngai's negative or ugly feelings are amoral, non-cathartic and do not lend themselves to emotional release. They are meta-feelings 'in which one feels confused about what one is feeling'.[14] This emphasis on the productivity of ambiguity is indeed characteristic of the affective turn in cultural feeling more broadly (in the context of cinema, Steven Shaviro's theory of 'post-cinematic affect' deals with the productivity of an audiovisual aesthetics that heightens ambiguous cultural structures of feeling quite extensively).[15] Working within another strand of affect theory, Brian Massumi has specifically differentiated affect from emotion by understanding emotion as 'captured' affect, named, identified and delimited after the fact.[16]

It can be argued that in their attention to affect, Ngai, Shaviro and Massumi all underscore the feeling of potential that ambiguity provides. There is an ethical responsibility at work in making potential visible or felt. Castaing-Taylor and Paravel's film has a similar affective orientation. Although the documentary's horror aesthetics and reference to monstrosity in its title suggest a narrative arc built around fear and terror, the unsettling audiovisual material never quite reaches the level of evoking a definable feeling or reaction in the viewer. Without a narrative climax or an identifiable agent behind the cameras through whose perspective the main threat can be defined, the image and sound tracks pull the viewer into the centre of a nighttime carnival of massacre on a raging ocean of micro-affects, which deprive them of a clear footing or interpretation. The deliberately dense and noisy soundtrack amplifies (if not establishes in the first place) the sense of affective and epistemological confusion, with the mix of machinic clamour and muffled sounds of the GoPros rendering any dialogue unintelligible. Karel states, contrary to MacDonald's interpretation of how the film leaves the audience 'exhausted and happy', that they tried to create through the soundtrack 'an intense and unpleasant experience in the theater' to convey the unpleasant time the filmmakers had on the boat. Adding that he is not sure whose benefit the simulation of such an experience serves, he continues:

> Usually you're not trying to make it unpleasant, and we weren't really *trying* to make it unpleasant, but then again I've done a lot of stuff in my own sound work that's loud and harsh and intense. That feeling of being disrupted or disturbed from your normal life can be a useful one.[17]

Karel seems to be describing 'irritation', the sense of feeling disturbed, which Ngai categorises as a negative, ambivalent and non-cathartic affect in this statement. The irritable mood that the soundtrack summons suggests that rather than merely amplifying the negative affective aesthetics of the film, *Leviathan*'s sound design effectively produces or establishes it as a milieu. Indeed, part of the effect of the milieu-building function is that irritation, as a disruption to smooth and habituated perception, can also shift from a negative state to one that reopens the perceptual field.

Noise as Milieu

The idea of 'doing anthropology in sound' is not new. In a 2004 interview, Steven Feld and Donald Brenneis discussed the renewal of interest in sound by social theorists, historians, folklorists, science and technology studies researchers, and visual, performative and cultural studies experts in the late 1990s.[18] Following the example of the anthropologist-filmmaker Jean Rouch, Feld called to blend the agendas of sound and the senses, leading to the proliferation of projects undertaking the 'anthropology of the senses', including research in film. In some of the earlier work, sound was celebrated for its capacities for place-making, preservation and the mediation between humans and their environment. However, it can be argued that the foregrounding of sound within the cinematic move toward immersive environments in the digital era has both strengthened and complicated the sound-image relations in sensory ethnographic filmmaking, with immersion no longer associated with precision and clarity in the soundtracks, signalling distinct locations, actions and events.[19]

In her recent study on the rising interest in 'dirty' soundtracks in the body-centred films of European cinema, Lisa Coulthard associates the coming to prominence of noise in the contemporary era with the emergence of new sensory modes of filmmaking, initially made possible by the acoustic innovations introduced by Dolby digital sound. Echoing Michel Chion, she suggests that, while Dolby digital surround sound has offered sonic immersion, increased precision and noise reduction, certain filmmakers deliberately celebrate noise and sonic imperfections, finding in the dirty aesthetics of digital soundtracks the possibility of a different type of immersive, haptic cinema:

> Chion anticipates this link between Dolby digital and a more haptic, tactile cinematic noise when he argues that Dolby stereo heralded a "new sensory

cinema" focused on the sound effects associated with everyday actions of the body (breath, skin touches, cloth movements, footsteps), technology (machine hums, traffic noise, engine rumbles) and the environment (animal cries, bird songs, cricket chirps). This new sensory cinema communicates sensations of physical, bodily life through an intensification of its sounds. This last point is crucial: we hear not only with our ears, but our entire bodies.[20]

The highly intricate sound mix of *Leviathan*, achieved by SEL-affiliated Karel and Hollywood-native sound-designer Jacob Ribicoff, has received a great deal of positive recognition due to its haptic and tactile use of cinematic noise. It has a sculptural quality, in that the sonic indistinction makes the recording process felt as a material abstraction from the environment. By abstraction, we mean not a reduction of sonic relations, but instead a making-felt of virtual potential, an attention to the coming-into-being of a sound in excess of its functional recognisability. With little dialogue, no music, caption or narration, the documentary is nevertheless immersed in a sound bath that assails the audience from the start, evoking (if not risking) a sense of sonic chaos. One of the most distinctive aspects of the 5.1 sound mix is the use of the poor quality and muffled recordings from the GoPro cameras with built-in microphones. Encased within waterproof housing, the cameras provide even lower precision sound when used underwater. Interestingly, *Leviathan* does not take the poor quality of the record, full of digital artefacts, as a flaw to be erased or avoided; instead, technological noise is rendered a critical component of the film, establishing a sonic landscape that is seemingly 'low-fidelity' – with weak auditory cues regarding the source and hierarchy of sounds – yet sophisticated as an acoustic ecology, produced by new machinic agents.[21] In several scenes, the cameras toggle between under and above water with the rise and fall of the boat, with the quality of the sound changing dramatically with each boundary crossing and continually drawing attention to the tiny machine in the ocean's swell. As with the newer sense of immersion, this self-referential quality of sound, retained and even highlighted in the mix complicates perception well beyond a simple self-reflexive exposure of the medium. The reminder of recording rather adds another body to the mix and in so doing, remixes the bodily assemblage as a whole. Additionally, when layered with other effects, frequencies and simultaneous tracks, the multi-directionality of the sounds that make up the film's sonicscape helps establish it as an acoustic space rather than a visual one. As Erik Davis argues, following Marshall McLuhan's formulation:

> Simply put, acoustic space is the space we hear rather than the space we see ... Acoustic space is multi-dimensional, resonant, invisibly tactile, "a total and simultaneous field of relations". Where visual space emphasises linearity, acoustic space emphasises simultaneity – the possibility that many events can occur in the same holistic zone of space-time.[22]

Leviathan's sound composition does not follow the Euclidian model of space serving as a container, a construct embraced by continuity as well as intensified-continuity cinema; rather, it extends beyond the limitations of visual editing and allows a simultaneity of relations, through folding sounds from multiple sources as well as footage captured at different times and locations onto each other. By doing so, it functions as a spectral milieu prefiguring experience, an 'acoustic envelope' (Didier Anzieu) or ocean 'upon which the images bob, pitch, and drown' (Max Goldberg).[23] Paradoxically, it is the general lack of intentionality behind images, sounds and affects in the film that gives *Leviathan* its distinctive embodied feel. In place of human intentionality, we find a relational ecology of rhythm, sometimes conveyed via the motion of the ship in a double visual rise and fall and sonic beat, and sometimes as an affective temporality (in the sense that Gaston Bachelard sets molecular or quantum level vibrations of matter as a foundation for understanding the discontinuous and arrhythmic temporalities we find in nature – like the interminable slowness of a quiet night and the changing intervals between consequent bursts of lightning in a thunderstorm), serving as a connecting milieu.[24] This latter, 'rhythmanalytic' approach to ecology finds expression in the film through the tension between the felt slowness of long-take shots and the changing temporal patterns/cadences of layered sounds. Rhythmic ecology is not merely a sonic representation, but rather an immersive, materialist holding together of the film's elements without a teleological arc. *Leviathan* actively works to disrupt temporal and spatial points of orientation, contagiously infecting the viewer with the experiential conditions surrounding the fisherman and filmmakers, including those actants (underwater and above the ship) that fall outside their reach. Within such a context, the distinctions between inside and outside, machines and nature, the sea and the sky and fishermen and fish get blurred, with each human and nonhuman agent becoming a fold in the larger assemblage of a liminal, monster-like audiovisual ecology.

The Audiovisual Folds

In his book on Michel Foucault, Gilles Deleuze evokes a topological image to describe how the questions of interiority – of the body, thought, or knowledge – become instead a reformulation of the inside as a fold of the outside in Foucault's work: that of a ship as a 'folding of the sea'.[25] A ship is a form of interiority in radical contact with the outside and a mode of individuation that cannot be separated from its associated milieu, the sea. This processual mode of subjectivation enacted through the fold has an explicitly political dimension for Deleuze. Refoldings are both the creative impetus of non-standardised political feeling and that which must be continuously generated to be effective. The fold of subjectivation is simultaneously a kind of mastery of the swarm of forces, the relations of 'speeds and slownesses' that compose any subject and one that, as with Deleuze's image of the boat, is a tenuous and continually-reconfigured relation of vulnerability.

An intensive folding of subjectivities and materialities is precisely the political feeling conveyed by Castaing-Taylor and Paravel in *Leviathan*, which enacts practice-based research grounded in an emergent critique of biopolitics. Here, the film's biopolitical intervention lies in its blurring of the boundaries between human, animal and machinic bodies, making them a part of a mutant and monstrous assemblage of audiovisual materialities, micro-rhythms and micro-affects. The sensationally rich document of the social, mental and environmental ecologies held together on the ship activates a strong sense of the 'ethico-political' through aesthetic practice, which places it within a new materialist framework. The use of the GoPro cameras is symbolic in this regard. The film produces and is produced through distributed embodiment with body-mounted technologies purporting to provide 'intimate' shots/sounds of bodily experience (suggesting interiority) while mounted on various bodily surfaces and machinic extensions. All shots in the film, save four, were hand held or produced by GoPros. The effect is frequently that of impossible objective shots (objective since unattributable to a specific character in the film; yet subjective due to the bodily apparatus), which appear incredibly, intimately embodied by human and machinic agents: as if the cameras are a folding of the human, the animal, the ship and the sea (figure 11.2). This produces a mode of cinematic subjectivation that, as Thomas Elsaesser and Malte Hagener have described in their sensory reorientation of film theory, 'seems poised to leave behind its function as a medium (for the representation of reality) in order to become a "life form" (and thus a reality in its own right)', a cinema that proposes 'besides a new way of knowing the world, also a new way of being in the world'.[26]

Figure 11.2 The front of the boat, in *Leviathan*.

Despite the heavy and industrial nature of the ship's machinery, the film effectuates the precarity of existence at every level in the audiovisual portrayal of a world always about to fall apart. It mobilises an 'operative map', or a biogram, as an analytical methodology. Biogram, a term Massumi develops from the work of Deleuze and Guattari on the diagram, articulates a new materialist focus on the small differences, or molecular revolutions, that an attention to becoming makes in studies of non-human becomings of animals, plants and machines.[27] The biogram reimagines bodies in terms of a becoming that is not a fully delimited and determined entity, but rather within a relational ecology of forces. As such, rather than imagining viewers as spat out 'exhausted and happy' from within this whale of a film, the film's discomfort lies in the precise ambiguity of what difference has been made by this journey through Leviathan's relational ecology.

The monstrous body depicted in Leviathan is also a body of virtuality and potentiality then. Its monstrosity lies in the paradox (à la Ligotti) of its being neither one thing nor another, which offers new possibilities for ethnography. The monster's liminality and the biogram's topological aesthetics offer us a way to articulate an experience of the twisting and folding of information into perception. Our perceptions are not interior representations of a world, but immediately part of it, in a space-time that changes as we move through it in an immanently relational configuration. Biograms are intensive mappings or productions of space-time that are temporally contingent, samples that are not simply archived tel quel, but involuntarily lived. Rather than starting from identity as a point, which is then displaced, in a regularised Cartesian grid, a biogram experiences space as immanently variable in time, based on a self-referential sense of displacement. Such displacement is a key part of the film's efficacy, in the non-habitual and eccentric nature of handheld shots decoupled from the usual synthesis of the hand's motion as intentional precursor to the operations of the eye. In the GoPro aesthetic, hand-shots do not necessitate a framing eye or vision for their capture of reality.[28] Further, the cameras, when mounted on boom poles or sticks, get linked up with audition, recalling boom poles' traditional use as extensions for sound recording (so the haptic separation between the image and sound recording disappears). Similarly, the mixing of multi-directional, multi-temporal sounds and persistent machinic noise perform a decoupling between hearing, listening and perception (one hears but does not necessarily comprehend the sounds, as they border on unintelligibility, cocooned in noise). Rather than first person perspective, the biogrammatic effect is an audiovisuality of what Foucault terms the 'anonymous murmur'.[29] Biograms are intersensory sound-images, fully real in their virtuality despite not being assignable to a particular object or single point of audition, not merely 'hallucinations' or subjective perceptions as we might imagine. Rather than an inert object, a biogram is a fold in place of temporal and spatial encounters, a simultaneity of multiple temporalities and experiences. It is an experience, as Massumi describes it, of 'the body minding itself': '(t)he biogram is a perceptual reliving, a folding back of experience on itself', where immediate perception is doubled by memory as virtual potential, an archive doubled by forces.[30]

This is the potential of a film like *Leviathan* and one of the reasons why the 'documentary' has continually been fringed by other generic descriptors, 'more thans' in the critical reception of the film, including the horror film. It produces an effect of the 'singular-generic', the singular eventness of the encounter that makes relationality immediately felt. Perhaps the strongest effect of *Leviathan* is that the film increasingly builds and sustains intensity; despite the long takes, the delimited field of consideration and a certain consistency of rhythm across the work, any exhaustion by the end of the film is that of a habitual way of seeing the world. The film's sonic ecology and attention to the monstrous embodiments emergent between the individuated figures and actants of the film, means that we are more than just spat out at the end, our own nature intact. We might recall Donna Haraway's assessment that the promises of monsters put the lie to any 'nature' outside artefactualism. The monstrous in this film names an immersive approach that does not seek to represent the world of commercial fishing, but to make a world out of the violent and disjunctive intimacies of documentary subjects, senses and materials.

Notes

1 Thomas Ligotti, *The Conspiracy Against the Human Race: A Contrivance of Horror* (New York: Hippocampus Press, 2011), 18.
2 Ibid., 13.
3 Scott MacDonald, 'Conversations on the Avant-Doc: Scott MacDonald Interviews', in *Framework: The Journal of Cinema and Media*, 54:2 (Fall 2013), 330.
4 Sarah Pink, *Doing Sensory Ethnography* (London: Sage, 2009).
5 'The Sensory Ethnography Lab (SEL)', at http://sel.fas.harvard.edu/index.html (accessed 9 February, 2014).
6 MacDonald, *American Ethnographic Film and Personal Documentary: The Cambridge Turn* (Berkeley: University of California Press, 2013), 335.
7 Selmin Kara, 'The Sonic Summons: Meditations on Nature and Anempathetic Sound in Digital Documentaries', in *The Oxford Handbook of Sound and Image in Digital Media*, ed. Carol Vernallis, Amy Herzog and John Richardson (Oxford: Oxford University Press, 2013), 582–598.
8 Trevor Johnston, 'All at Sea', in *Sight & Sound*, 23:12 (December 2013), 44.
9 Steven Shaviro, *The Cinematic Body* (Minneapolis, MN: University of Minnesota Press, 1993).
10 Johnston, 'All at Sea', 44.
11 Trinh T. Minh-Ha, *The Digital Film Event* (New York: Routledge, 2005), 7.
12 Lisa Cartwright, 'My Hero: A Media Archaeology of Body-Mounted Camera Technologies of the Self' (public talk presented at the iSchool Colloquia Series, University of Toronto, Toronto, January 30, 2014).
13 Thomas Hobbes, *Leviathan* (Lexington, KY: Seven Treasures Publications, 2009).
14 Sianne Ngai, *Ugly Feelings* (Cambridge, MA: Harvard University Press, 2005), 14.
15 Shaviro, *Post Cinematic Affect* (Winchester: Zero Books, 2010).

16 Brian Massumi, *Parables for the Virtual: Movement, Affect, Sensation* (Durham: Duke University Press, 2002).

17 Karel quoted in Max Goldberg, 'Signal to Noise: An Interview with Ernst Karel at the Harvard Sensory Ethnography Lab', in *Moving Image Source* (February 28, 2013), at http://www.movingimagesource.us/articles/signal-to-noise-20130228 (accessed 2 February, 2014).

18 Steven Feld and Donald Brenneis, 'Doing Anthropology in Sound', in *American Ethnologist*, 31:4 (2004), 461–474.

19 Mark Kerins, *Beyond Dolby (Stereo): Cinema in the Digital Sound Age* (Bloomington: Indiana University Press, 2011); William Whittington, 'Lost in Sensation: Reevaluating the Role of Cinematic Sound in the Digital Age', in *The Oxford Handbook of Sound and Image in Digital Media*, 61–77.

20 Lisa Coulthard, 'Dirty Sound: Haptic Noise in New Extremism', in *The Oxford Handbook of Sound and Image in Digital Media*, 118.

21 R. Murray Schafer, *The Tuning of the World* (New York: Knopf, 1977); Steven Feld, 'From Ethnomusicology to Echo-Muse-Ecology: Reading R. Murray Schafer in the Papua New Guinea Rainforest', in *Soundscape Newsletter*, 8 (1994), 9–13; Trevor Pinch and Karin Bijsterveld, 'New Keys to the World of Sound', in *The Oxford Handbook of Sound Studies*, ed. Trevor Pinch and Karin Bijsterveld (Oxford: Oxford University Press, 2012), 3–39.

22 Erik Davis, '"Roots and Wires" Remix: Polyrhythmic Tricks and the Black Electronic', in *Sound Unbound: Sampling Digital Music and Culture*, ed. DJ Spooky That Subliminal Kid (Cambridge, MA: MIT Press, 2008), 54.

23 Didier Anzieu, *The Skin Ego* (New Haven: Yale University Press, 1989); Goldberg, 'Signal to Noise.'

24 Gaston Bachelard, *Dialectic of Duration*, trans. Mary McAllester Jones (Manchester: Clinamen Press, 2000).

25 Gilles Deleuze, *Foucault* (New York: Continuum, 2006), 81.

26 Thomas Elsaesser and Malte Hagener, *Film Theory: An Introduction Through the Senses* (New York: Routledge, 2010), 12.

27 Massumi, *Parables for the Virtual*.

28 Cartwright, 'My Hero.'

29 Deleuze, *Foucault*.

30 Massumi, *Parables for the Virtual*, 194.

Afterword

Anahid Kassabian

Film music scholarship has a long and intriguing history. During the silent period, there were various writings, including both guides for musicians, such as Ernö Rapée's *Encyclopedia of Music for Pictures*, as well as critical writings.[1] At the advent of sound-on-film, there was a small blossoming of writing, most famously (at least in English) books by Kurt London (*Film Music*, 1936; a historical analysis and predictions for future developments) and Leonid Sabaneev (*Music for the Films*, 1935; addressed towards practicing composers and musicians).[2] But after those early years, there is much less critical and theoretical interest in film music: in fact, there are hardly any academic offerings, except for Zofia Lissa's *Music and Film: Study on the Borderline of Ontology, Aesthetics and Psychology of Film Music* (in Polish, 1937 and may have been translated into German) and *Ästhetik der Filmmusik* (1964 in Polish, translated into German in 1965).[3] As other authors in this volume have pointed out, there were resources for composers, arrangers and musicians such as George Antheil's columns in *Modern Music* and periodicals (*Film Music Notes* and *Film Music Notebook*).[4] Among longer works for composers, Theodor Adorno and Hans Eisler's *Composing for the Films* (1947) and Roy Prendergast's *Film Music: A Neglected Art* (1977) come closer to the kinds of thought and analysis that are useful for academic approaches.[5] But no sustained, sophisticated academic conversation developed until relatively recently.

As is by now widely acknowledged, Claudia Gorbman's *Unheard Melodies* (1987) is the first of a series of works through the 1990s – Caryl Flinn's *Strains of Utopia* (1992) and Kathryn Kalinak's *Settling the Score* (1992), Royal S. Brown's 1994 *Overtones and Undertones* and Jeff Smith's *The Sounds of Commerce* (1998).[6] But it wasn't until later in this millennium that the field began to really come into its own, with volumes on particular genres (e.g. *Music in the Horror Film* [Neil Lerner, 2010] and *The Gendered Score* [on 1940s Hollywood melodrama, Heather Laing, 2007]) and cinematic practices outside of Hollywood (Annette Davison's *Hollywood Theory, Non-Hollywood Practice* [2004] and Miguel Mera and David Burnand's 2006 collection *European Film Music*).[7] It is in this decade, however, that the field has really come into its own, becoming a wide ranging, multi-disciplinary area of both criticism and theorising, and this volume is an outstanding example of that.

While the field has indeed been developing in all kinds of important directions, until now there has been too little work on sound and music in documentary films, the few important articles notwithstanding.[8] That fact makes this volume a long-awaited touchstone that will set the conversation for some time to come, not only because it is the first volume on documentary sound, but also because of the range of its contributions. There are a number of essays on early documentaries, as well as several on contemporary works and others on the many years in between. There are chapters on John Grierson and the GPO Film Unit (Carolyn Birdsall and Thomas F. Cohen) as well as others on Chris Marker and the essay film (Orlene Denice McMahon). Whatever future scholars may want to say about music in documentary films, they will need to think through at least some of the essays in this book. Moreover, some themes emerge through the book that will, I am certain, generate more new scholarship on documentaries.

In Birdsall's essay, she focusses on the ways in which early filmmakers approach the aesthetics of sound in the city. At the time when the city was being aestheticised from various directions, Birdsall hears filmmakers experimenting with formal structures taken from orchestral compositions, especially the symphony, as a way to structure their films. In another work on early film, James Deaville considers sound and music in the first generation of sound newsreels. The fascination with sound-on-film meant not only that diegetic music appeared often in newsreels, but also that the makers of newsreels liked filming a wide range of musical performances. And in another essay on the city, McMahon discusses two of Chris Marker's earlier films, *Dimanche à Pékin* (1956) and *Lettre de Sibérie* (1958), to show how his use of sound serves his interest in critiquing the objective posture that documentaries so often take on. Relatedly, Julie Hubbert's essay details how music in American World War II documentaries signifies race and place. While the composer of the music for the recently found 1940 film *One Tenth of Our Nation*, Roy Harris, thought he could create an autogenetic compositional practice that made the music he used American rather than black or Southern, many of his contemporaries believed that such an evacuation of the history of musical fragments brought with it its own set of problems.

Several of the essays (Mervyn Cooke, Carolyn Birdsall and Kevin Donnelly) notice how some documentaries use musical instruments or other post-production practices to recreate real-world sounds. Such practices would be interesting in any film, but in documentary, they highlight the challenge of discerning what exactly is being 'documented'. Documentaries perforce confront such questions, whether they try to hide them or bring them up to the surface for shared contemplation by audience and filmmakers alike. Many of the essays here discuss this problematic to a greater or lesser extent, which reflects its centrality to scholarship on documentaries more generally. John Corner, for example, discusses some very high profile contemporary works and how the uses of sound and music open new arenas for exploring this problematic in a number of varied feature documentaries.

Unpredictably, another theme that arose in this volume is a watery one. The essays by Cooke, Selmin Kara and Alanna Thain and Donnelly all deal with sounds of and in water, which is a fascinating topic. Whether the question is point of audition sound (see for example several of the essays in Jay Beck and Tony Grajeda's edited collection *Lowering the Boom: Critical Studies in Film Sound*, 2008), subjective sound, or any of the several genres in which water features significantly (e.g. disaster films), water is an important feature of distinctive sound experiences.[9] Similarly, there is a long history of musical compositions that invoke water from which film composers have drawn ideas and approaches. Whether the water appears in a film like the 2012 documentary *Leviathan* (Kara and Thain) that has no narration and minimal language use, or in an 'ethnofiction' like Robert Flaherty's 1934 *Man of Aran* (Donnelly) that has a thick orchestral score, or in the soundtrack to the 1956 French documentary by Jacques-Yves Cousteau and Louis Malle, *Le Monde du Silence* (Cooke) that has a thinner, partly modernist score, there are shared strategies of treating music that invoke water across all these very different films, and those differences and similarities are clear in the essays that discuss them. And all of these films might be put into conversation with Cohen's consideration of educational films. In particular, he considers how government-issued documentaries teach us ideas about the orchestra, which could be useful to compare, in terms of sound and music strategies, with the uses of musical tropes of water and their uses in fiction films. Another theme that emerges in this collection is the relationship between art film practices and documentaries. It is clear even from the trailers on YouTube that *Leviathan* is not what we normally imagine a documentary to be; for starters, there is no commentary to lead us to the 'correct' interpretation. Similarly, the films that Rob Strachan and Marion Leonard focus on – *sleep furiously* (Gideon Koppel, 2008) and *Silence* (Pat Collins, 2010) – are poetic landscapes, dealing in an entirely different filmic language, a part of which is a different treatment of ambient sound. They argue that the soundtrack both heightens realism while at the same time creates an uncanny distanciation effect for listener/viewers.

Through Jamie Sexton's essay, the volume also points towards a whole range of problems that is just coming into focus. From the fan videos of concerts that are uploaded to YouTube that he discusses in his essay, to vloggers (video bloggers) like Jenna Marbles, to YouTube series such as Hannah Hart's *My Drunk Kitchen* or Rhett and Link's *Good Mythical Morning*, to documentary videogames such as the UN's *My Life as a Refugee*, to partly autobiographical fictional short video series such as Felicia Day's *The Guild* and Issa Rae's *Misadventures of Awkward Black Girl*, new forms are blossoming that will require at least extensions, if not whole cloth changes, to our approaches to sound and music in documentary audiovisual works.[10] *Awkward Black Girl*, for example, is the story of a young African-American woman who is unhappy at her job and when the series begins she has just broken up with a long-time lover. Rae has often said that the main character, J, is based on herself and she uses events from her life as inspiration for plot developments. While not strictly speaking a documentary, the similarity in camera style in significant moments to vlogs helps to blur its status, especially when she looks and speaks directly into the camera (Rae has been outspoken about how online video hosting sites and affordable cameras and editing software have made it possible for a wider and more diverse range of creative people to make videos. Her YouTube channel serves as a platform for her several web series by and about black people).[11]

The raps that the main character of ABG writes are one of the primary ways that the series expresses her awkwardness, with lyrics like:

> I go by J, Ce Ce is my bestie
> My job is dumb, sell pills to fatties
> I hate this shit. I am not happy
> So I write rhymes, word to your Daddy.
> Know I need to quit and my job got worse
> Just got a new boss – I will put him in a hearse
> Working on my anger, though, one day at a time
> I hope they all die but I won't commit the crime.[12]

Her raps are profoundly uncomfortable, making the listener squirm by enacting awkwardness in a very palpable way. Of course, the raps are not the only way J's awkwardness is demonstrated, but they are one of the main ones (it is interesting to note that the style of these sequences points towards a certain music video aesthetic, perhaps best known in Spike Jonze's hand-held, lo-fi camera work.) Any attempt to think about this series would certainly need to take her rapping into account. But there are other uses of music throughout the series that invite consideration as well, uses more similar to fiction film and television and that are one of the ways the series helps make listener-viewers comfortable with an uncomfortable story told in a new medium.

These new forms point towards the ever-deepening complexity of separating documentary from fiction. To take the UN game as one example, each of the characters that you can play as is fictional and each character can take many different paths in her/his attempt to escape the difficulties of local life. So by many standards, this is a fictional game, not different from, say, *Sonic the Hedgehog*. And yet the game is released by the UN High Commissioner for Refugees as an educational tool and as a way to get people involved in refugee issues. Insofar as it explains real conditions in specific parts of the world, it is at least as much a documentary work as a fiction. Peculiarly, there is no sound or music in the game, making the experience quite dry. The first time I played it, I felt manipulated by the choices – the format is a kind of decision tree in which many options lead to the arrest or death of the characters you are playing and/ or their family members. But the use of music would have drawn us into more affective relationships with the characters and the story, which would have served the game's purpose better. Moreover, certain sounds, such as gunshots, would have brought players into more intense relationships with the events.

If games become, as is predicted, one of the primary educational tools of the near future, then sound and music will have an important place in them.

One last example of the uses of music in newer forms of cultural production. There are a host of genres of videos that circulate on video sharing sites that are about music in a variety of ways. One of these is the 'literal video', the most well-known of which is made from the video for Bonnie Tyler's 'Total Eclipse of the Heart' (1983). In a literal video, the maker removes the original vocal track in a video and replaces it with a description of what's happening on screen. So, for example, in the opening of the 'Total Eclipse of the Heart' literal video, the lyrics are:

> Pan the room,
> Random use of candles, empty bottles and cloth,
> And can you see me through this fan?
> Slo-mo dove,
> Creepy doll, a window, and what looks like a bathrobe.

What intrigues me about the literal videos is that they adopt an approach to videos that is very much like what we, as teachers, ask of our students. They notice every (in this case visual) detail. The literal videos are a wonderful preparation for an analysis of the visual track of any given music video. In fact, it also highlights the auditory details as well, partly because the vocals are always amateurish, but also because the entire project makes the listener-viewer consciously aware of all the details of the video. While there isn't an audio equivalent yet, I'm sure there will be soon (if not, I may assign students to make such a thing as an assignment). But even though its emphasis is on the visual aspects of the video, the literal videos make listener-viewers aware of details in a way that is funny and enjoyable, but also scholarly.

There is another aspect to the literal video, which is that it shares a kind of status with 'The Making of…' documentaries. In highlighting so many details of the video, it gives listener-viewers a much more vivid sense of art, costume and set design, as well as choreography, than one might ordinarily have while watching a music video. In preparation for writing this afterword, I watched several literal videos, including one I had not seen before of 'Let it Go' from Disney's *Frozen* (2013). Now, I had seen and enjoyed the film, but the literal video made me see things I genuinely did not notice when watching the film, despite the radical difference in screen size. If such videos point out visual details, are they documentaries? Are they analyses? What tools would we reach for in order to begin studying them?

In this sense, some of the thinking here will offer approaches to these new kinds of objects, as scholars begin to consider these questions. This volume not only includes the state-of-the-art in documentary film music scholarship, but it also offers a lot of signposts to what the next generation scholarship on sound and music in documentary films and other audiovisual texts will be like. The future of thinking in this field will be fundamentally altered by the publication of this book, which is all that the contributors and editor can have hoped for.

Notes

1 Ernö Rapée, *Encyclopaedia of Music for Pictures* (New York: Belwin, 1925). For more on early criticism, see Clifford McCarty, 'Introduction: The Literature of Film Music', in *Film Music 1* (New York and London: Garland Publishing, 1989), ix–xv. For more on silent film music practices, see Martin Miller Marks, *Music and the Silent Film: Contexts and Case Studies, 1895–1924* (New York: Oxford University Press, 1997) and Rick Altman, *Silent Film Sound* (New York: Columbia University Press, 2007).

2 Kurt London, *Film Music*, trans. Eric S. Bensinger (London: Faber and Faber, 1936); Sabaneev, however, had a cynical view of the art, claiming that 'the ability to borrow wisely and opportunely, to imitate good and suitable examples, is a valuable endowment in his [the composer's] case, though these qualifications by no means add lustre to the ordinary composer'; *Music for Films: A Handbook for Composers and Conductors*, trans. S.W. Pring (London: Pitman, 1935), v.

3 Zofia Lissa's two books about film music have never been translated into English. As far as I know, hers is the first music philosophical study of film music, preceding Theodor Adorno and Hans Eisler's *Composing for the Films* (London and New York: Continuum, 2007 [originally published in 1947]) by seven years. The German translation(s) are only occasionally cited by scholars writing in English, most often by Philip Tagg. The absence of English translations of these works is an enormous hole in our understanding of the history of film music thinking.

4 There were also, of course, fanzines, such as that issued by the Max Steiner Music Society, 1965-76 and (what McCarty calls 'lamentable') amateur reviewing and criticism from the 1970s on; 'Introduction', xii.

5 Adorno and Eisler, *Composing for the Films*; and Roy Prendergast, *Film Music: A Neglected Art* 2nd Edition (New York: New York University Press, 1977 [originally published 1977]).

6 Claudia Gorbman, *Unheard Melodies: Narrative Film Music* (Bloomington and Indianapolis: Indiana University Press, 1987); Caryl Flinn, *Strains of Utopia: Gender, Nostalgia, and Hollywood Film Music* (Princeton, NJ: Princeton University Press, 1992); Kathryn Kalinak, *Settling the Score: Music and The Classical Hollywood Film* (Madison, WI: Wisconsin University Press, 1992); Royal S. Brown, *Overtones and Undertones: Reading Film Music* (Berkeley and Los Angeles: University of California Press, 1994); Jeff Smith, *The Sounds of Commerce: Marketing Popular Film Music* (New York: Columbia University Press, 1998).

7 Neil Lerner, *Music in the Horror Film: Listening to Fear* (New York: Routledge, 2010); Heather Laing, *The Gendered Score: Music in 1940s Melodrama and the Woman's Film* (Aldershot: Ashgate, 2007); Annette Davison, *Hollywood Theory, Non-Hollywood Practice: Cinema Soundtracks in the 1980s and 90s* (Aldershot: Ashgate, 2004); Miguel Mera and David Burnand, *European Film Music* (Aldershot: Ashgate, 2006).

8 See, for some examples: John Corner, 'Sounds Real: Music and Documentary', in *Popular Music*, 21:3 (2002), 357–366; Lerner, 'Musical Texture as Cinematic Signifier: The Politics of Polyphony in Selected Documentary Film Scores', in *Film Music II*, ed. Claudia Gorbman and Warren M. Sherk (Sherman Oaks, CA: Film Music Society, 2004), 1–25; and Jeffrey Ruoff, 'Conventions of Sound in Documentary', in *Cinema Journal*, 32:3 (Spring, 1993), 24–40.

9 Jay Beck and Tony Grajeda, *Lowering the Boom: Critical Studies in Film Sound* (Champaign, Urbana and Chicago: University of Illinois Press, 2008).

10 *My Drunk Kitchen* premiered in March 2011 and uploads on Thursdays. It was followed by a second series that uploads on Tuesdays, which includes collaborations with other YouTube personalities, documentary footage of Hart's national and then

international tour to shoot episodes of *MDK* in other people's kitchens making recipes of their choice. Rhett and Link, among the most popular YouTube celebrities, began their internet career making comedy advertisements. *Good Mythical Morning* debuted in January 2012; see the GMM channel at https://www.youtube. com/channel/UC4PooiX37Pld1T8J5SYT-SQ (accessed 22 February 2014). One of the earliest, best known vloggers is Jenna Marbles (https://www.youtube.com/ user/JennaMarbles/featured, accessed 22 February 2014), whose channel includes everything from commentary on gender roles to parody impressions. *My Life as a Refugee* was released in June 2012 by the United Nations High Commissioner for Refugees. *The Misadventures of Awkward Black Girl* debuted in February 2011 on YouTube; its wild popularity has led to a book contract and HBO series contract (for both co-writing and starring), a talk show and more. *The Guild* premiered in July 2007 (making it one of the earliest web series) and concluded in 2013; its star, Felicia Day, has gone on to do a number of things, many of which appear on her premium YouTube channel 'Geek and Sundry', including the series *The Flog*, *Vaginal Fantasy* (a book club), *Felicia's Ark* and *Co-Optitude*.

11 See https://www.youtube.com/issarae (accessed 22 February 2014).
12 Season Two trailer: https://www.youtube.com/watch?v=vEcsam8zonc (accessed 22 February 2014).

List of Contributors

Carolyn Birdsall is Assistant Professor in Media Studies at the University of Amsterdam. Her publications and research interests are in the fields of media and cultural history, with a particular focus on radio, film and television sound, nonfiction genres and urban studies. Her monograph *Nazi Soundscapes* (2012) examines the significance of radio and sound systems in urban environments in National Socialist Germany. Birdsall is also co-editor of *Sonic Mediations: Body, Sound, Technology* (2008) and *Inside Knowledge: (Un)doing Ways of Knowing in the Humanities* (2009). In her current research, Birdsall is investigating emergent concepts of 'documentary sound' in radio broadcasting and sound film in interwar Europe.

Thomas F. Cohen is Assistant Professor of Communication at the University of Tampa. He is the author of *Playing to the Camera: Musicians and Musical Performance in Documentary Cinema* (Wallflower 2012) as well as several essays on documentary film and music.

Mervyn Cooke is Professor of Music at the University of Nottingham. He is the author of *A History of Film Music* (CUP, 2008) and editor of *The Hollywood Film Music Reader* (OUP, 2010). He has also written and edited several volumes on the life and music of Benjamin Britten and the history of jazz. He is currently co-editing (with Fiona Ford) *The Cambridge Companion to Film Music* and writing an analytical study of the ECM recordings of jazz guitarist Pat Metheny.

John Corner is a Visiting Professor at the University of Leeds and Emeritus Professor of the University of Liverpool. He has written widely on media form and particularly on aspects of documentary, including in his monograph *The Art of Record* (1996) and in a number of journal articles and book chapters. Among his recent publications is *Theorising Media: Power, Form and Subjectivity* (2011).

James Deaville is Professor in the School for Studies in Art and Culture: Music at Carleton University, Ottawa. He has published in the *Journal of the American Musicological Society, Journal of the Society for American Music,* and *Music and the Moving Image* (among others), has contributed to books published by Oxford University Press, Cambridge University Press, Princeton University Press, Ashgate, and Routledge (among others), and is editor of *Music in Television: Channels of Listening*

(Routledge, 2011). He has published about music, television news, and war in *Music in the Post-9/11 World* and *Echo*. His article "The Changing Sounds of War: Television News Music and Armed Conflicts in Vietnam and the Persian Gulf" appeared in 2012 in the Wesleyan University Press anthology *Music, Politics, and Violence*, while 'The Envoicing of Protest: Occupying Television through Sound and Music' was published in the *Journal of Sonic Studies* in 2012.

K.J. Donnelly is reader in film at the University of Southampton. He has written *Occult Aesthetics: Synchronization in Sound Cinema* (Oxford University Press, 2014), *British Film Music and Film Musicals* (Palgrave, 2007), *The Spectre of Sound: Film and Television Music* (British Film Institute, 2005), *Pop Music in British Cinema: A Chronicle* (British Film Institute, 2001) and the edited collections *Film Music: Critical Approaches* (Edinburgh University Press and Continuum, 2001), *Music in Science Fiction Television: Tuned to the Future* (co-edited with Philip Hayward, Taylor and Francis, 2012) and *Music in Video Games: Studying Play* (co-edited with Will Gibbons and Neil Lerner, Taylor and Francis, 2014).

Julie Hubbert is an Associate Professor of Music History at the University of South Carolina. Her articles on a variety of film music topics have appeared in journals such as *American Music, The Musical Quarterly* and *The Moving Image* as well as in a variety of essay collections. In 2011 she published *Celluloid Symphonies: Text and Contexts in Music History* (University of California Press.) She is currently working on a book on the intersection of sound reproduction technology and compilation scoring practices in film since 1968.

Selmin Kara is an Assistant Professor of Documentary and New Media at OCAD University in Toronto Canada. She has critical interests in the use of new technologies, tactical media and sound in documentary, as well as post-cinematic aesthetics and new materialist approaches in film. Her work has appeared and is forthcoming in *Studies in Documentary Film, Poiesis: A Journal of the Arts & Communication, Sequence* and the *Oxford Handbook of Sound and Image in Digital Media*. Selmin is currently co-editing a special theme issue on 'Unruly Documentary Artivism' for *Studies in Documentary Film*, and working on her book project *Reassembling Documentary: From Actuality to Virtuality*, which offers a new materialist framework for understanding sound-image relations in contemporary documentary media.

Anahid Kassabian is the James and Constance Alsop Chair of Music at the University of Liverpool and the author of *Ubiquitous Listening* (2013) and *Hearing Film* (2001). She co-edited two volumes, *Ubiquitous Musics* (2013) and *Keeping Score: Music, Disciplinarity, Culture* (1997). She is a past editor of 'Journal of Popular Music Studies' and 'Music, Sound, and the Moving Image' and she is a past chair of the International Association for the Study of Popular Music (IASPM). She has also co-curated several Armenian diasporan film festivals and she serves on the Board of Trustees of the Liverpool Arabic Arts Festival and Aunt Lute Books.

Marion Leonard is a senior lecturer in the School of Music at the University of Liverpool. She is author of *Gender in the Music Industry* (2007) and co-editor of *The Beat Goes On: Liverpool, Popular Music and the Changing City* (2010) and *Sites of Popular Music Heritage* (forthcoming). She has recently completed a research project funded, by the AHRC, which investigated the practical and theoretical issues involved with collecting and representing popular music in museums. Her research focuses on popular music and she has published on a wide range of topics including gender, identity, material culture and the rock documentary.

Orlene Denice McMahon is a musicologist specialising in film and media music. She received her doctorate from the University of Cambridge and is now teaching as an Associate Lecturer in Musicology at Paris-Sorbonne University (Paris IV). Her first book, *Listening to the French New Wave: The Film Music and Composers of Postwar French Art Cinema*, is forthcoming from Peter Lang Oxford. Current research projects include a monograph on French composer Jean-Claude Eloy as well as research into the evolution of French electronic dance music from the 1980s onwards, looking in particular at the house music phenomenon 'French Touch'.

Bill Nichols is Professor Emeritus of Cinema at San Francisco State University. He is the author of a general introduction to the cinema that stresses film's social significance, *Engaging Cinema* (2010), and of the widely used *Introduction to Documentary* (2nd ed., 2010). His other books include *Blurred Boundaries: Questions of Meaning in Contemporary Culture* (1994), *Maya Deren and the American Avant-garde* (2001) and the seminal anthologies, *Movies and Methods*, vols 1 and 2 (1976, 1985). These works helped establish film studies as an academic discipline. He has given over 100 lectures around the world and published numerous essays on a wide variety of topics. He has served on film juries at festivals in many countries from Brazil to South Korea and he is a consultant to a number of documentary filmmakers on their current projects.

Holly Rogers is senior lecturer in music and director of the Research Centre for Audio-Visual Media at the University of Liverpool. She has published on many aspects of audiovisual culture, including film music, experimental cinema sound, composer biopics and video and interactive media. She is author of *Visualising Music: Audiovisual Relationships in Avant-Garde Film and Video Art* (Verlag, 2010) and *Sounding the Gallery: Video and the Rise of Art-Music* (OUP, 2013). Her work has been funded by the Irish Research Council for the Humanities and Social Sciences, the Fulbright Commission and Trinity College Dublin.

Jamie Sexton is senior lecturer in Film and Television Studies at Northumbria University, UK. His publications include a co-authored book, *Cult Cinema* (Wiley-Blackwell, 2011) and a co-edited collection, *No Known Cure: The Comedy of Chris Morris* (BFI 2013). He is currently working on a book examining the interconnections between American independent cinema and independent music.

Robert Strachan is a lecturer in music at the University of Liverpool. He has published numerous articles on a variety of aspects of music and sound including DIY cultures, electronic music, digital technologies and audiovisual media. His artistic work includes installations exhibited at the Wordsworth Trust, Liverpool Biennial and the Foundation for Art and Creative Technology

(FACT) and one-off hybrid audiovisual performances at venues including the FutureEverything and Abandon Normal Devices festivals, Tate Liverpool and the National Review of Live Art.

Alanna Thain is an Associate Professor of World Cinemas and Cultural Studies at McGill University in Montreal, Canada. She co-directs the Moving Image Research Laboratory, devoted to studying relations between bodies and moving image media. Her research connects affect, media and the body, focusing on contemporary cinema, animation and screendance. Her book, *Bodies in Time: Suspense, Affect, Cinema* is forthcoming from the University of Minnesota Press. Having written about questions of time, embodiment and cinema in David Lynch, William Kentridge and others, she is currently completing two books, on Norman McLaren and on 'Anarchival Cinemas', exploring dance performance in post-cinematic production.

Index

PEFC Certified

This product is
from sustainably
managed forests
and controlled
sources

www.pefc.org

PEFC™

PEFC/16-33-415

#0222 - 040116 - C0 - 229/152/12 - PB - 9780415728669